OXFORD STUDIES IN AFRICAN POLITICS
AND INTERNATIONAL RELATIONS

General Editors
NIC CHEESEMAN, PEACE MEDIE, AND
RICARDO SOARES DE OLIVEIRA

Oxford Studies in African Politics and International Relations is a series for scholars and students working on African politics and International Relations and related disciplines. Volumes concentrate on contemporary developments in African political science, political economy, and International Relations, such as electoral politics, democratization, decentralization, gender and political representation, the political impact of natural resources, the dynamics and consequences of conflict, comparative political thought, and the nature of the continent's engagement with the East and West. Comparative and mixed methods work is particularly encouraged. Case studies are welcomed but should demonstrate the broader theoretical and empirical implications of the study and its wider relevance to contemporary debates. The focus of the series is on sub-Saharan Africa, although proposals that explain how the region engages with North Africa and other parts of the world are of interest.

Controlling Territory, Controlling Voters

The Electoral Geography of African Campaign Violence

MICHAEL WAHMAN
Michigan State University

OXFORD
UNIVERSITY PRESS

OXFORD
UNIVERSITY PRESS

Great Clarendon Street, Oxford, OX2 6DP,
United Kingdom

Oxford University Press is a department of the University of Oxford.
It furthers the University's objective of excellence in research, scholarship,
and education by publishing worldwide. Oxford is a registered trade mark of
Oxford University Press in the UK and in certain other countries

Published in the United States of America by Oxford University Press
198 Madison Avenue, New York, NY 10016, United States of America

British Library Cataloguing in Publication Data

Data available

Library of Congress Control Number: 2023937955

ISBN 9780198872825

DOI: 10.1093/oso/9780198872825.001.0001

Printed and bound by
CPI Group (UK) Ltd, Croydon, CR0 4YY

MIX
Paper | Supporting
responsible forestry
FSC
www.fsc.org   FSC® C013604

Acknowledgments

Writing this book took me a long time, seven years to be precise. I made multiple trips to Malawi and Zambia and changed employers several times, in that period. Along the way, I have made new friends and acquaintances who have influenced me in profound ways. I have also relied on the wisdom and support of old friends and colleagues who continue to inspire me. This book may have my name on the spine, but the generosity of a large community of outstanding scholars enabled it.

The initial idea for this book came from my research project on *Elections and Electoral Corruption in New Democracies*, financed by the Swedish Research Council (SRC) (VR DNR 2012-6653). I developed the grant proposal and many of the foundational ideas with great support from some of my most influential early mentors, including Sarah Birch, Staffan Lindberg, and Jan Teorell.

My closest colleague in Malawi is Nandini Patel. I have gathered so much of my knowledge about Malawian politics from numerous conversations with Prof. Patel over a decade. I am also more than grateful for her hospitality and generosity in providing an institutional home for me at the Institute for Policy Interaction (IPI). Apart from Prof. Patel, I am also grateful to the late Rafiq Hajat, the Director of IPI and a legendary Malawian Human Rights defender. IPI was my partner in fielding the Malawi Election Monitor Survey (MEMS). I want to thank all enumerators at IPI and all the participants in the surveys and focus groups. I particularly want to thank my good friend Felix Chauluka, who has contributed to this book in multiple ways through years of excellent research assistantship. MEMS was also enabled by the amazing institutional support of the National Initiative for Civic Education (NICE). I am particularly grateful to the Director Ollen Mwalubunju and Deputy Director Gray Kalindekafe. I also want to thank Sangwani Mwafulirwa at the Malawi Election Commission (MEC). During my fieldwork in Malawi, I benefited greatly from conversations with many colleagues, including Joseph Chunga, Boniface Dulani, Sean Dunne, David Kayuni, and Happy Kayuni.

I am beyond grateful for all the support that I received from the community at the Southern African Institute for Policy and Research (SAIPAR) during all my trips to Zambia. The Director, Marja Hinfelaar, has provided endless support and multiple lessons about Zambian politics. The Zambian Election Monitoring Survey (ZEMS) was enabled by a wonderful collaboration with the Forum for Democratic Process (FODEP) and the Southern African Center for the Constructive Resolution of Disputes (SACCORD). I am grateful for all the support from the executive directors at these two institutions, Chimfwembe Mweenge and Boniface Cheembe. An excellent group of enumerators in Lusaka carried out ZEPS. I particularly want to thank Josephine Chanda for managing the project and Beauty Nalwendo for her support during the focus groups. I am also grateful to all the participants in the survey and focus groups. My fieldwork and data collection in Zambia was enabled by two additional grants from the Magnus Bergvall Foundation (2015-00698) and the University of Missouri Research Council (URC-16-023). There are many more colleagues in Zambia that deserve special mention for all their input and support, including Tinenenji Banda, Lister Madubansi, Manenga Ndulo, O'Brien Kaaba, Owen Sichone, and Neo Simutanyi.

I base Chapter 5 on data from the Zambia Election Panel Survey (ZEPS). I benefited from a fantastic collaboration with The Governance and Local Development Institute (GLD) at University of Gothenburg and the Institute for Democracy, Citizenship and Public Policy in Africa (IDCPPA) at University of Cape Town in collecting these data. I am particularly grateful for the astonishing leadership of Ellen Lust. Nicole Beardsworth, Matthias Krönke, and Jeremy Seekings were excellent partners in ZEPS and have provided steadfast support throughout the years. The collection of the ZEPS data was enabled by a Swedish Research Council Recruitment Grant (E0003801) and funding from the University of Cape Town. Erica Metheney and Kirk Ammerman provided data collection support. The survey was implemented masterfully by Ubuntu Research and Rural Development Company. The Director of Ubuntu, Fison Mujenja, was such a tremendous resource.

Catherine Boone has been an extraordinary colleague and mentor. It is fair to say that no one has made a greater intellectual contribution to this book. She has been my foremost intellectual sparring partner in the last ten years and has taught me so much about African regionalism and political geography. Cathy was also kind enough to invite me to be part of her Economic and Social Research Council (ESRC) project *Spatial Inequalities in African Political Economy* (ES/R005753/1). Much of the constituency-level data used in the empirical analysis were collected within this project, and I am also grateful to Stephan Kyburz for compiling much of these data. During my time at the

London School of Economics (LSE), I also benefited from input from generous colleagues, including Elliot Greene, Ryan Jablonski, Tomila Lankina, and John Sidel.

I particularly want to highlight the contributions of two outstanding collaborators contributing to different parts of the argument and analysis presented here. First, Edward Goldring was an excellent research assistant during my fieldwork in Zambia. More importantly, we collaborated on an article published in *Journal of Peace Research* in which we developed many modelling strategies used in Chapters 4 and 7. I also want to thank Inken von Borzyskowski. We co-authored an article in the *British Journal of Political Science* in which we compared MEMS and ZEMS with other possible datasets. Inken was a great collaborator and inspired much of my thinking on election violence data.

I want to thank colleagues at my former department at University of Missouri, particularly Moisés Arce, Sheena Chestnut Greitens, Audra Jenkins, Jonathan Krieckhaus, Bryce Reeder, and Laron Williams. I also want to thank my current colleagues at Michigan State University. I have particularly relied on the support and advice from Ana Bracic, Eric Chang, Erica Frantz, Nikolaos Frantzeskakis, Christian Houle, Andrew Kerner, Nazita Lajevardi, Shahryar Minhas, and Li-Hong Weng. Few people have contributed more to this book than Jeffrey Conroy-Krutz. Having one of the best Africanists down my MSU hallway has been a privilege.

I spent a formative period as a visiting scholar at University of Cape Town's IDCPPA. During this period, I interacted closely with some of the most knowledgeable scholars on Malawian and Zambian politics. I am grateful to Diana Cammack, Joseph Chunga, Hangala Siachiwena, and Sishuwa Sishuwa for numerous inspiring conversations.

I organized a book conference at MSU in the fall of 2021. The comments I received at this occasion completely transformed how I articulate many of the ideas presented here. The book became infinitely better from all the excellent feedback that I received from Jaimie Bleck, Michael Bratton, Justine Davis, Anne Pitcher, and Scott Straus. In connection with the book conference, Kristine Höglund also read the entire manuscript and provided excellent comments. I have presented parts of the manuscript at seminars at University of Bergen, University of Michigan, and the London School of Economics; I thank participants on all these occasions.

Two long-time collaborators, Nicholas Kerr and Merete Bech Seeberg, also deserve special mention for their input. I also received invaluable comments from several other colleagues. I want to thank Leonardo Arriola, Laia Balcells,

Sarah Brierley, Johan Brosché, Ursula Daxecker, Augustina Giraudy, Adrienne Lebas, McDonald Lewanika, Kelly McMann, Muna Ndulo, George Ofosu, Manuela Travaglianti, Megan Turnbull, Lise Rakner, Peter VonDoepp, and Nicolas van de Walle. Nic Cheeseman has been an outstanding editor and a great supporter of my work. I am also truly indebted to the excellent comments from three anonymous reviewers and to Dominic Byatt and Karen Bunn at Oxford University Press.

Lastly, I want to thank my family and friend. Thank you to my mother, Åsa Wahman, and sister, Sophia Wahman, for all your support and encouragement. I am also lucky to have parents-in-law as wonderful as Drs. Constance and Lafayette Price. My father, Bengt Wahman, sadly passed away in the most intense phase of writing this book. He is the reason I do what I do; he inspired my interest in politics, a cosmopolitan worldview, and my relentless stubbornness. I miss him every day.

I dedicate this book to the two most important people in my life, my extraordinary wife, Charis Wahman, and my beautiful son Samuel Wahman. Charis has extended more love and tolerance than I could possibly have asked for and Sam makes every day so much brighter. Finishing this book was our collective achievement.

To Charis and Samuel

Contents

List of Figures

List of Tables

List of Abbreviations

Armed Conflict Location and Event Data Project (ACLED)
Alliance for the Restoration of Democracy (AFORD)
African National Congress (ANC)
Chama Cha Mapinduzi (CCM)
Democratic Progressive Party (DPP)
Electoral Commission of Zambia (ECZ)
Election Management Bodies (EMB)
Forum for Democratic Development (FDD)
Foundation for Democratic Process (FODEP)
Institute for Policy Interaction (IPI)
Kenyan African National Union (KANU)
Modifiable Areal Unit Problems (MAUP)
Malawi Broadcasting Cooperation (MBC)
Malawi Congress Party (MCP)
Malawi Electoral Commission (MEC)
Malawi Election Monitor Survey (MEMS)
Malawi Election Support Network (MESN)
Multiparty Liaison Committee (MPLC)
Movement for Multiparty Democracy (MMD)
Mudzi Transformation Trust (MTT)
Malawi Young Pioneers (MYP)
National Democratic Alliance (NDA)
National Initiative for Civic Education (NICE)
Patriotic Front (PF)
Party for National Unity (PNU)
Public Order Act (POA)
Peoples' Party (PP)
Republican Party (RP)
Southern African Center for Constructive Resolution of Disputes (SACCORD)
Social Conflict Analysis Database (SCAD)
Single Member District (SMD)
United Democratic Alliance (UDA)
United Democratic Front (UDF)
United National Independence Party (UNIP)
United Party (UP)
United Party for National Development (UPND)
United Progressive Party (UPP)
United Transformation Movement (UTM)

Zimbabwe African National Union–Patriotic Front (ZANU–PF)
Zimbabwe African People's Union (ZAPU)
Zimbabwe Congress of Trade Unions (ZCTU)
Zimbabwe Electoral Commission (ZEC)
Zambian Election Monitor Survey (ZEMS)
Zambian Republican Party (ZRP)

1

Introduction

I would like to thank you people for welcoming us and patronizing our
function in large numbers. You have shamed the devil of stone pelting.
Some people think this area belongs to them.
                    Saulos Chilima, Malawi Opposition Leader, June 7, 2020[1]

In a functioning democracy, everyone should feel free to wear party
regalia and there should be no such thing as a no-go area.
              Hakainde Hichilema, Zambia Opposition Leader, June 13, 2016[2]

Thyolo district in southern Malawi is perhaps an unlikely hotspot for election
violence. Thyolo is not a buzzing cosmopolitan center; sitting on the border
with Mozambique on the outskirts of Malawi's Southern Region, it is a rural
district without major cities. Economically, the district is dominated by subsistence farming and no major natural resources are within its borders. Nor
are there any large-scale communal land disputes fueling conflicts between
rival groups. The population is ethnically homogenous; almost 75% of the district's population belongs to the Lomwe ethnic group.[3] Politically, the district
could not be any less competitive. Two presidents, Bingu Mutharika and later
his brother, Arthur Peter Mutharika, hail from here. Since the creation of the
Democratic Progressive Party (DPP), the party has carried the district with
great margins. In the three elections between 2009 and 2019, DPP won on
average 91% of the district's presidential vote. Nevertheless, serious violence
broke out when President Joyce Banda and her People's Party (PP) arrived in
the district in March 2014 to hold an early election rally at Goliati Community
Ground. Two people lost their lives that day as supporters of the DPP attacked
the rally. Party leaders within PP were fast to make their analysis known to
the public: DPP was trying to create a "no-go zone" in Thyolo. In the mind of

[1] Quoted in Majawa (2020) from an election rally in Mangochi.
[2] Quote from a statement published on Hichilema's Facebook page (2016).
[3] 2008 Malawi Census.

Controlling Territory, Controlling Voters. Michael Wahman, Oxford University Press.
© Michael Wahman (2023). DOI: 10.1093/oso/9780198872825.003.0001

leaders within the locally strong party, the area belonged to them and the mere presence of rival parties was seen as a sign of aggression.

The term "no-go zone politics" is frequently evoked in Malawian politics and its meaning is well understood among voters and politicians alike, but the term has also been associated with elections in other African countries. For instance, in the 1996 Ghanaian election, Jerry Rawlings declared Ho constituency in the Volta region his "vote world bank" and a "no-go area" for the opposition (Asante and Gyimah-Boadi 2004). In Zimbabwe's 2013 election, the Zimbabwe African National Union–Patriotic Front (ZANU–PF) designated a no-go zone in Mount Darwin in order to "protect" voters from "outsiders." (Lewanika 2019: 202). The notion of parties "owning" space is antithetical to any reasonable understanding of democracy, where voters are entitled to autonomously make electoral decisions with free access to information.

In this book, I will focus on the political geography of campaign violence in Africa. While much election violence literature has focused on cross-national variations (Hafner Burton et al. 2014; Burchard 2015; Fjelde and Höglund 2016; Taylor et al. 2017; von Borzyskowski 2019), the focus in this book is subnational variations in campaign violence. The decision to study violence from an electoral geography perspective derives from a fairly simple observation: elections in many African countries are highly structured around regional cleavages and the support for political parties is rarely nationalized (Wahman 2017; Boone et al 2022). Although African countries have become increasingly competitive nationally, such competitiveness is rarely reflected at the local level where election campaigns take place. I will refer to countries with high levels of electoral competition at the national level, but low levels of competitiveness at the subnational level as *geographically polarized electoral systems*. The study of campaign violence in geographically polarized electoral systems raises important questions that I attempt to answer in this book: How does campaign violence affect political competition and campaigns in electoral systems where regionalism serves as the structuring cleavage for political competition? More practically, how does the nature of political competition in such geographically polarized electoral systems translate into subnational variations in campaign violence?

I introduce the concept of territoriality to the study of campaign violence. That is a "spatial strategy to affect, influence, or control people by controlling space" (Sack 1986:1). My main argument in this book is that political campaigns in geographically polarized electoral systems are contests over the mobilization of regional cleavages. Voters form their electoral expectations and interpretations locally and parties use campaigns to create a sense of local viability and advocacy. Campaign violence in this environment is utilized by parties as a territorial tool to shape local electoral environments. It is used to regulate access to space, both to enforce and contest territoriality.

Using a multi-method approach and unique and innovative data, the book studies geographic patterns of violence in Malawi and Zambia. Both countries are clear examples of geographically polarized electoral systems. The choice of cases may seem surprising. Neither one of them have featured prominently in the election violence literature. Instead the literature has been dominated by cases like Kenya (e.g. Kanyinga 2009; Boone 2011; Mueller 2011), Nigeria (Omotola 2009; Onapajo 2014; Angerbrandt 2018), and Côte d'Ivoire (Daddieh 2001; Straus 2011; Klaus and Mitchell 2015) where election violence has been more large-scale and resulted in thousands of deaths. Indeed, in Malawi and Zambia few people have periled due to violence in electoral campaigns. By selecting two cases that do not feature extreme levels of deadly violence in elections, I want to diverge from much of the conflict literature and instead focus on the way that campaign violence shapes electoral competition. I want to illustrate how pervasive and important campaign violence is for the quality of elections in African geographically polarized electoral systems, even beyond the most extreme examples. Even seemingly unremarkable and everyday expressions of coercion can have profound consequences for political competition and participation. In essence, even low-scale violence can serve to uphold subnational authoritarianism.

1.1 Defining Campaign Violence: Not Always Lethal, Always Devastating

Violence in election campaigns is common across the African continent and beyond. According to some estimations, most African elections contain some degree of violence and most of this violence happens before elections, during the election campaign (Straus and Taylor 2012; von Borzyskowki 2019). Campaign violence does not necessarily manifest itself in large-scale lethal violence, but it always threatens the integrity of elections. Campaign violence distorts political competition by creating an uneven playing field tilted towards actors with repressive capacity. Violence also deprives voters of a meaningful opportunity to participate in the electoral process. It restricts citizens' political agency, enhances political inequalities, and reduces voters' ability to form their political opinions through an open political campaign.

Campaign violence is an expression of conflict, but it is also a form of electoral manipulation (e.g. Birch 2011; Norris 2013; Asunka et al. 2019; Birch et al. 2020; Birch 2020; Fjelde 2020; Gonzalez-Ocantos et al. 2020;

Gutiérrez-Romero and Lebas 2020). That is, it is a strategic tool for political actors to affect electoral outcomes, similar to other forms of manipulation such as vote buying and tabulation fraud (Schedler 2002; Birch 2011; van Ham and Lindberg 2015). The word "strategic" is not meant to imply that every incident of violence is premeditated and sanctioned by the highest central authority. Nevertheless, parties send signals, promote cultures, and create repressive capacity to enable violence as they see fit to advance their electoral goals. In this book, I adopt the theoretical lens of violence as a strategic form of manipulation and accept the definition of campaign violence provided by Höglund (2009: 417) as an act of physical violence carried out before an election to influence the electoral process and, in extension, the outcome.

The term "election violence" has been used to describe a wide-ranging menu of violence occurring in and around elections, including violence between political parties, state repression of opposition supporters, terrorist attacks against democratic targets, or fighting by antigovernment militias. Staniland (2014) trying to organize the large literature on election violence, suggests that we ought to distinguish between intrasystemic and antisystemic election violence. Intrasystemic violence refers to violence used by various actors to affect the outcome of the election, while antisystemic violence refers to violence used by various actors to overthrow the institutions and the status quo. Höglund's (2009) definition and the focus on election violence as electoral manipulation calls for a focus on intrasystemic violence. Indeed, as Staniland (2014) suggests, we should not assume that the causes and consequences of intra- and antisystemic violence are the same.[4] Apart from the focus on intrasystemic violence, the other limitation in Höglund's definition is the focus on the physical act of violence, partly due to its observability. It is, however, important to note that actual violent events are often the tip of the iceberg in environments entrenched in fear and intimidation.

These limitations apart, the definition provided here is relatively broad. It does not put limits in terms of perpetrators or victims. Actors involved in election violence can include parties, voters, election officials or the state apparatus itself through the violence by the police or military (Levitsky and Way 2010; Mueller 2011; Bob-Milliar 2014). While the government party is the most common perpetrator of violence, the opposition can also use violence to achieve electoral goals (Taylor et al. 2019).

---

[4] For a useful empirical application of the terms antisystemic and intrasystemic election violence see Harbers et al. (2023).

Importantly, the definition also is not restricted to violence with lethal outcomes. Indeed, one of the main contributions of the book is to appropriately theorize and empirically measure low-scale violence. Violence in elections is often low-scale and may include forms of violence such as beatings, use of teargas, or destruction of property, to mention a few examples. In fact, for many citizens living in African democracies, where violence has been a part of election campaigns, lethal violence is not the sort of violence they are the most likely to encounter in their day-to-day life. For instance, in a survey fielded in April 2022 in Lusaka, we asked 2964 randomly selected respondents to give examples—in their own words—of violence that happen during elections. Among the respondents, only 19% mentioned killings or death as an example of election violence, while 68% mentioned fighting or beatings (von Borzyskowski and Wahman 2022).[5]

The literature has often been assumed that the more lethal the violence, the more it will affect electoral outcomes. However, we cannot a priori assume that only violence that result in the most serious consequences affects electoral outcomes. In fact, it is reasonable to expect that fatal violence is suboptimal for violent perpetrators. Electoral manipulation is most effective when it shapes behavior without incurring high reputational costs for the perpetrator (Cheeseman and Klaas 2019). High-scale lethal violence comes with great costs for perpetrators and risk to erode the legitimacy of governments involved (van Ham and Lindberg 2015). It can result in criminal charges, as in Kenya after the 2007 election (Brown and Sriram 2012), or international sanctions, as in the case of brutal election violence in Zimbabwe 2008 (Grebe 2010).[6] Low-scale violence does not come with the same reputational cost. Most commonly it goes unnoticed by the international community.

1.2 Existing Approaches to the Study of Campaign Violence

The literature on campaign violence has grown considerably in recent years (e.g. Birch et al. 2020); still the field remains somewhat fractured in two main traditions. On the one hand, part of the field has studied violence during elections as a case of conflict (e.g. Davenport 1997; Reno 1998; Dunning 2011; Brancati and Snyder 2013; Goldsmith 2015; von Borzyskowski 2019). This

---

[5] The data were coded from the open-ended responses. The exact question in the survey was: "When you think about 'intimidation and violence' that happens during elections, can you tell me one or two examples that you think about?"

[6] The more dramatic and internationally visible the trigger event, the higher the likelihood of democratic sanctions (von Soest and Wahman 2015).

literature has highlighted how elections exacerbate existing conflict and political grievances, particularly in post-conflict environments. In this strand of work, researchers have focused more on the physical costs of conflict (most particularly the number of fatalities) than the electoral or democratic consequences. A second tradition—more inspired by comparative politics literature on electoral integrity—has focused on election violence as a case of electoral manipulation (Hafner-Burton et al. 2014; van Ham and Lindberg 2015; Fjelde and Höglund 2016; Taylor et a. 2017; Birch 2020; Fjelde 2020). This literature has found great inspiration in conflict theories for understanding the nature and consequences of violence, but remained more focused on the ways that violence directly affects electoral behavior.

While we are gaining a better understanding of the behavioral consequences of campaign violence, the literature would still benefit from a closer dialog with the literature on parties and elections. Indeed, although campaign violence remains one of the most important forms of electoral manipulation, it is still one of the most poorly understood. In particular, more research is needed to understand how particular modes of political campaigns and mobilization create specific incentives for election violence. This is one of the main ambitions of this book.

Quantitative work on election violence has traditionally been mostly cross-national, studying the correlates of election violence. In Africa and elsewhere, two factors stand out as particularly associated with higher prospects of violence. First, violence is more likely when electoral stakes are high. Regimes are more likely to engage in violence when the president stands for re-election (Taylor et al. 2017) when they have been involved in grand corruption (Birch 2020), when alteration in power is rare (Ruiz-Rufino and Birch 2020), or when elections are contested in the context of deep economic or ethnic grievances (Boone 2011; Dercon and Gutiérrez-Romero 2012). Second, violence is more likely when the election outcome is uncertain (Hafner-Burton et al. 2014; Salehyan and Linebarger 2015; Fjelde and Höglund 2016). The costs make actors more likely to use violence when faced with higher uncertainty. However, while the relationship between uncertainty and election violence in Africa is robust at the national level, this research has not typically acknowledged that most African countries are electorally uncompetitive at the subnational level. More emphasis is needed on the within-country electoral dynamics promoting election violence as an electoral strategy.

Traditionally, most existing subnational research on election violence in Africa has been qualitative and aligned more with the conflict literature than the literature on electoral manipulation. Also, most of this work has focused on particular violent hotspots where elections are contested in the context of deep intergroup political conflict. Foundational research from countries such as Kenya and Côte d'Ivoire has described how politicized property rights have led to large-scale violence in regions with communal conflicts over competing claims to land ownership (Kanyinga 2009; Boone 2011; Klaus and Mitchell 2015; Klaus 2020). These studies offer a highly convincing explanation for electoral violence in specifically violent hotspots within some of the most violent elections in recent African electoral history. However, with a singular focus on the most extreme hotspots, such theories are not necessarily broadly applicable to explaining subnational variations in electoral violence within a broader set of countries and across the territory.

There has been a recent surge in more election-related quantitative literature on subnational variations in election violence (e.g. Fielding 2018; Choi and Raleigh 2021; Müller-Crepon 2021; Harbers et al. 2023). Much of the subnational research has again focused on the importance of political competition. Similar to cross national literature, this research has mainly argued that local-level competition enhances the incentives for election violence (e.g. Bangura and Söderberg Kovacs 2018; Reeder and Seeberg 2018). However, this conclusion is highly conditioned on modes of political mobilization and incentives created by institutional arrangements. For instance, in his argument about ethnic violence during elections in India, Wilkinson (2004) argues that election violence can be used to foster ethnic voting cohesion in Indian elections where social class acts as a cross-cutting cleavage. However, since violence is costly, parties will be mostly incentivized to engage in violence in subnational units where elections are close. Although Wilkinson's argument is convincing in the Indian case, the thesis does not travel well to the context of African geographically polarized electoral systems. Cross-cutting cleavages are generally absent and constituencies are more likely to vote uniformly in line with mobilized regional cleavages. Moreover, while national majorities in the parliamentary democracy of India are secured by winning minimum winning coalitions in a majority of the country's Single Member District (SMD) electoral districts, majorities in most African presidential elections are won by mobilizing a party's regional base and winning regional strongholds with great margins (Chapters 3 and 6).[7]

A third and final strand of research has adopted a more behavioral lens to understanding subnational variations in campaign violence across

---

[7] Also see Malik (2018) on the importance of electoral institutions for the geographical distribution of election violence.

the territory. This strand of research is most directly relevant for the themes discussed in this book. Most of the research in this tradition has been inspired by micro-level research on the behavioral consequences of electoral violence (e.g. Gonzalez-Ocantos et al. 2020; Gutiérrez-Romero and Lebas 2020; Young 2020; Rosenzweig 2021). Extrapolating from micro-level studies, researchers have produced hypotheses about the sort of locations that should be most conducive to violence. A key insight from this literature is that campaign violence may be conceived as the mirror image of vote buying; while vote buying is used to drive supporters to the polls, campaign violence is used to demobilize the support of rival parties (Collier and Vicente 2012; Gonzalez-Ocantos et al. 2020). According to this logic, parties will use violence in their opposing parties' strongholds to deter turnout (Rauschenbach and Paula 2019). However, engaging more deeply with research on African electoral sociology, I argue that most behavioral approaches to election violence have underestimated the consequences of campaign violence in fundamentally shaping electoral environments. Space has been ascribed, at best, secondary importance and used simply as a stand-in for other spatially clustered cleavages, such as ethnicity or partisanship. In extension, this literature has not directly addressed the potentially detrimental effect of violence on the quality of local-level democracy.

1.3 The Argument in Brief

A central tenant in this book is that election violence can be understood as a form of electoral manipulation (Birch 2007). Seen in this light, a theory of election violence cannot be separated from theories of voting and elections. Parties will use violence and other forms of manipulation strategically to further their electoral goals corresponding to the structure of electoral competition. Contextual factors such as electoral system design, social cleavages, and party systems will shape incentives and how violence features into the electoral process. Therefore, theories of campaign violence will often be restricted in generalizability. In this book, I will particularly focus on the dynamics of election violence in African countries where regionalism functions as a major political cleavage. I here present an electoral geography theory of campaign violence, a theory stressing the importance of space and territoriality. In this theory, parties are the main actors that actively use violence in a strategic manner to control territory in order to control voters. The argument laid out here is descriptive rather than causal. The main task of the book is not to prove a unidirectional causal chain between local-level competition and electoral violence. Instead, I want to map the occurrence of violence across space to make a broader argument about the role of violence within local electoral markets. This task is important in order to better grasp how electoral violence works as a form of electoral manipulation in contemporary Africa. To summarize the argument, I provide Figure 1.1. The figure illustrates how the theory moves from arguments about the nature of political competition to the structure of political competition, subnational variations in campaign violence, and micro-level consequences.

The theoretical foundation of the main argument is presented in the first box (to the left) in Figure 1.1. Regional patterns in African voting have often been considered a reflection of underlying cleavages, particularly spatial clustering of ethnicity (e.g. Arriola 2013; Horowitz 2016; Seekings 2020). However, an alternative view has argued that regional cleavages, beyond individual-level ethnic identity, shape much of partisan politics in Africa (e.g. Kalipeni 1997a; Kim 2017; Boone et al. 2022). My analysis of Zambia and Malawi confirms the fundamental importance of regional cleavages. However, while regional cleavages may structure political competition in lasting and predictable ways, parties still need to translate cleavages to political mobilization (Lipset and

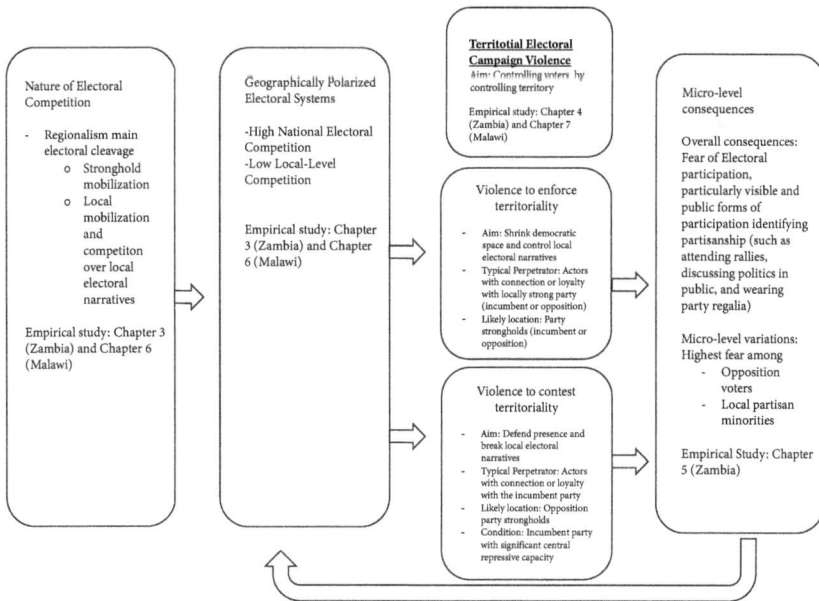

Figure 1.1 Illustration of Main Argument.

Rokkan 1967). African party systems, both locally and nationally, have been characterized by high levels of volatility (Wahman 2014; Weghorst and Bernhard 2014; Kuenzi et al. 2019) and individual party organizations often do not have strong and long-lasting connections to particular regions. Instead, a party's position in the local electoral market needs to be constantly and actively cultivated. Parties attach themselves to regional cleavages by controlling local electoral narratives.

For parties to affect local electoral narratives, local presence is key. Narratives and interpretations of elections are formed locally, perceptions of viability are interpreted largely based on local presence, and the translation of regional cleavages to partisan politics is negotiated in the local electoral market place (Horowitz and Long 2016; Letsa 2019). This interpretation of electoral competition has been referred to as *localism* in the electoral geography literature (Agnew 1987). To boost local presence, parties in Africa have been known to devote huge amounts of resources to local-level campaigns (Horowitz 2016; Paget 2019; Gadjanova 2021). Local campaigning allows parties to attach themselves to locally important issues, create expectations of future advocacy, and build trust. National elections in such environments are often not won by winning swing voters in swing districts (Rauschenbach 2015; Horowitz 2016). Instead, parties that effectively capture local electoral narratives can dominate local electoral markets. The fate of political campaigns will be decided by the extent to which parties can mobilize voters in strongholds and win them with great margins.

The resulting structure of political competition is one where parties create alternate national coalitions by mobilizing opposing local supermajorities (second box of Figure 1.1). In this book, I use the term *geographically polarized electoral systems* to refer to electoral systems that combine high levels of national-level competition with low levels of local competition. This form of mobilization has been particularly common in African electoral systems that combine SMD plurality elections with national presidential elections. In such systems, parties have been incentivized to build distinct regional bases and win national majorities through stronghold mobilization. Prominent examples of geographically polarized electoral systems include Kenya, Malawi, Zambia, Ghana, Zimbabwe, Cotê d'Ivoire, Sierra Leone, and Nigeria.

In geographically polarized electoral systems, electoral competition is real. However, most voters will experience little of this competition in their local environments. The term geographically polarized electoral systems should not be confused with the term "political polarization", often used to describe a process in which voters and parties move to more extreme positions on the political policy spectrum (Somer et al. 2021) or increased conflict between parties (Lebas 2006). Instead, the term geographically polarized is taken from the electoral geography literature to refer simply to the geographic distribution of votes (Johnston et al. 2020).

Geographically polarized electoral systems are different than systems that are more competitive both nationally and subnationally, such as Cape Verde, Senegal, Liberia, and the Seychelles. They are also different than more hegemonic regimes such as Uganda, Tanzania, Cameroon, and Rwanda. Hegemonic regimes may have opposition enclaves, such as the Northwest region of Cameroon (Letsa 2019) or the Kilimanjaro region of Tanzania (McLellan 2020). However, these opposition enclaves are few and do not threaten the incumbent party's grip on national power, at least in the short term.

How does the nature of localized campaigns in geographically polarized electoral systems affect how parties engage in campaign violence across subnational locations (third box of Figure 1.1)? This is the main question of the book. In an electoral system largely shaped by localism and highly structured around regional cleavages, but where local political allegiances can shift, campaign violence becomes an important tool in parties' attempts to restrict and gain access to local electoral market places. In other words, we can think of election violence as a territorial tool.

Campaign violence can relate to territoriality in two ways. First, locally strong parties can use violence to enforce territoriality. While local volatility has been high in many African elections and regional cleavages need to be constantly activated, violence can be an important tool to shrink the democratic space. The opening anecdote from Thyolo in the Southern Region of Malawi is an illustrative example of this sort of violence. When the locally strong party (DPP) used violence to shut down the local challenger (PP), it did so to enforce its monopoly on the local electoral narrative. Violence significantly curtailed the government party's ability to campaign in the district, resulting in DPP maintaining its role as the uncontested promoter of regional interests.

A noteworthy feature of the Thyolo incident is that the attack was perpetrated by the opposition party. While the literature suggests that government parties and their associates are the most common perpetrators of election violence (Taylor et al. 2019), this is not necessarily the case when it comes to violence designed to enforce territoriality. Opposition parties mostly lack central capacity for violence. They do, however, typically have repressive capacity within their strongholds. In other words, both opposition and incumbent parties can use violence in their strongholds to enforce territorial control. Parties perpetrating violence within their strongholds is puzzling from the perspective of most existing theorizing about election violence, but empirical descriptions from Zambia and Malawi will show that this is not at all uncommon. The concept of territoriality helps us theoretically grasp the motivations that may explain such incidents of violence. We can imagine territorial motivations for election violence also in more competitive sublocations, especially if sublocations are divided into discrete political zones with varying allegiances (e.g. across different neighborhoods in a city or different traditional authority zones in a more rural constituency). However, in most cases, such territorial dynamics would be less likely in competitive subunits and campaign violence would be less effective as a tool to establish territorial control.

Second, election violence can be used to contest territoriality held by locally strong parties. Parties able to create a foothold in rival parties' strongholds can upset the rival's momentum within key geographic areas. As opposed to violence used to enforce territoriality, violence to contest territoriality often requires central repressive capacity. Most commonly, such capacity overwhelmingly rests with the ruling party. Indeed, the ruling party often uses violence in opposition strongholds to display its central repressive capacity and undermine the impression that the opposition has enough territorial control in its strongholds to shield its supporters from the possible negative consequences of mobilizing on behalf of the opposition.

The highest central capacity for violence will be found in cases where the ruling party holds a strong command of central institutions, most importantly repressive institutions such as the police and military, but also the institutions that are assigned with the important task of overseeing and adjudicating elections, such as Election Management Bodies (EMB) and courts. Without strong and neutral institutions, the ruling party can use the state as a repressive resource, often with impunity (Hassan 2017).

The combination of a government party with high central repressive capacity and an opposition with high local repressive capacity has often rendered opposition strongholds hotbeds for election violence (Rauschenbach and Paula 2019). In this book, I particularly focus on the importance of central repressive capacity for subnational patterns of violence. Empirically, I contrast Zambia and Malawi in this regard. While Zambia had a strong government party with significant central repressive capacity, Malawi had a remarkably weak ruling party. In Zambia, opposition strongholds were particularly prone to election violence, but in Malawi strongholds of the government and opposition party were equally likely to experience violence.

I have argued that parties mostly use election violence to affect electoral environments. However, environments change because individuals change their behavior (right-most box in Figure 1.1). I argue that the territorial election violence described above will make local partisan minorities particularly fearful of violence in elections. The most fearful will be partisan minorities inside another party's stronghold. Dominant parties will attempt to quell local minorities' political participation to protect territoriality. I also argue that local minority voters will be particularly fearful of participating in highly visible forms of partisan participation. Such forms of participation are particularly challenging for parties trying to assert territoriality. While reluctance to participate in visible forms of participation, such as wearing party regalia, discussing politics in public, and attending campaign rallies may have little consequence for particular individuals' (particularly strong partisans) vote choice or likelihood to vote, such engagement is crucial for the local political environment. In the localized electoral market described above visibility and local presence is key for forming local electoral narratives.

The argument presented here will be fleshed out throughout the book. The theory will be explained in greater detail in Chapter 2 and the nature of election competition will be developed in Chapter 3 (Zambia) and 6 (Malawi). Chapters 4 (Zambia) and 7 (Malawi) will analyze subnational patterns of election violence, while Chapter 5 will look into micro-level consequences. The argument presented here suggests that election violence may be perceived as an important tool in the subnational authoritarian toolbox (McMann 2006; Gibson 2013; Giraudy 2015). While few voters will experience violence directly, the fear of violence and the electoral environment created as a product of such fear is antithetical to a vibrant democracy. In countries like Zambia and Malawi, few people die as a consequence of electoral violence, but violence is still a major concern for ordinary voters.

1.4 Case Selection and Scope Conditions

This book will focus on two particular cases, Zambia and Malawi. Both of these countries are clear examples of geographically polarized electoral systems, but neither one of them have featured prominently in the election violence literature (some important exceptions include Höglund 2017; Brosché et al. 2020; Kapesa et al. 2020). They are, however, not the only examples of geographically polarized electoral systems on the African continent. To obtain a snapshot of the relationship between national-level and local-level competition, I collected subnational-level electoral data for as many African countries as possible. I used 2015 as my baseline year and used this year or the closest previous election year[8] (with available disaggregated data) to gauge differences between national-level and local-level election results.[9] To calculate the difference between local-level competition and national-level competition, I calculated the average vote share at the local-level (constituency or district) for the locally most popular presidential candidate. I then divided this vote share with the vote share for the winning candidate at the national level.[10] The resulting data are displayed in Figure 1.2. Values below 1 indicate higher levels of competition at the subnational level than at the national level.

Figure 1.2 shows that most African countries are significantly more competitive nationally than subnationally. The prominence of geographically polarized electoral systems in Africa illustrates the prevailing importance of regionalism in African electoral politics. The focus on geographically polarized electoral systems can be understood as a scope condition for the argument

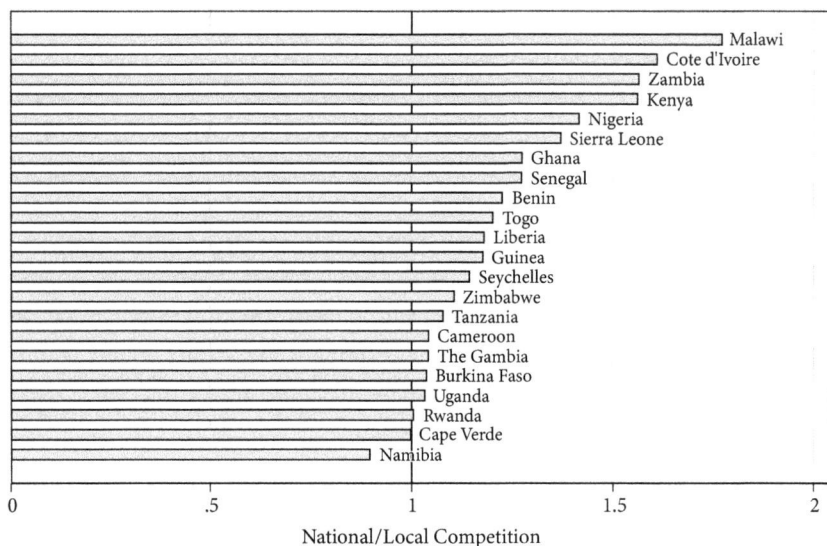

Figure 1.2 Ratio National/Local Level Competition.

Note: The figure shows the ratio between the average national-level competition and the local-level for presidential elections.

[8] I here use data for Benin 2011, Burkina Faso 2015, Cameroon 2011, Cape Verde 2011, Cote d'Ivoire 2010, Ghana 2012, Guinea 2015, Kenya 2013, Liberia 2011, Malawi 2014, Namibia 2014, Nigeria 2015, Rwanda 2010, Senegal 2012, Tanzania 2010, The Gambia 2011, Togo 2015, Uganda 2011, Zambia 2011, Zimbabwe 2013.

[9] If possible, I used constituency-level presidential election data. However, disaggregated election data is hard to find for many African elections, particularly in presidential elections (Fridy 2009). If such data were not available, I used district (admin 2-level) data. If no such data were available, I excluded the country from the sample.

[10] In the case of multiple election rounds, I use data from the first round of voting.

formulated in this book. However, it is also possible that some of the dynamics described here could be applicable to some hegemonic multiparty regimes as heavy-handed incumbent regimes attempt to suppress election campaigns in opposition enclaves.[11]

Before laying out the rationale for selecting Malawi and Zambia among other possible African geographically polarized electoral systems, it is useful to illustrate how they compare to other African countries in terms of the dependent variable (election violence). Figure 1.3 scatters two vital variables, the cumulative number of fatalities from election violence and reported fear of election violence among voters. The data on fatalities are collected from the Deadly Electoral Conflict Dataset (DECO), a dataset based on events collected in news media and election reports (Fjelde and Höglund 2022). It reports the total number of fatalities in a country 1990–2017. Data on fear of violence are collected from the 7th round of the Afrobarometer. I here concentrate on the share of voters expressing the highest level of fear, stating that they fear election violence "a lot."

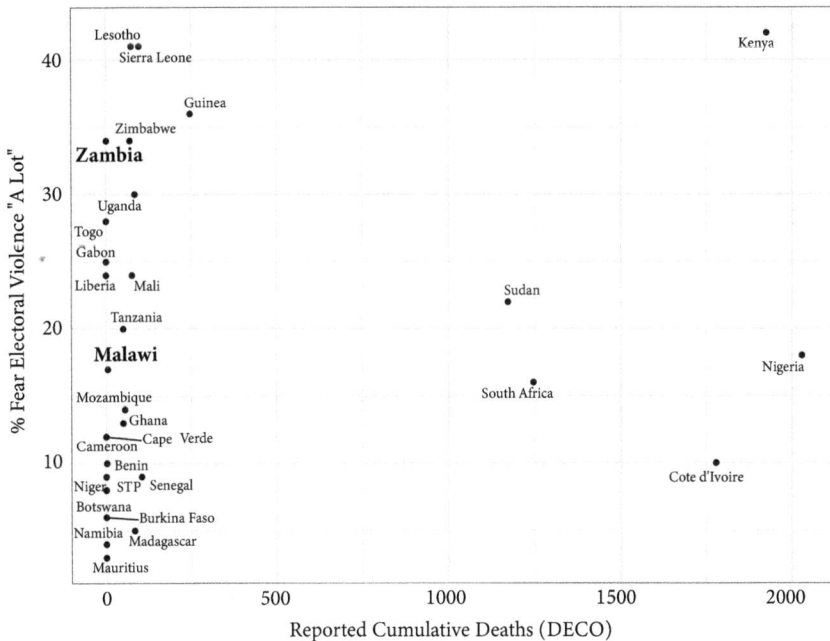

Figure 1.3 Election Violence in Africa.

Note: Data from Afrobarometer Round 7 and Fjelde and Höglund (2022).

---

[11] For instance, such dynamics have been observed in cases such as Uganda (Abrahamsen and Bareebe 2016).

Measured in terms of fatalities, elections in Zambia and Malawi do not stand out as particularly affected by violence. According to the DECO data, Zambia has only one recorded death, while Malawi has five. Although more deaths have been documented in other sources, it is undeniably the case that both Zambia and Malawi have had relatively few fatalities due to election violence.

Despite few lethal events of election violence, fear of election violence is significant in both countries. In fact, Zambia is one of the countries in Africa where voters fear election violence the most. In Zambia, as much as 36% of voters fear election violence "a lot." If we also consider voters that fear election violence "somewhat" and "a little," we find that 64% of voters in Zambia have some level of fear during elections. To put this in perspective, only 17% of Zambians stated that they had been exposed to vote buying at least once (in the same Afrobarometer survey).[12] While fear of violence in Malawi is lower, 17% still say they fear election violence "a lot", and 43% say that they fear election violence to some extent. The share of Malawian voters having a high level of fear is similar to the levels reported in Nigeria, the country with the highest number of reported fatalities (2,029 killed). In fact, looking at the data in Figure 1.3, there is almost no correlation between the extent to which voters fear election violence and the number of reported cumulative deaths due to election violence.

It is noteworthy that almost all writing on election violence in Africa has concentrated on cases far out on the x-axis in Figure 1.3. Cases such as Côte d'Ivoire, Kenya, and Nigeria (e.g. Kanyinga 2009; Omotola 2009; Angerbrandt 2018; Klaus 2020; Smidt 2020) have received almost all attention in the election violence literature. All these countries are geographically polarized electoral systems, but most of these cases also have deep underlying conflicts not directly related to elections. Much less is known about the nature and function of violence in other cases such as Sierra Leone, Lesotho, Guinea, and Zambia, where election violence is a major concern for voters but where the number of fatalities is less extreme.[13]

Low fatalities make Zambia and Malawi "hard cases" for showing the impact of election violence on elections. Nevertheless, illustrating the patterns of low-scale violence is essential for expanding our understanding of election violence

---

[12] It is, however, important to keep in mind that survey questions about acceptance of bribes may suffer from social desirability bias, as respondents may be reluctant to admit that they received a gift in exchange for a vote (Gonzalez-Ocantos et al. 2012)

[13] The main exception is probably Zimbabwe, a well documented country in the election violence literature (e.g. Lebas 2006; Young 2020). However, while Zimbabwe has only mid-levels of documented electoral violence deaths in DECO (70), the violence in the country has still been severe and highly visible.

as a form of electoral manipulation in Africa. The data in Figure 1.3 suggest that cases like Zambia and Malawi are far more representative of the continent than cases such as Nigeria and Côte d'Ivoire. In most cases where election violence is a prominent factor in the mind of voters, the number of fatalities is relatively low and violence tends to be mostly low-scale.[14]

Zambia and Malawi also serve as a good pair of comparative cases. Subnational research requires significant investment in data collection. For this reason, most subnational work tends to focus on only one national context and, consequently, suffers from limited external validity (Snyder 2001). Perhaps more importantly, there is an emerging recognition in the conflict literature that macro-level (e.g. county), meso-level (e.g. subnational), and micro-level (e.g. individual) factors interact in complex ways (Balcells and Stanton 2021). In this book, I will particularly focus on how centralized repressive capacity shapes subnational patterns in election violence. While Zambia and Malawi share many similarities, the government party in the 2014 Malawi election was significantly weaker than the government party in the 2016 Zambian election. Important literature on electoral manipulation has suggested that the institutional strength of incumbent parties is vital for their capacity to manipulate elections and that the forms of manipulation used by incumbents will be contingent on their strength and institutional control (Levitsky and Way 2010; van Ham and Lindberg 2015; Seeberg 2018). The comparison between Zambia and Malawi allows me to study how central capacity plays into subnational variations in election violence and how central and local political dynamics interplay in producing varying preconditions for violence.

Besides focusing on African geographically polarized electoral systems, there are also two additional scope conditions of the argument to clarify. First, it is not clear that the book's argument is applicable to countries with radically different electoral systems than Malawi and Zambia. One important component of the argument is that parties try to win supermajorities inside their strongholds to win national majorities. However, violent dynamics may look rather different in systems where parties have to win subnational majorities, for instance to win a majority of parliamentary seats in parliamentary democracies (Wilkinson 2004; Müller-Crepon 2022). Second, as discussed in the section on definitions of election violence, I am here focusing on intrasystemic

---

[14] Levels of fear shown in Figure 1.3 establish that election violence is not a marginal phenomenon in Africa and plays a significant role, even in cases where violence does not result in many casualties. Figure 1.3 only exhibits the share of voters with the highest level of fear, those that fear violence "a lot." However, if we also consider voters that express "some" or "a little" fear of becoming victims of election violence, we learn that more than 40% of respondents feel some level of fear in 22/32 sub-Saharan African countries in the sample of Afrobarometer's 7th round.

violence, i.e. violence intended to affect the outcomes of elections (Staniland 2014). The theory presented here would not be applicable to environments where much of the violence is antisystemic, for instance, in elections held in contexts with significant insurgent or terrorist activity (Harbers et al. 2023).

1.5 Data

One of the major contributions of this book is the multitude of data that it brings to bear on the theme of subnational variations in campaign violence. The book relies on multiple rounds of fieldwork in both Malawi and Zambia during seven years, including three unique surveys, multiple focus groups, and qualitative interviews with local-level domestic observers as well as secondary analysis of newspaper articles, election reports, and court records. The main ambition with the data collection strategy is to study the topic of election violence from the bottom up, but to do so in a systematic manner to avoid regional biases in the data collection. I wanted to access both nationwide quantitative data and local-level narratives about elections and the use of violence. One of the main challenges was to design data collection strategies that did not miss out on reports of low-scale violence. Throughout the process, I have worked closely with domestic civil society in Zambia and Malawi, most importantly the domestic election observers the National Initiative for Civic Education (NICE) in Malawi and the Foundation for Democratic Process (FODEP) and the Southern African Center for Constructive Resolution of Disputes (SACCORD) in Zambia.

The most challenging empirical task is to map the dependent variable, campaign violence, across space. This is also where this book makes its most important methodological innovation. I introduce two new datasets on constituency-level election violence: the Malawi Election Monitor Survey (MEMS) and the Zambian Election Monitor Survey (ZEMS). The surveys utilize the experience of domestic election observers and treat them as experts to collect detailed event narratives about election violence in the constituency they monitored throughout the election. In a separate article, co-authored with Inken von Borzyskowski (von Borzyskowski and Wahman 2021), we describe in detail the methodological benefits of this approach and compare it to the most feasible alternative, media-based event data provided by sources such as the Armed Conflict Location and Event Data Project (ACLED) (Raleigh et al. 2010) and the Social Conflict Analysis Database (SCAD) (Salehyan et al. 2012). Media-based event data have become the standard for studying subnational variations in election violence (e.g. Reeder and Seeberg 2018; Daxecker 2020; Choi and Raleigh 2021; Müller-Crepon 2022); for research studying violence over time or across many countries, there might not be many other options than to rely on such more easily accessible data. Nevertheless, media-based event data suffer from serious biases, most importantly because the media is most likely to pick up on serious incidents of violence, particularly if they happen in urban areas with greater penetration of media and civil society. In my article with von Borzyskowski (von Borzyskowski and Wahman 2021), we find several benefits with the observer-based approach used here: it is more able to capture low-scale violence, it is less prone to underreporting of violence in rural areas, and more likely to pick up on violence outside anticipated violence hotspots. In the end, we conclude that the data used for most subnational research on election violence may have biased the results of earlier research.

The data collection strategy adopted here is resource-intense but necessary if we hypothesize that much violence will happen in strongholds far away from national attention and commonly be low-scale. To complement the MEMS and ZEMS data, I also use geocoded data from the Afrobarometer and a new voter survey from the 2021 Zambian election. Although voter surveys have been used before in other important work on election violence (e.g. Bratton 2008; Rauschenbach and Paula 2019; von Borzyskowski and Kuhn 2020), I particularly use geocoded data on election violence to understand how individual-level characteristics interact with location characteristics to increase the fear of election violence.

1.6 The Organization of the Book

This book wishes to make contributions both to the African electoral geography literature and the literature on election violence. It aims to empirically study regional patterns of African elections and macro-electoral trends and particularly discuss how subnational political dominance shapes African elections. In particular, it will describe the way that campaign violence varies across space and how electoral geography shapes such subnational variations.

Chapter 2 fleshes out the theoretical argument of the book. I start this chapter by discussing the nature of political competition in geographically polarized electoral systems. I discuss the electoral dynamics that promote regionalization of politics and discuss different potential explanations for geographic polarization. I move on to discuss how such campaign incentives will affect the use of violence in geographically polarized electoral systems. I argue that electoral geography is key for understanding the use of campaign violence in electoral systems with strong regional cleavages.

In Chapter 3, I introduce the history of multiparty elections and electoral geography in the case of Zambia. I use constituency-level election results from presidential elections to show how elections in Zambia have become increasingly regionalized. Although regionalism is a major cleavage in Zambian elections, parties also attempt to actively mobilize regional cleavages. National elections in Zambia have historically been won by strongly mobilizing regional cleavages and boosting turnout and vote margins in regional strongholds. In such an environment, controlling space is crucial for the prospects of winning national electoral contests.

Chapter 4 empirically analyzes campaign violence in the Zambian 2016 election. The chapter uses both qualitative data collected from focus groups with domestic election observers and quantitative data from ZEMS. The chapter describes the nature of election violence in the 2016 campaign, map violence across space, and analyzes the characteristics of constituencies most affected by violence. The qualitative analysis shows the pervasiveness of low-scale campaign violence in the 2016 election and highlights how such violence was organized and employed in a territorial way. In the quantitative part of the chapter, I employ the data from ZEMS to establish broader correlational trends between electoral geography and campaign violence. The analysis reveals that campaign violence was concentrated in party strongholds. Both opposition and incumbent party strongholds were affected by campaign violence, but especially those that drew many votes for the opposition.

Chapter 5 studies the micro-foundations of election violence in Zambia. Using geocoded Afrobarometer data and data from the Zambia Electoral Panel Survey (ZEPS) (Lust et al. 2021), I show two main findings: (i) that partisan minority voters residing in party strongholds, particularly strongholds held by the government party, are the most fearful of election violence; and (ii) that fear of election violence is more associated with forms of political participation such as attending rallies, wearing party regalia, and discussing politics in public, than voting. Fear of such activities is especially pronounced among opposition party supporters and local partisan minorities. These findings support the claim made in this book that violence can be used as a territorial tool to shape local campaign environments.

Chapter 6 introduces the case of Malawi, by focusing on the history of democracy and electoral geography. Like Zambia, Malawian elections are highly characterized by electoral regionalism. However, unlike Zambia, most successful parties competing in Malawian elections have been largely monoregional. The chapter also particularly introduces the rather unique 2014 election and discusses how the government lacked many of the incumbent advantages usually associated with new African democracies. I argue that a lack of central repressive capacity will reduce the government party's ability to use violence to contest territoriality in opposition party strongholds.

Chapter 7 extends the empirical analysis to the Malawi 2014 election. Although violence has not been quite as widespread in Malawi as in Zambia, it has still played a crucial role in elections. I use qualitative accounts to illustrate the pervasiveness of no-go zone politics in Malawi, not only in 2014 but throughout Malawian electoral history. The chapter models subnational election violence using the MEMS data. As in Zambia, I find that campaign violence is particularly common in party strongholds. However, contrary to Zambia, I do not find that opposition strongholds were particularly affected. I argue that the government party's limited centralized repressive capacity restricted their ability to use violence to contest territoriality.

Chapter 8 places the Zambian and Malawian cases in a wider context and probes the generalizability of the theory in other African geographically polarized electoral systems. First, using descriptive data of electoral polarization across the continent, I show that geographically polarized countries tend to have higher levels of violence than more subrationally competitive or nationally non-competitive countries. I also introduce two additional cases, Kenya and Zimbabwe, and show that, while different from Zambia and Malawi in many ways, campaign violence has still been highly territorial.

Chapter 9 offers conclusions and discusses further implications of my findings. I particularly emphasize the implications for cross-national research on election violence, electoral manipulation, and the study of subnational authoritarianism. Lastly, I discuss potential policy implications of the book and argue for more investment in maintaining quality data on subnational variations on electoral violence. I also particularly argue for a deeper appreciation of the possibly devastating effect that low-scale violence may have on the quality of elections and argue for bottom-up intervention strategies to solve electoral disputes locally.

2

An Electoral Geography Theory of Campaign Violence

In African democracies, electoral regionalism has often given rise to a geographically polarized electoral system; although national-level competition is high, political support is highly clustered spatially. Most of the cross-national research on African election violence has disregarded the importance of geographic electoral polarization and instead focused on aggregate levels of competition. In the subnational literature, previous scholars have paid some attention to electoral geography by acknowledging the existence of geographic electoral strongholds. However, such strongholds are a product of specific modes of political mobilization and indicative of the deeper nature of political competition. The use of campaign violence should be explicitly theorized in relation to such mobilization processes.

This chapter introduces an electoral geography theory of campaign violence. The theory is developed for the context of African geographically polarized electoral systems and builds from a particular understanding of voting and political mobilization. In contrast to much earlier work on this topic, I argue that geographic polarization cannot simply be understood from the geographic distribution of different ethnic groups but is also a consequence of the electoral campaign itself. Space is not merely a stand-in for the geographic clustering of segmental cleavages, but an important factor in political mobilization. I evoke the concept of localism to describe how electoral expectations and interpretations are created locally and argue that parties compete over the mobilization of regional cleavages. This understanding of elections in geographically polarized electoral systems suggests that election campaigns are not simply designed to win the support of individual voters but also entire local communities. In this context, the importance of violence goes beyond the individual-level effect on voting behavior among directly targeted voters. Instead, it shapes entire local electoral environments. Political actors can use violence to regulate space, limit local political pluralism, and challenge prevailing local electoral narratives about viability and advocacy. This view of election

Controlling Territory, Controlling Voters. Michael Wahman, Oxford University Press.
© Michael Wahman (2023). DOI: 10.1093/oso/9780198872825.003.0002

violence suggests that violence, even the low-scale type that remains most common in African elections, has the potential to distort political competition. When local electoral environments are entrenched in violence and coercion, political pluralism suffers and violence becomes an essential instrument for upholding a form of subnational authoritarianism.

2.1 The Origin of Geographically Polarized Electoral Systems

Figure 1.2 of the introduction chapter shows how African countries, in general, have remained far more competitive at the national than at the local level. This pattern has persisted despite a general continent-wide trend towards increased national-level competition. In Figure 2.1, I measure levels of competition in presidential elections in 1989–2016. I measure competition in two ways, first the turnover rate (i.e. whether there was executive turnover as a consequence of the election) and, secondly, the level of competition, measured as the ratio of the second vote-getter to the first vote-getter. Data are collected

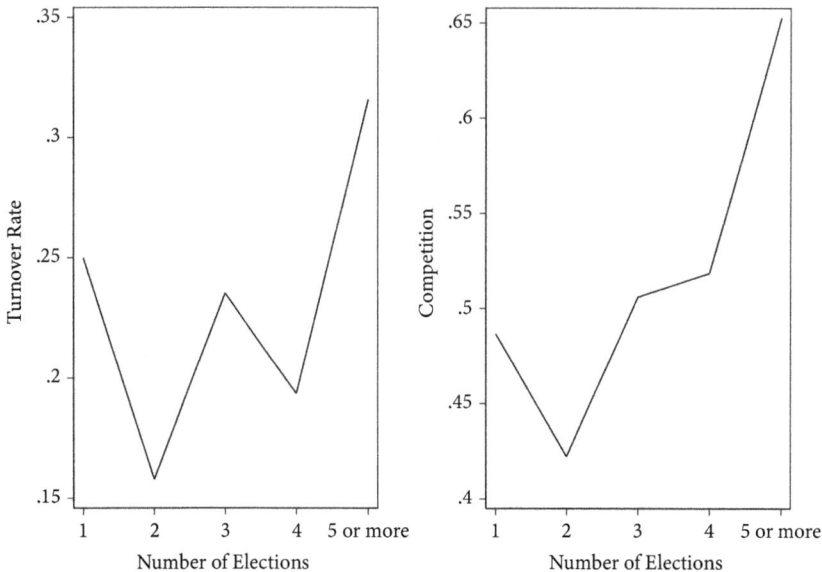

Figure 2.1 National Competition in African Presidential elections 1989–2016.

Note: Left panel shows the percentage of all elections resulting in a turnover. Right panel shows the level of competition measured as the ratio of second vote-getter to first. Data collected from the V-Dem dataset.

from the V-Dem dataset. Figure 2.1 shows that, regardless of measurement, Africa has experienced a significant increase in electoral competition nationally.

However, increased national-level competition has not necessarily been coupled with higher levels of subnational competition. In fact, looking at many African geographically polarized electoral systems, we see no relationship at all between national-level competition and local-level competition. In some cases, even the opposite; the more the opposition has been able to mobilize its regional base the more nationally competitive elections have become. For instance, Figure 2.2 shows the relationship between national-level and local-level competition in four geographically polarized electoral systems: Ghana, Kenya, Malawi, and Zambia. Here, I contrast the national-level competition for presidential elections with the average constituency-level presidential competition.[1] There is no relationship between local and national-level competition. In some cases, like Zambia, the relationship even appears inverted.

The literature has mainly understood increased national-level electoral competition as a product of ethnic coalition building (Arriola 2013). However, while such explanations provide a possible answer for increased national-level competition, they do not explain why local-level competition has often declined. Moreover, to understand the nature of political competition in geographically polarized electoral systems we need a deeper understanding of how geographic building blocks in national competition have remained so cohesive. Below, I will review different theoretical explanations for geographic clustering of vote choice in African politics. I will find inspiration in the nationalization literature and draw heavily on various accounts of electoral geography from Africa and the rest of the world. I will focus particularly on the importance of social cleavages (mainly ethnicity) and their distribution across space, regionalism, clientelism, and electoral institutions. Although all these various accounts of political nationalization in Africa have their distinct merits, I will argue for an approach where space matters in more intricate ways than a heavily deterministic understanding of electoral geography would suggest. Structural variations between regions matter in structuring the electoral map, but besides this basic structure, local organization, mobilization, and

---

[1] Competition is measured as the ratio between second vote-getter and first vote-getter. Nationally, this implies the ratio between the votes of the runner-up and the winner. Locally, this implies the ratio between the presidential candidate that won the second most votes in the constituency and the one that won the most votes.

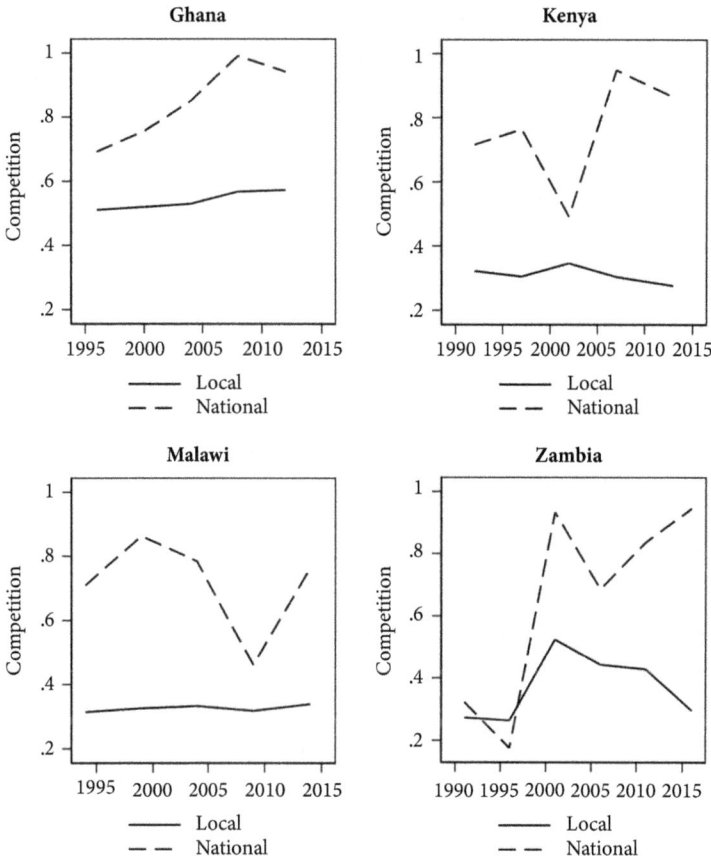

Figure 2.2 Local and National-level Competition over Time for Ghana, Kenya, Malawi, and Zambia.

Note: The figure shows the local average level of competition, measured as average ratio between constituency-level second vote-getter and the constituency-level first vote-getter, and the national-level competition measured as the ratio between the national first vote-getter and the second vote-getter. Presidential election results are used, as reported by national electoral commissions, with the exception of Malawi 1994, 1999, and 2004, where local competition is measured using parliamentary election results.

contestation of territorial control are also important for understanding electoral geography in Africa. Space matters, not only because spatial units vary along important national fault lines, but also because voters, particularly in non-nationalized and volatile party systems, make sense of elections within a predominantly local space. This is an important first step in establishing the connection between electoral geography and campaign violence in geographically polarized electoral systems.

2.1.1 Social Cleavages, Regionalism, Clientelism, and Electoral Institutions

The African voting literature has mostly attempted to explain the clustering of African vote choice with four sets of explanations: social cleavages, regionalism, clientelism, and electoral institutions. Below, I will review these different explanations, but also explain why in themselves they are unsatisfactory for understanding the nature of political competition in geographically polarized electoral systems.

Social Cleavages

More than anything else, the polarization of African vote choice across territory has been understood as a direct consequence of subnational variations in demographic composition. Building on research focusing on individual-level vote choice (e.g. Bratton et al. 2012), the dominant argument has assumed that individual-level determinants of vote choice, more or less neatly, aggregate to the subnational level to explain regional variation in vote choice. In this way, the dominant account of African electoral geography has much in common with earlier accounts of electoral geography in Western Europe, where scholars understood regional variations in vote choice as a reflection of the uneven distribution of groups across territory (Butler and Stokes 1969; Galli and Prandi 1970). Whereas most accounts of Western European electoral geography have concentrated on the uneven distribution of functional cleavages (predominantly social groups), African electoral studies have instead been concentrated almost exclusively on segmental cleavages, most importantly ethnicity, but also, to a lesser extent, a division based on urban/rural differences (Resnick 2014; Nathan 2019; Harding 2020).

It is hardly surprising that so much of spatial variation in voting in Africa has been explained by ethnicity. By global standards, African countries have extremely high levels of ethnic segregation (Alesina and Zhuravskaya 2011; Robinson 2020). After all, ethnic categories are themselves often regional identities reconstructed over time to fit political purposes (Posner 2005). Economic institutions, such as land rights, have also been constructed to reinforce local, ethnic identities (Boone 2014).[2]

---

[2] Indeed, de Miguel (2017) showed a strong relationship between ethnic segregation and the territorialization of politics in a global sample, particularly among countries with highly disproportionate electoral systems. Ishiyama (2012) finds that ethnic groups in Africa that are geographically concentrated are more prone to ethnic bloc voting.

Although, analytically, it is hard to completely dismiss the idea that the spatial distribution of social cleavages causes geographic polarization, there are several reasons to question that ethnic clustering alone determines geographic polarization. A growing literature in African politics has acknowledged that the predictive power of individual characteristics is highly contingent of contextual factors. For instance, Ichino and Nathan (2013) find that local minority populations in the case of Ghana have a high propensity to vote for the party associated with the local majority, even if this means "crossing the ethnic line."[3] Indeed, in related work, my coauthors and I found that geographical vote concentration is often higher than ethnic concentration in African democracies. The permanent regional voting blocs that structure African politics transcend the geographical area of traditional ethnic homelands (Boone et al. 2022). In other words, ethnicity seems to underdetermine the level of geographic clustering observed.

Regionalism

Much of the literature on African voting behavior has evoked the term "ethno-regionalism" without making much effort to disentangle the two composite terms *ethnicity* and *regionalism*. It is, however, possible that the two terms have become, at least partially, conflated. In their famous account of Western European party systems, Lipset and Rokkan (1967) describe the process of nationalization as one in which functional cleavages find priority over territorial cleavages. In earlier periods of the European nation-state, opposition to the nation-building project came from the territorial periphery, remote areas that struggled against the hegemony of the center. With low integration across regional entities, politics became a game of regional representation.

In African politics research, the fixation with ethnicity and the priority of individual-level research over approaches more sensitive to electoral geography has muted the emphasis on regionalism in most election research. Authors have either prioritized ethnicity over regionalism or simply surrendered to the fact that, empirically, the two are very hard to disentangle given their strong covariance and endogenous nature. For instance, in an analysis of individual-level voting behavior in nine different African countries, Basedau et al. (2011: 475) find that including regional dummies in a regression analysis drastically reduces the predictive power of ethnicity on voting.

---

[3] This pattern is also reaffirmed in the case of Malawi in a study by Dulani et al. (2021).

However, they conclude that "it is empirically difficult to disentangle ethnic from regional effects with the available sample."[4]

The absence of regionalism in most theorizing on African voting behavior is, perhaps, somewhat surprising. In Hetcher's (1975) understanding of British politics, ethnic divisions are largely contingent on uneven economic development across the territory. Economically marginalized groups in the periphery use ethnicity to mobilize against economic exploitation from the center.[5] Nevertheless, compared to most of the industrialized world, African regional economic inequalities are extraordinarily high. Such variations exist not only between rural and urban areas, but also between rural areas of high and low economic productivity. Summarizing different forms of data capturing spatial inequality, such as subnational GDP data, nightlight data, and survey-based poverty data, Boone and Simson (2019) show that African countries in general exhibit extremely high levels of spatial inequality by every indicator. Such differences in economic development may stem from historical variations in political institutions, infrastructure, and natural endowment. It is also often, at least partially, a product of regional politics itself and the regional priorities of political elites that have captured the power of the central state (Kasara 2007; Briggs 2012; Franck and Rainer 2012; Jablonski 2014). Economic marginalization of certain regions has led to demands for political decentralization and tension between the center and periphery on issues related to the institutional organization of the state (Kapesa et al. 2020).

Apart from variations in economic productivity, African regionalism is also fueled by sectoral interest. Research on African politics in the one-party era acknowledged such interests, perhaps most apparent in the relationship between the urban industrial proletariat, subsistence farmers, and producers of cash crops (e.g. Bates 1981). In the case of Zambia, Momba (1985) acknowledged a form of peasant differentiation developing after independence, where regional economic interest became crucial for interest formation and political mobilization. Other, more recent, contributions to these discussions have highlighted how multiethnic, regional coalitions have been created around similar sectoral interests, such as different types of regional crop production, in the multiparty state. Given local political economies, voters and regional

---

[4] Most individual-level analysis focusing on the effect of ethnicity on vote choice does not include controls for regionalism or employ any other more geographically sensitive estimation strategy (e.g. Bratton and Kimenyi 2008; Bratton et al. 2012; Hoffman and Long 2013; and Weghorst and Lindberg 2013).

[5] Related arguments have been made in the African politics literature, Houle et al. (2019), for instance, argue that intragroup political inequality enhances ethnic voting. This argument was, however, not directly related to electoral geography.

elites have come to favor varying economic policies and institutional solutions (Kim 2017; 2018).

Clientelism

Clientelistic, place-bound, politics has been regarded as the antithesis of political nationalization. In lieu of developed nationalized functional cleavages, Lipset (1960) argued that elections in nonintegrated democracies often take the form of regional competition for centralized resources. Much of the African literature on regional politics has developed along similar ideas. The African postcolonial state was one characterized by weak central authority. Indeed, the weak national institutions set up by colonial European powers were not designed to effectively control the entire territory and subnational authority was delegated to local intermediaries (Mamdani 1996; Herbst 2000). For Africa's post-independence leaders, establishing territorial control was a mammoth task. According to van de Walle (2007), a system of prebendalism (in combination with institutional centralization) became an essential governing strategy for African leaders in poorly integrated states. In the prebendal African state, central leaders could use centralized economic resources to incorporate local elites, with large local popular following, into the central winning coalition. Some African regimes were more regionally inclusive than others, but few states could be ruled from one region or ethnic group alone (Arriola 2009; Roessler 2011; Albrecht 2015).

Local intermediaries embedded in complex clientelistic networks have been central to much theorizing of local bloc voting in Africa and elsewhere. For instance, important literature on the role of African chiefs and other local intermediaries has argued that African regimes have created strong relationships with (predominantly) rural elites and used them as important vote-brokers (Beck 2008; Baldwin 2013; 2014; Koter 2013). Chiefs, particularly those with great power in the distribution of local resources, including the granting of customary land rights, hold great authority over their subjects. Moreover, Baldwin (2013) has argued that voters see great benefits in harmonious relationships between chiefs and politicians. Creating strong relationships with local vote-brokers has enabled African leaders to win great local vote margins even outside the areas traditionally seen as party strongholds or areas that are part of an incumbent president's ethnic homeland (Koter 2017).

However, the strength of local vote-brokers varies greatly across space and is highly dependent on the strength of local political institutions and regional political economies (Boone 2003; Ziblatt 2009; Koter 2013) For instance, Conroy-Krutz (2018) finds a strong relationship between land tenure regimes and local bloc voting in Uganda. Variations in the strength of local vote-brokers will vary not only between urban and rural locations but also between rural locations of varying economic development. Voters will have significantly more autonomy vis-à-vis local vote-brokers in regions with higher economic development (Wahman and Boone 2018).

Not only does the clientelistic argument hold varying merit across space. We may also expect that vote-brokers themselves will be affected by local electoral environments and assessments of political viability. Local vote-brokers, like other political elites, engage in complex tipping games where the ambition is to maintain the position within nationally successful coalitions that grant access to nationalized political and economic resources (van de Walle 2006; Beck 2008; Wahman and Seeberg 2022). In other words, it is hard to completely divorce local power brokers from the local political environment created by political campaigns.

Electoral Institutions

Underlying subnational variations in voting are likely to be reinforced or mitigated by electoral institutions. The seven countries with the highest level of geographic polarization according to Figure 1.2 combine two important institutional traits (i) Single Member District (SMD) elections and (ii) a strong directly elected president. In earlier research, I showed a strong relationship between average district magnitude and the level of party nationalization in African democracies (Wahman 2017). African countries with lower district magnitude tend to have significantly lower levels of nationalization. These findings also align with other studies on party nationalization globally or within other regional contexts (Morgenstern et al. 2009; Golosov 2016). SMD elections incentivize parties to build strong local majorities and for local elites to consolidate around fewer locally viable parties. To win parliamentary representation, a party needs at least one regionally defined stronghold. Particularly for opposition parties, with limited resources, this creates incentives to stack their electoral support and develop strong territorial identities (Wahman 2017). Although opposition parties may not have enough strength to win national elections, they may still be able to win a sizeable number of parliamentary seats by running a more geographically restricted campaign and mobilizing voters on regional grievances against the political center. In other words, SMD has been highly beneficial for mobilizing territorial opposition.

However, in order to understand the institutions that have proven conducive to the creation of geographically polarized electoral systems in African democracies, we also have to consider the interaction between legislative and presidential elections. It has often been said about African elections that the presidency remains the grand prize. Indeed, power and resources tend to be heavily concentrated on the executive and local elites have been eager to join winning coalitions with realistic expectations to capture the presidency (Bratton and van de Walle 1997; Rakner and van de Walle 2009). Much literature on the creation of nationalized parties has argued that coordination between districts is facilitated when local elites see higher incentives to coordinate in the pursuit of nationalized resources (Aldrich 1996; Chhibber and Kollman 1998; Hale 2010; Hicken and Stoll 2011; Stoll 2015).

More opposition coordination in many African countries has led to enhanced national competition. Elections in the early period of African multipartyism were characterized by significant regional fragmentation among uncoordinated opposition parties (Howard and Roessler 2006; Arriola 2013; Wahman 2011; 2016; Beardsworth 2019). With increased electoral experience and wavering support for incumbents, opposition parties increased their level of coordination often through the creation of loosely organized opposition coalitions. Arriola (2013) understands such coalitions as ethnic marriages of convenience where regional leaders pool their resources to mount a credible national threat to the incumbent government. Note that such increased national competition is not necessarily enabled by challenging the incumbent party on its own turf, but by stacking regional blocs on top of each other.

An important feature of most African presidential systems is that they do not put any serious restrictions in terms of the geographical distribution of votes across the territory. Instead, in most countries, a president is elected by a national plurality or a majority (in a two-round system). Although some countries, like Kenya, require presidential candidates to have support in a minimum number of geographical subunits, such rules still do not require much national presence.[6] This system puts most African democracies in great contrast to for instance the US electoral college system, where elections are decided completely in a handful of swing states (Powell 1986; Shaw 1999). In countries like Malawi, Liberia, Kenya, and Zambia, a vote secured within the party stronghold is as much worth as a vote secured in a competitive district or within a rival party stronghold. These structures make elections a numbers game, where parties secure national victories by enhancing turnout and registration within their own strongholds and by winning their "home areas" with crushing margins.

---

[6] In Kenya, a winning candidate only needs at least 25% support in 24 out of 47 counties.

2.1.2 From Regionalism to Political Mobilization: The Importance of Localism

Social cleavages, regionalism, and clientelism are important for structuring the African political landscape. They create a sense of political alignment and shared regional interests. In other words, they shape fundamental political identities among voters. However, there is no one-to-one relationship between identities and political mobilization. For instance, although a particular Zambian voter may think of herself as first and foremost a Northwesterner, it is not a given whether a voter wishing to promote the interests of Northwestern Province should vote for the Patriotic Front (PF) or the United Party for National Development (UPND). Most supposed links between certain parties and regions or ethnic groups are made after the fact, based on the way that various parties perform within a specific subgroup of voters or in a particular area. However, most analyses of regional or ethnic voting gloss over the process of political mobilization.[7]

The way that African parties create and maintain regional links is important given that parties are rarely institutionalized and lack deep roots in the regions they are said to represent. Party volatility is high both nationally and locally (Wahman 2014; Kuenzi et al. 2019). While certain regions of a particular country may be described as a "stronghold" for a particular party, this party may not have even existed a year before the election. For instance, in Malawi's 2019 election, Northern region was considered a stronghold of the United Transformation Movement (UTM), a party that did not exist until 2018 (Wahman and Brooks 2022). In 2014, the very same region was considered a stronghold of the People's Party (PP), a party completely unrelated to UTM (Patel and Wahman 2015). What is more, political parties in Africa have often been known to reconfigure their geographic coalitions. For instance, while the Movement for Multiparty Democracy (MMD) in the early days of Zambian multipartyism was an urban party with its roots in the Copperbelt, it slowly eroded its urban base to incorporate new regions, including the rural Eastern Province, the only province to vote against the MMD in the founding 1991 election (Cheeseman and Hinfelaar 2010).

---

[7] Lipset and Rokkan have been famously criticized for asserting that European party systems were "frozen" in the 1960s (Mair 1997). Later periods of high party volatility seem to suggest change rather than stability. Nevertheless, one might argue that although political parties have changed in popularity, the fundamental cleavages have remained the same. For instance, class consciousness may still be strong, although many voters perceive populist right parties to be the representatives of the working class rather than Social Democratic parties.

In order to understand elections in geographically polarized electoral systems and, in extension, the way that election violence features into such contests, we need to focus on the process in which politicians attempt to forge linkages between their parties and regions. Politicians attempt to shape interpretations, expectations, and perceptions of elections using existing political identities. Such processes tend to happen locally in non-nationalized party systems. In highly volatile electoral systems such linkages have to be actively maintained, renewed, and manufactured on an election-by-election basis. This fundamental view of territorial mobilization is in concurrence with Lipset and Rokkan (1967), who argue that territorial opposition is not structurally determined, but that political organization needs to translate cleavages into partisanship.

In his 1986 seminal book on the role of space in politics, Agnew argues that subnational units in non-nationalized political systems are not simply composite parts of the greater political system. In his theorizing, Agnew makes an argument for the importance of *localism* in the formation of politics. Agnew argues that (1987: 6): "The social contexts provided by local territorial-cultural settings (neighborhoods, towns, cities, small rural areas) are viewed as crucial in defining distinctive political identities and subsequent political activities, from votes, to strikes to street violence." Indeed, the very definition of territorial politics is that politics take divergent expressions across subnational locations.

The fundamental assumption in the localist understanding of electoral politics is that electoral campaigns are distinctly local: Information is local, electoral narratives and expectations are shaped locally, local issues that do not register nationally may be decisive for political alignment. The interpretation of national issues is filtered through a local lens and political socialization happens within a local organizational context. This line of thinking had broad resonance in much of the electoral geography literature from non-African contexts (Rokkan and Valen 1962; Butler and Stokes 1969; Agnew 1995; Wuhs 2016).

In much of the original literature on nationalization, scholars emphasized the importance of national communication and transportation. Pre-industrial Europe in particular was characterized by distinct local entities with little communication in between. Mass communication did not bring about perfectly nationalized political systems but did shift political conversations towards more unifying national themes (Agnew 1996; Caramani 2004). In terms of national integration through infrastructure and mass communication, most African countries appear less integrated than countries in the developed world where local politics still have remained important factors. Cultural and linguistic barriers restrict access to nationalized information and media land-scapes are often dominated by local radio stations (Ismail and Deane 2008; Chiyamwaka 2015).

Electoral campaigns in Africa have a distinctly local flavor, and mass rallies have remained arguably the most important tool for political mobilization and persuasion (Paget 2019; Brierley and Kramon 2020). Campaign rallies insert political parties into the local conversation and allow them to communicate directly with the local concerns felt by ordinary citizens. They also send impor-tant signals about local connections and local presence. Similar dynamics have been noted elsewhere in the developing world. For instance, Muñoz (2019) notes how political parties in Peru buy audiences for local rallies in an attempt to create the illusion of a strong local presence.

While several accounts of elections in Africa have stressed the distinctively local character of the electoral campaign in specific regions (e.g. Carrier and Kochore 2014; Sishuwa 2016), others have highlighted localism in a more comparative way. In a study of Kenya's 2007 election, Horowitz and Long (2016) show that information about candidate viability is shaped locally. Voters living within local party strongholds often fail to realize the limited national electoral support of their locally strong candidate. Similarly, Letsa (2019) shows that incumbent and opposition voters alike in Cameroon are more likely to recognize national democratic deficits in localities dominated by opposition parties. The presence of opposition parties facilitates the spread of information about the government's authoritarianism. Hern (2019) argues that the mobilization of the electorate in Zambia is highly contingent on citizens' experience of local service delivery.

In electioneering, national politicians have adopted distinct local appeals when addressing various audiences. Several authors analyzing the electoral strategy of the PF noted how the party differentiated its message and appeal to rural and urban audiences and how local development was often a cornerstone in electoral campaigns (Resnick 2014; Sishuwa 2016). Apart from generalized local appeals, promising local development, and portraying cultural affinity, there are also concrete local issues that tend to animate strong feelings within geographically confined parts of the electorate. For instance, for politicians trying to establish support in Malawi's Northern region, it has become com-monplace to promise the abolition of regional educational quotas (that have disadvantaged the well-educated north). In Zambia's Western province, the issue of increased autonomy for Barotse Land has a similar attraction (Sumbwa 2000).

For political actors, maintaining control over local political narratives and "owning" space is imperative for electoral success. Under the form of electoral institutions that have prevailed in much of Africa, where majoritarian electoral systems are combined with strong presidentialism, this mode of mobilization will lead to parties that win national elections by strongly mobilizing its geographic bases with an uncontested regional link. Regionalism, clientelism, and social cleavages help to explain polarized electoral geography in African countries, but localism is an important key for uncovering the link between regional interest and partisan mobilization. It is from localism and a locally shared understanding of the stakes involved in elections and the viable paths toward promoting regional interests that local dominance is born. Political parties will do their utmost to protect local consensus or disturb local narratives. As I will argue in the rest of this chapter, the realization that the electoral marketplace is local rather than national has important consequences for theorizing the meaning of campaign violence in geographically polarized electoral systems.

2.2 Campaign Violence as a Form of Strategic Electoral Manipulation

So far, this chapter has highlighted the modes of political mobilization conducive to regionalized politics in contemporary Africa. How can campaign violence affect elections within this context? A central theoretical tenant in this book is that electoral manipulation can be understood as a strategic form of electoral manipulation; political elites are likely to promote it in ways that serve their electoral purposes. The evolution of the study of electoral violence, with arguments evolving both in the conflict literature and the electoral manipulation/democratization literature, has created an uneasy, often implicit, tension within the field (Birch et al. 2020). Much of the early literature on violence in elections emerged out of the study of conflict, attempting to understand the ways in which elections may exacerbate already existing conflict (e.g. Snyder 2000; Mansfield and Snyder 2005; Salehyan and Linebarger 2015 Goldsmith 2015). In the conflict literature, low-scale violence was of little interest, as non-lethal violence did not typically appear in the datasets commonly used in the conflict literature (Fjelde and Höglund 2022). Concentrating particularly on contexts with deep political divisions and grievances, the conflict literature on election violence also tended to be divorced from the democratization and election literature. This literature has helped us understand the grievances that may be mobilized for political purposes but not necessarily the electoral purposes of violent mobilization. Yet, the literature on conflict and violence provides important insight into how violence shape political identities fundamental to political mobilization (Kalyvas 2006; Lebas 2006).

More recently, researchers focused on electoral manipulation and electoral integrity have taken an interest in election violence. Indeed, the definition of campaign violence used in this book, "an act of violence carried out before an election to influence the electoral process and in extension the outcome" (Höglund 2009), explicitly conceptualizes campaign violence as a form of electoral manipulation.[8] In Schedler's (2002) classic work on electoral authoritarianism, he uses the metaphor of a "menu of manipulation" to describe the many manipulating options available to autocrats organizing competitive elections (see also Birch 2007). Some have argued that different forms of manipulation are substitutional, i.e. that parties engaged in one form of manipulation (e.g. ballot stuffing) may be less inclined to engage in other forms of manipulation (e.g. repression and violence) (Van Ham and Lindberg 2015). However, it is noteworthy that African countries known for problems with forms of manipulation such as ballot stuffing, registration fraud, and vote buying, such as Nigeria, Zimbabwe, and Côte d'Ivoire, have also had exceptionally high levels of violence during elections (Cheeseman 2015; Bogaards and Elischer 2016; Bleck and van de Walle 2018). Indeed, Birch (2020) argues that violence forms a central role in electoral manipulation, not only as a form of manipulation in its own right but also as a way to support other forms of election manipulation, vote buying in particular.

The differentiation between election violence as a form of conflict and as a form of manipulation is vital for theorizing and measurement. First, theoretically, an underlying assumption in the literature understanding election violence as a form of manipulation is that violence can largely be understood as strategic rather than spontaneous and aimed at affecting electoral outcomes. The conflict literature has acknowledged that violence may be both expressive and strategic (E.g. Horowitz 2001; Kydd and Walter 2006). However, as far as violence is strategic, the strategic goal is not necessarily to affect electoral outcomes. The word *strategic* should here be understood broadly. Strategic use of violence does not necessarily imply that political elites sanction and organize every incident of violence. Instead, strategic use of violence implies that politicians actively encourage and enable violence. However, they may

---

[8] As opposed to, for instance, definitions that categorize all forms of conflict occurring during the electoral cycle as a form of electoral violence.

not always control exactly when or where such violence will occur or what the ultimate consequences will be. For instance, while an individual politician may not give explicit orders to their party foot soldiers to kill members of the opposing party while campaigning, she can still have built organizations with significant violent capacity, armed her supporters, and asked them to create a hostile environment for the rival party's supporters. Elites can also strategically increase group conflict to enhance the chances that followers will engage in violence against outgroups (May 1991). The empirical chapters will show how political parties and candidates, either at the national or local level, were clearly related to a majority of the incidents of electoral violence reported. As a consequence, we can think of temporal or spatial patterns of election violence as largely a consequence of electoral incentives and reflective of the way that politicians understand the process of electoral mobilization.

Second, empirically, when studying election violence as a form of manipulation, we cannot simply disregard low-scale violence. If our ultimate interest is to understand how political actors use violence to affect elections, there is no a priori reason to believe that only fatal violence will affect the electoral environment or the behavior of voters. One illustration of this point is found in Figure 1.2 of this book's introduction chapter. There is little correlation between the level of lethal election violence in a political system and the level of fear voters perceive during election campaigns.

While electoral violence is increasingly studied within the context of electoral manipulation, it is arguably the least understood form of manipulation. The purpose of other forms of manipulation, such as media censorship, ballot stuffing or malapportionment and gerrymandering is often fairly obvious (Lehoucq and Molina 2002; vonDoepp and Young 2013; Boone and Wahman 2015). In some cases, it is even possible to measure the effect of such forms of manipulation with some accuracy (Myagkov et al. 2009; Wong 2019). The intended purpose of campaign violence is much more complicated and subject to considerable debate. In this way, the study of campaign violence has much in common with the study of electoral clientelism and vote buying. However, while the study of electoral clientelism has matured considerably through vital discussions about the role of electoral clientelism under conditions of the secret ballot and limited monitoring capacity (Nichter 2008; Stokes et al. 2013; Kramon 2018; Muñoz 2019, Hicken and Nathan 2020), the literature on campaign violence is still at a much more nascent stage. In particular, more discussion is needed on how electoral violence may be used for varying purposes in diverse electoral environments. To this end, we need to integrate a theory of election violence with a theory of voting in geographically polarized electoral systems. Most researchers trying to understand election violence from the perspective of voting theories have gravitated towards various individual-level behavioral approaches, hypothesizing the way in which election violence may alter individual-level political behavior. However, I will argue that there are limits to the individual-level behavioral approach to election violence in geographically polarized electoral systems.

2.2.1 The Limits of the Micro-Level Behavioralist Approach to Election Violence

With increased focus on the mechanisms of violence as a deliberate and strategic form of electoral manipulation, researchers started to ask some new fundamental questions: Why do parties and candidates engage in electoral violence? What do they try to achieve? And, given these objectives, who are the people that are most likely to be the victims of election violence? In trying to answer these questions, most scholars have gravitated towards micro-level behavioral approaches, either theorizing micro-level behavioral change and measuring empirically observable consequences at the aggregate-level (subnational or national) or by studying individual-level behavior or attitudes using observational or experimental data.

The behavioralist approaches have focused particularly on two individual-level outcomes: vote choice and turnout. Most research in this tradition has remained skeptical that election violence will gain a party or candidate new voters. Most voters consider election violence morally reprehensible (Bratton 2008) and in an election with a secret ballot it is often not possible to use coercion to force a voter to vote for a certain party or candidate. Indeed, some recent research has suggested that voters dislike violence to such an extent that they may avoid voting for known perpetrators of election violence (Gutiérrez-Romero and Lebas 2020). For this reason, election violence targeted at the wrong category of voters may turn out devastating for the perpetrating party. Election violence to sway swing voters may be particularly ineffective (Gonzalez-Ocantos et al. 2020). Rosenzweig (2021), using experimental data from Kenya, goes as far as to argue that political elites misjudge the effectiveness of election violence and that it is likely to have negative consequences for the electoral returns of the perpetrating party.

While violence is unlikely to successfully win over swing voters, there are more reasons to believe that campaign violence could be used as a demobilization tool and reduce turnout among rival party voters. In this way, election violence can be understood as the strategic mirror image of clientelism: While clientelism can be used to mobilize swing voters and core supporters, election violence can be used to demobilize rival party supporters (Collier and Vicente 2012; Rauschenbach and Paula 2019; von Borzyskowski and Kuhn 2020; Gonzalez-Ocantos et al. 2020). This thinking has also affected much of the research on subnational variations in election violence. Collier and Vicente (2012) argue that election violence will be used to discourage softcore voters supporting rival parties (i.e. those supporting the rival party with less conviction) from turning out to vote. They argue that violence can be used by both the opposition and the incumbent, but that parties need to use violence with caution. Violence may also have the adverse effect of turning off the perpetrating party's softcore voters from participating. Consequently, Collier and Vicente argue that violence will be mostly used by parties with little softcore support.

Similarly, recent work has built on micro-level behavioral research to make predictions on subnational variations in election violence. Rauschenbach and Paula (2019) argue that election violence should be particularly common in opposition party strongholds. They argue that parties are incentivized to use violence in their rival party strongholds to discourage turnout, but that incumbents are most likely to use this tool. They base this argument on earlier research showing that the bulk of election violence in Africa is conducted by incumbents (Straus and Taylor 2012; Taylor et al. 2017). Using Afrobarometer data, they show that voters living in opposition strongholds are the ones most fearful of violence. Voters living in incumbent party strongholds are the ones least afraid. Rauschenbach and Paula's work is a great corrective to much of the national-level research that has failed to acknowledge subnational variations in election violence. However, like most micro-level behavioral research on election violence in Africa it lacks an underlying theory of voting and campaigns appropriate for this context.

To some extent, the lack of engagement with the African voting literature in research on election violence may be an artifact of the literature's origin within conflict research. Some of the literature has engaged with ethnic identity and questioned how it conditions the behavioral consequences of violence (Gutiérrez-Romero and Lebas 2020), but mostly as a way to proxy partisan attachment. In most of the behavioral micro-level research, electoral participation is seen as an individual-level process in which voters weigh individual-level perceived costs against individual-level benefits of engaging. There is no theorizing about the interdependency of voters' political behavior and limited recognition that violence indirectly affect political behavior.

As far as political participation is concerned, most behavioral research has maintained a rather narrow understanding of political participation, concentrating only on voting itself. Nevertheless, participation ought to be understood in a much broader sense. The focus on localism presented above suggests that other forms of electoral participation shaping local electoral environments are crucial for mobilizing regional political cleavages. The literature on clientelism has gone further in embracing a more space-sensitive approach to manipulation. Authors such as Kramon (2018) and Muñoz (2019) have argued that vote buying is more accurately understood as a way to boost a sense of local presence than a direct way to "buy" votes.

There are several unanswered puzzles left by recent work on micro-level behavior and election violence. If violence is counterproductive, why is it still so widely spread? Daxecker (2014) shows that most election violence does not happen on election day or shortly before the election, but earlier in the election cycle. How could this be if the main objective is to scare voters from turning out to vote? Similarly, most research has shown that relatively few voters are directly affected by election violence (Bratton 2008; Gutierrez-Romero 2014). If so, how would we expect violence to make any real impact in elections? Violence may not only affect those directly affected by it but also other people who may become afraid of political participation, but if so, how can perpetrators be sure to restrict such changes in behavior to voters that would show up to vote for the rival party? Lastly, there is very little real-world empirical evidence, beyond survey experiments and hypothetical voting, to claim that violence reduces election turnout. On the contrary, observational research has struggled to find strong correlations between violence and lower levels of turnout (Bekoe and Burchard 2017; Martínez i Coma and Morgenbesser 2020).

In the next section, I will introduce an electoral geography theory of election violence that is particularly suitable for understanding election violence in geographically polarized electoral systems. This theory extends my earlier discussion on localism in African voting. It diverges significantly from most of the micro-level behavioral research by theorizing local contextual factors in understanding election violence and de-emphasizing autonomous vote choice by individual voters. This theoretical lens for understanding election violence questions some recent attempts at understanding the behavioral consequences of election violence using randomized survey treatments. Such approaches treat electoral contexts as noise and strive to keep contextual factors constant. However, my argument suggests that such experiments may have little external validity. Indeed, if election violence is more a tool to shape the local electoral

context than an instrument to alter the rational calculations of individual voters directly, it may be of little use to know how individual voters alter their
behavior when exposed to information about violence. The next section will
introduce an approach to election violence that does not treat electoral context
as noise but instead the very thing that violence tries to affect.

2.3 An Electoral Geography Theory of Campaign Violence in Geographically Polarized Electoral Systems

An electoral geography understanding of campaign violence does not necessarily contest hypotheses from behavioral theories. Indeed, it is true that
violence is likely to change political behavior of the individuals targeted. Still,
the electoral effects of violence are much greater than such theories would lead
us to believe. As discussed earlier in this chapter, local political dominance is
not created by voters making autonomous decisions on vote choice, independent of the local political environment in which they reside. It is also not simply
a local sum of individual-level attributes, as would be argued in, for instance,
the "ethnic head count" account of African politics. It is instead a product of
the emerging local electoral narrative, where parties compete over mobilizing
regional cleavages.

Violence in this context can be an incredibly powerful tool. It can alter not
only individual-level behavior but entire local electoral environments. This is
key to understanding how violence serves as an electoral strategy in geographically polarized electoral systems. In cases where regional modes of political
mobilization prevail and electoral systems incentivize parties to create local
supermajorities, violence may be an integral tool in electoral strategies for
achieving national majorities.

Fundamentally, I argue that violence can be understood as a tool for what
Robert Sack (1986: 1) labels "territoriality," that is, "a spatial strategy to affect,
influence, or control resources and people, by controlling area." The spatial
understanding of conflict has greatly influenced the study of civil war. Most
notable, Kalyvas (2006) foundational book on violence in civil war argues that
authority tends to be fragmented or segmented in such contexts.[9] The extent
to which an actor (a government or an insurgent) in an ongoing conflict can
foster collaboration among the population is heavily dependent on its level
of control, i.e. the extent to which actors are able to establish exclusive rule

---

[9] See also Siqueira and Sekeris (2012), Tao et al. (2016), and Rueda (2017) for some other examples
of research emphasizing territorial control in civil conflict.

in a territory. The way that territoriality plays out is different in civil war and electoral politics. In civil war, collaboration would mean active involvement in the conflict on behalf of the controlling actor or compliance providing information to the same actor. In electoral politics, control will instead be related to political participation, such as visiting rallies, working on campaigns, discussing politics in the community, or voting. In electoral politics, control is not dependent on formal decision-making power but on the influence that a party has on the campaign environment. However, in both civil war and electoral politics, violence is one of several tools to uphold control and can be highly effective to this end. Moreover, in both civil war and violent electoral politics, different actors will have varying capacities for violence across space depending on their level of previous control. This applies to all actors involved in elections, including incumbent parties, opposition parties, and the state's coercive institutions. In countries characterized by regionalism, control will vary greatly across space.[10]

The electoral geography theory of campaign violence presented here emphasizes violence as a way to preserve and contest local control. Such violence can be orchestrated by central actors, most likely parties in power with central coercive capacity, to reassert power in areas where their control of the electoral process is seriously threatened. However, violence can also be used by those already in local control, most commonly the locally strong party, to manifest its power and shrink the democratic space. Such violence will most likely be locally organized. In this book, I refer to these two manifestations of election violence as violence to *contest* or *enforce* territoriality. Although these two forms of violence are conducted by different actors, they both serve to affect the local electoral environment.

The consequence of this approach is that violence, or the credible threat of violence, could play a central role in electoral competition, even in countries where violence is predominantly low-scale and few individuals are directly affected. Violence restricts the ability for voters to freely engage in elections within their local communities, it limits the access to information, enhances political inequalities, and creates undue advantages to actors with repressive capacity both locally and centrally. Violence has the potential to effectively dismantle local democracy and promote a form of local hegemony or, if you want, subnational authoritarianism.

---

[10] The uneven reach of the African state has been the object of study in several foundational books in African politics (e.g. Mamdani 1996; Herbst 2000; Boone 2003).

In the following sections, I will develop the ideas of election violence to both enforce and contest territoriality. I will develop the purpose of these different forms of territorial violence, discuss how local and central electoral incentives are conducive to such forms of violence, and what actors are likely to be involved in the perpetration. I will argue that violence will be most effective as a territorial tool in noncompetitive sub-locations. Operationally, any empirical analysis will suffer from modifiable areal unit problems (MAUP). That is, different subunits like provinces, districts, or constituencies may be competitive at the aggregate level, but contain several pockets of political dominance (e.g. certain neighborhoods in a city or traditional authority areas of a rural constituency). In such pockets, territorial dynamics could still be in play. However, we would expect that violence as a territorial tool would be less effective in more competitive areas and far riskier for the perpetrator.

2.3.1 Violence as a Tool to Enforce Territoriality

Locally strong parties can use electoral violence to preserve and reinforce local electoral narratives. When violence is used against perceived "outsiders," it can reduce such parties' access to local political campaigns and their ability to contest existing narratives about local viability and advocacy. It can also serve to entrench existing regional polarization by inserting a sense of conflict into local perceptions of elections.

What I refer to as violence to *enforce* territoriality, is a form of violence used by locally strong parties and their affiliates against those associated with locally weak parties. Local strength creates authority and coercive capacity that can be used strategically by political parties to assert territoriality. This violence is likely to occur in party strongholds but could be perpetrated both by the ruling party *and* the opposition. Most of the election violence literature has assumed that the opposition has limited coercive capacity (Rauschenbach and Paula 2019; Taylor et al. 2017). However, such assertions cannot easily be extrapolated to every single subnational jurisdiction. Locally strong parties, even those in national opposition, command significant popular support and organize most local elites and resources. They also have superior access to local party foot soldiers and other crucial agents for the perpetration of violence (Bob-Milliar 2014). This local resource advantage can be translated into local coercive capacity.

The idea of violence as a tool to enforce territoriality has been popularized in African political discourse by the frequent use of the term "no-go zone politics."

No-go zones are geographical areas claimed by a political party. Violence is not the only tool available for political elites that wish to assert local control (Kalyvas 2006), tools such as clientelism, monitoring, and social pressure can also be used for these purposes, but credible threats of violence are often a precondition for such tools to function effectively (Birch 2020).

Needless to say, the idea of political parties "owning" space is completely antithetical to any reasonable interpretation of democracy. In a democracy, parties should be free to campaign across the territory without fear of repression. Voters, on their behalf, should be equally free to access information from varying political sources, even though they reside within an area where political competition is nearly non-existent. In a no-go zone, political parties interpret even the existence of a rival party as a form of aggression akin to an "invasion" of a foreign power. Parties can enlist local elites, including chiefs in upholding such territorial control. In some cases, no-go zones can be enabled by the mere threat of violence. In other cases, parties are forced to use actual force to assert this territorial control. In this sense, actually manifested violence is just the tip of the iceberg in a political order entrenched in coercion.

Violence within a party's stronghold is arguably the most effective way to shrink the local democratic space and fend off any fear of defection or confusion about what party supposedly "represents" the region. With the effective use of violence, parties can minimize the visibility of the rival party in the area and dissuade any contestation of locally dominant electoral narratives. For instance, parties can use violence against locally weak parties to deter the party from organizing rallies or making voters fearful of attending such campaign events.[11] Ultimately, voters will be left with the impression that there is no effective competition and no reason to entertain the idea of defection. Complete political dominance projects power and shapes the behavior of various political actors. When localism prevails, such perceptions of power will be formed at the subnational level (Horowitz and Long 2016; Letsa 2019).

Violence cannot only freeze local understandings of political mobilization of regional cleavages but also reinforce such cleavages and minimize the risk of cross-cutting cleavages emerging and threatening local dominance. When locally weak parties are perceived as "outsiders," escalation of violence can benefit the locally strong party. Inserting conflict into the electoral campaign can increase perceived electoral stakes and entrench regional identities. Although not focusing specifically on subnational dynamics, Lebas (2006) describes how

---

[11] In other parts of the developing world, researchers have suggested that failed campaign rallies may prove costly for political parties. If parties cannot draw large crowds to campaign events it leaves voters unsure about the party's viability and clientelistic ability (Langston and Rosas 2018).

violence has enhanced polarization in the case of Zimbabwe. She claims that Zimbabwean political parties used violence to strengthen their mobilization capacity and reduce the risk of defection. Similarly, locally strong political parties can use violence to create cycles of violent confrontation between local actors and outsiders during election campaigns. While the main perpetrator of such violence is often hard to identify for local population, violence may be perceived as political conflict against regional lines and a reminder for voters to remain loyal to regional interests.

Much of the literature assuming that violence is mostly used to deter turnout has precluded the possibility of parties perpetrating violence in their own strongholds. In accordance with this logic, violence perpetrated in a party's own stronghold would make little sense. After all, if voters are afraid to engage in the electoral process they may decide not to turn out at all (Collier and Vicente 2012; Rauschenbach and Paula 2019). However, the logic described above, where violence is mostly used to shape electoral environments, offers a possible explanation for why parties nevertheless would engage in such violence. Indeed, the empirical chapters will provide numerous examples of violence perpetrated by locally strong parties (both ruling parties and opposition) in Malawi and Zambia. Such examples are not, however, restricted to these two cases. For instance, Lewanika (2019) describes such strategies frequently used by the Zimbabwe African National Union–Patriotic Front (ZANU–PF) in Zimbabwe. In this case, violence was systematically targeted against opposition candidates, sympathizers, or believed sympathizers within ZANU–PF strongholds. According to Lewanika (2019): "the violence acted not only as a punishment for belonging to the opposition, but also a destabilizing strategy that forced the opposition to scatter, and go into hiding, which resulted in them failing to organize themselves openly and meaningfully in the area."

2.3.2 Violence as a Tool to Contest Territoriality

Opposition areas have often been described as violence-hotspots in literature on African campaign violence (Borzyskowski and Kuhn 2020; Rauschenbach and Paula 2019; Choi and Raleigh 2021; Daxecker and Rauschenbach forthcoming). Most commonly, such patterns have been understood as a consequence of ruling party repression. Ruling parties have used their superior coercive resources to strike down on opposition areas and reduce the willingness of opposition voters to turn out on election day. While I acknowledge that the resource asymmetry between opposition and ruling parties in most African electoral regimes is important for understanding geographical patterns of campaign violence, I contend that this form of violence fills a much broader role than previously argued. The patterns observed in much of the literature may more accurately be understood as a manifestation of power struggles between central political forces and peripheral opposition. While the ruling party strives to control the electoral process, its powers is significantly challenged inside opposition enclaves. Opposition parties within their strongholds strive to uphold territorial control and dominate local perceptions of elections, but ruling parties can equally use their central coercive capacity to instill local doubt in such narratives and reassert the image of central control.

When opposition parties successfully maintain territorial control, such local dominance represents a great challenge to ruling parties and their authority (Kalyvas 2006). With prevailing localism, the total abdication of the central government would create an impression of opposition momentum and possibly even the inevitability of incumbent defeat. For this reason, ruling parties need local presence inside opposition strongholds. If challenged physically, they need to mobilize their own resources to remind voters that they are still in control. Government parties can use their resources to create a sense of viability within opposition strongholds. They can mobilize outside resources to organize election campaigns and ensure that the opposition does not get a monopoly on local electoral narratives. For instance, the empirical chapter on Zambia will show how the ruling party often used expensive campaign strategies such as bussing their supporters to attend large campaign rallies within key opposition areas. Such campaign events often led to spiraling violence.

The key to enabling violence as a tool to contest territoriality is access to centralized coercive resources. Such resources come primarily from two sources. First, parties with enough financial and organizational capacity can mobilize their party machinery to perpetrate violence across the territory. Incumbent parties, with their access to state resources and their ability to engage in state clientelism, are usually better equipped to enlist agents for election violence or other forms of electoral manipulation (Rundlett and Svolik 2016).

Second, the state itself has often been engaged in politically motivated violence during elections on behalf of the executive (Straus and Taylor 2012; Birch 2020). When ruling parties command strong control of central supposedly independent institutions, we are likely to see particularly high levels of centralized violence. Such institutions include repressive institutions such as the police and the military. For instance, Hassan (2017) shows how the ethnic profile of police officers under Moi's Kenyan African National Union (KANU) regime varied depending on electoral geography. Moi's co-ethnics were more likely to be posted in areas that were non-aligned with the president to bolster the regime's repressive capacity in such areas. Centralized capacity also includes the control of other institutions charged with overseeing the electoral process and keeping those responsible for election violence accountable, this includes Election Management Bodies (EMBs) and courts (Boone 2009; Mueller 2011). A common observation in many cases with high levels of violence is that government parties have been allowed to perpetrate violence with much impunity. Pro-government perpetrators are rarely arrested, election management bodies do not suspend government-party candidates involved in election violence or suspend campaigns (Omotola 2010; Opitz et al. 2013), and courts are unlikely to nullify elections characterized by government violence (Simati 2020; Kerr and Wahman 2021).

While the assumption that ruling parties can use central resources to reassert authority in opposition areas will hold for most African elections, it is not always true (Seeberg 2018; 2021). Weak incumbents without manipulating capacity will find it hard to engage in targeted violence against opposition areas. If parties do not have access to clientelistic resources, if agents believe that the government is destined for defeat, or the government does not control the coercive apparatus, we are unlikely to see much more violence in opposition areas than in ruling party areas.

In the empirical chapters, I will contrast the case of Zambia and Malawi to make this point. Whereas the Zambian ruling party had significant central coercive capacity, this was not the case for the weakened government under President Joyce Banda in Malawi. While countries with weak incumbent governments are unlikely to see much violence to contest territoriality, they are still likely to see violence to enforce territoriality. On aggregate, such cases are likely to see less violence as they will have fewer hotspots where spiraling violence occurs between locally dominant parties and outsiders keen to break the territoriality of their political rivals. Variations in centralized repressive capacity highlight the need to theorize the interaction between macro-level and meso-level factors when studying subnational variations in election violence (Balcells and Stanton 2021). If we assume that violence is, at least partially, centrally organized, we cannot assume that all countries will display the same subnational patterns of violence regardless of various actors' ability to perpetrate violence and make credible attempts to assert control across the territory.

2.4 Conclusion

This theory chapter has presented an electoral geography theory of campaign violence. The theory builds on a particular understanding of electoral mobilization in geographically polarized electoral systems. The gist of the theory suggests that in elections, where regionalism is the structuring political cleavage, political campaigns are a contest over local electoral interpretations. Election violence in this context can be used to contest and enforce territoriality and shape electoral environments. Ruling parties can use their superior resources to contest territoriality in opposition strongholds, and both opposition and ruling parties can use violence to enforce territoriality in their respective strongholds. The theory laid out in this chapter results in several empirical expectations that will be probed in the empirical chapters about the nature of mobilization, the location of violence, and the micro-level consequences of such violence.

Chapters 3 and 6 will examine the issue of political mobilization in Zambia and Malawi respectively. The chapters will study the nature of electoral cleavages, political geography, and political mobilization. The chapters will particularly concentrate on how we can understand political competition in these countries as regional and, if so, whether parties actively campaign to mobilize these cleavages. In both cases, I will also particularly focus on the importance of stronghold mobilization for winning national majorities. This analysis will be conducted using secondary accounts as well as two new longitudinal constituency-level election datasets.

Chapters 4 and 7 may be described as the main empirical chapters of the book. In these chapters, I will study subnational variations in campaign violence in Zambia and Malawi. The chapters will use constituency-level election violence data from ZEMS and MEMS, as well as various qualitative sources. The theory presented here suggests that we are likely to find more violence in party strongholds, both strongholds held by the opposition and the ruling party. I will also particularly contrast Zambia and Malawi, two countries with widely different levels of central coercive capacity. The theory above suggests that an increased propensity for violence in opposition strongholds will be particularly likely in cases like Zambia, where the ruling party has strong central coercive capacity. However, we may not find the same pattern in cases such as Malawi, where ruling party central coercive capacity is weak. It is important to note that the hypothesized correlation between party dominance and election violence is correlational and that I could not possibly claim unidirectional causation. Violence is part of the toolkit to maintain political dominance or break it, but political dominance also motivates political actors to engage in violence to maintain or break territoriality. As such, Chapters 4 and 7 are more interested in understanding the electoral environments in which violence is likely to occur than describing a simple causal link either between competition and violence or violence and competition.

Chapter 5 will look closer at the empirical micro-level implications of the theory in the case of Zambia. The theory above suggested that violence is more likely to be used as a tool to shape local electoral environments broadly than to deter turnout. The theory also suggests that voters belonging to local minorities may be particularly affected by violence as locally strong parties use violence to monopolize space. Chapter 5 will study how voter-level characteristics and local-level context interact to produce individual-level variation in fear of election violence, using geocoded Afrobarometer data. I will also use new data from the Zambian Election Panel Survey (ZEPS) to study what activities voters are most afraid of engaging in.

3

Democracy, Elections, and Electoral Geography in Zambia

The theory chapter of this book argues that any analysis of campaign violence (if understood as a form of electoral manipulation) needs to be in
close conversation with an analysis of electoral mobilization and competition. Contextual factors such as electoral system design, social cleavages, and
party systems underpin the strategic use of violence. Without appreciating
electoral dynamics in a given context we may misinterpret the strategic use
of violence.

This chapter introduces the case of Zambia. The chapter will focus on the
basic structure of Zambian electoral competition over time, specifically focusing on the 2016 election. I will mainly discuss the origin and effect of electoral
institutions, the general cleavage structure, and the emergence of the geographically polarized electoral system. The chapter will discuss how regional politics
has characterized Zambian campaigns since independence. I will also discuss
how the structure of the 2016 election and significant incumbent advantages
created centralized capacity for campaign violence. At the same time, electoral
closeness at the national level provided obvious incentives for a pressured
incumbent party to use all electoral tools, legal and illegal, to enhance its
chances for re-election.

For the theory presented in this book, two common misunderstandings,
simplifications, or stylizations about electoral competition in Zambia (and
many other geographically polarized electoral systems) will be particularly
important to correct. The first misunderstanding is that clustering of vote
choice in Zambia reflects predictable, predetermined, co-ethnic voting. If elections are no more than a structurally predetermined ethnic census, there would
be little need to use violence for other possible purposes than to dissuade
rival ethnic groups from voting. The second myth addressed in this chapter
is that national majorities are primarily won by winning swing districts in a
handful of non-aligned areas. If this is the case, there would be little reason
to engage in costly efforts to change or reinforce local electoral narratives in
party strongholds.

Controlling Territory, Controlling Voters. Michael Wahman, Oxford University Press.
© Michael Wahman (2023). DOI: 10.1093/oso/9780198872825.003.0003

Contrary to these common misunderstandings, the chapter will argue that the Zambian cleavage structure is much more intricate than an overdetermined focus on ethnicity would suggest. The chapter will introduce the deep regional cleavages that have structured Zambian politics since independence. I will argue that Zambian cleavages are complex constructions where popular perceptions of political and economic marginalization have interacted with sectoral and economic interest to forge regional identities that transcend ethnic boundaries. Equally important, parties actively attempt to mobilize regional political cleavages in an electoral environment where national majorities require multi-regional and multi-ethnic coalitions and where party volatility has been significant. While regional voting is substantial, it is not predetermined. The popularity of parties within certain regions has shifted over time, and certain regions have been more effectively mobilized by some parties than others.

I will also argue that the nature of Zambian localist electoral mobilization, in combination with the electoral institutions, has created strong incentives for regional stronghold mobilization. Historically successful parties, such as the PF and UPND, have often made electoral advances primarily by strengthening their hold of key strongholds rather than winning new territory or swing districts. The most successful strategy for opposition parties has been cultivating a strong regional basis rather than attempting a nationalized strategy.

3.1 The Origin of Zambian Political Cleavages: More than Ethnicity

How have regional cleavages in Zambia emerged over time? What continuity can be detected? Are regional identities more complex than a theoretical lens focusing on ethnicity would suggest? Indeed, the history of political cleavages in Zambia indicates that regional identities have remained strong since independence from British colonial rule in 1964. Many of the main cleavages identified in present-day politics can already be traced in the early multiparty years of independent Zambia and the subsequent one-party state under the United National Independence Party (UNIP).

Early Zambian multiparty elections were primarily a struggle between Kenneth Kaunda's United National Independence Party (UNIP) and Harry Nkumbula's African National Congress (ANC). Whereas UNIP was generally perceived to have its base in the urban Copperbelt, the industrial powerhouse of Zambia, the party's nationalization was enabled by its capacity for state patronage (Baylies and Szeftel 1992). Conversely, the ANC concentrated its support among the Tonga in Southern and Central Province. Nevertheless, political alignments in the 1960s were not purely ethnic. The ANC mobilized its Southern base on a pro-agrarian platform. The Southern Province had, in the colonial period, created an agricultural economy mainly built around the cultivation of cash crops. Consequently, the region developed a wealthy peasantry of small-scale farmers. This peasantry relied more on transportation, infrastructure, access to credits, and crop prices than their poorer compatriots in regions such as Northern, Luapula, and Northwestern Province. The interests of the wealthy agrarian south were also in stark contrast to those of the urban workers of the Copperbelt (Momba 1985). Macola (2008: 36) notes how the ANC frequently portrayed UNIP supporters as "poor 'thieves' whose political activities were solely designed to rob honest peasants of the hard-won fruits of their agricultural labor."

Kaunda had early expressed his preference for one-partyism but had maintained that UNIP would eventually become the single party through the ballot box. By the late 1960s opposition to UNIP had, however, still not withered away (Pettman 1974). Apart from ANC, the United Party (UP) emerged in 1966 as a vital entity in the Western or "Barotse" province. Barotseland had enjoyed a special agreement under colonialism as a protectorate separate from Northern Rhodesia. Barotse Province entered the Zambian nation with the Barotseland Agreement of 1964, an agreement designed to maintain much of the region's autonomy. However, the central government's failure to honor the agreement made Western Province prone to oppositional politics (Rasmussen 1969). The government banned UP in 1968, but the ban strengthened the ANC as former UP leaders aligned with the major opposition party in an anti-UNIP opposition representing politically marginalized regions (Bratton 1992).

In 1971, UNIP faced serious defections as Simon Kapwepwe, one of the foundational independence leaders and Kaunda's vice president, resigned from government. Kapwepwe had been associated with the new United Progressive Party (UPP), but formally joined the party at the time of his resignation. The defection presented an unprecedented challenge to UNIP rule. Kapwepwe articulated grievances among urban workers, particularly on the highly mobilized Copperbelt, and presented a veritable threat to UNIPs hold on its territorial base in Bemba-speaking regions (Sishuwa 2016: 106). The growth of UPP resulted in violent clashes between the opposition and the incumbent party on the Copperbelt. By 1972, the government banned the UPP. A month later, Kaunda announced a commission laying the foundation for a new one-party constitution (Pettman 1974). The new single-party UNIP was more national in its character than its multiparty version. Kaunda strategically used coalition building to appease varying factions of the party and introduced a strategy referred to as "tribal balancing." However, factions within UNIP emerged due to the party's inability to balance urban and rural interests and accommodate the interests of unionized urban workers, particularly on the Copperbelt (Bratton 1992).

Serious organized resistance against the one-party state emerged from the creation of the Movement for Multiparty Democracy (MMD). The MMD was formed as a coalition of diverse interests along some already well-established cleavages in Zambian politics. The coalition had its base in the Western region but grew to prominence with the incorporation of urban union interests on the Copperbelt. Urban workers and industrial interests had been severely hurt by the economic policies pursued under the structural adjustment programs led by the UNIP government (Baylies and Szeftel 1992; Lebas 2011). After the UNIP government was forced into arranging multiparty elections, MMD emerged as a broad pro-democracy coalition.

The strong regional cleavages that emerged in the pre-democracy era have never vanished in contemporary multiparty politics. In fact, such cleavages have grown stronger over time. Regional identities have been reinforced by contrasting sectoral interests (Kim 2017). Regionalism has also been reinforced by a sense of political inequality and integration with the state, what could be referred to as a "center and periphery" cleavage. While the economically advanced Southern Province was a traditional agricultural and educational frontrunner, the region has remained politically marginalized. Intellectuals from the region have failed to obtain top positions within subsequent government administrations (Kapesa at al. 2020). Other regions like the more impoverished Western Province have continuously sought independence or at least greater regional autonomy, creating a weak relationship with the center. While regional identities have created mobilizable cleavages for political parties, the history of Zambian multiparty elections will show that the allegiances between certain regions and particular parties have often been short-lived and the competition over regional mobilization has remained strong.

3.2 The Institutional Underpinning of Geographic Polarization

The theory chapter suggested that majoritarian electoral institutions will likely reinforce regional identities, especially as parties tailor electoral strategies to maximize their electoral returns. Indeed, electoral institutions in Zambia from the introduction of multipartyism have favored regionalized electoral strategies that accentuate regional cleavages. The electoral system introduced in the founding 1991 election was highly disproportional. Presidential elections were held in a single round and parliamentary elections were held using SMD in constituencies with high levels of malapportionment (Boone and Wahman 2015).

Shortly after getting into office, MMD consolidated power using its overwhelming legislative majority. The first multiparty constitution from 1991 was not a fundamental revision of the county's pre-democratic constitution. Apart from removing the privileged position of UNIP as the country's one legal party, it had not undone many of the excessive executive powers that had characterized the one-party state (Erdmann and Simutanyi 2003: 11; Hinfenlaar et al. 2020). A new amended constitution passed by parliament in 1996 further entrenched executive powers (Ndulo and Kent 1996).

The 1996 constitution did not fundamentally change the electoral system. The existing electoral system seemed beneficial for the ruling MMD, given its overwhelming strength, and served to starve out smaller challengers. With the SMD electoral system and national hegemony, the best bet for new opposition challengers was cultivating a regional following and win seats in restricted parts of the country. Zambia has not established any requirement forcing presidential candidates to win votes across the territory.

Scarritt (2006) noted that the institutional context of Zambia, combined with the ethnic geography, has necessitated multiethnic and multiregional coalitions to win national elections. MMD from the get-go, fits this mold and subsequent nationally viable parties have all drawn on broader coalitions. This means that monoethnic or monoregional parties in the Zambian context would only have limited success. Parties have to appeal to multiple regional identities to win elections. The most favored parties would be those that draw on multiple regional strongholds to maximize parliamentary representation by geographic vote concentration while simultaneously enabling a plurality of votes in presidential elections.

3.3 From a Hegemonic to a Geographically Polarized Electoral System

Figure 3.1 shows national and local competition for every regular Zambian presidential election (excluding the by-elections of 2008 and 2015). The noteworthy takeaway from Figure 3.1 is that Zambia has become *more* nationally competitive and subnationally *less* competitive over time. The increased

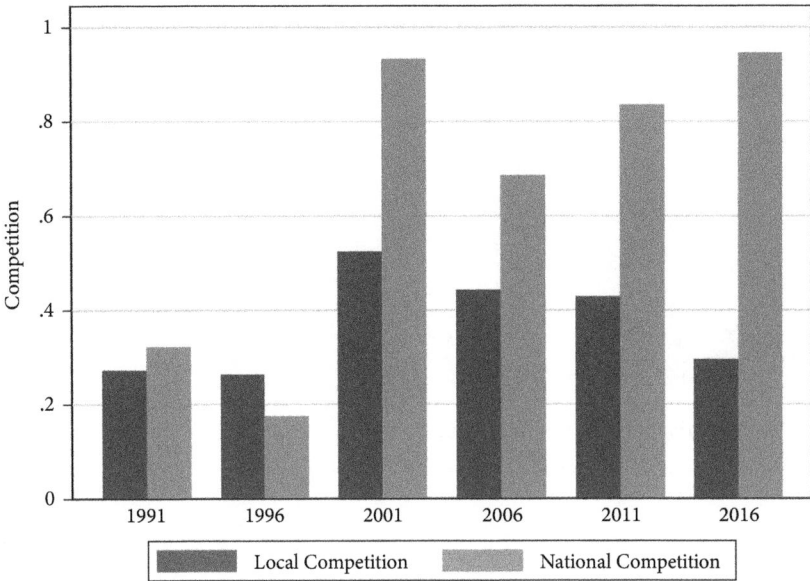

Figure 3.1 Local and National Competition in Zambia 1991–2016.

Note: Local Competition shows the number of votes won by the runner-up presidential candidate divided by the winner's number of votes as an average across all constituencies. National competition shows the national runner-up's number of votes divided by the national winner's number of votes.

regionalization of politics is not primarily an effect of more pronounced regional identities. The identities described above have been constant features of Zambian politics. Instead, the increased regionalization of Zambian politics has been an issue of supply rather than demand. As factions within political parties have occurred they have often (as in the early period of Zambian independence) followed distinct regional logics. As MMD's hegemonic position was eroded and space was opened for political elites to advance outside the MMD, most successful opposition parties adopted a regionalized strategy to challenge the incumbent by mobilizing various regional interests against the center.

The strong regional character of Zambian politics was obscured in the founding 1991 election (see Figure 3.2). In an election that could be primarily understood as a referendum on UNIP, a strong regime cleavage took priority over regional cleavages as the opposition united against the ruling party (Burnell 2001; Rakner and Svåsand 2004). The only region that did not follow the national trend, but remained loyal to the ruling party, was Eastern Province. This province had generally been favored under the one-party state (Lindemann 2011).

MMD vote share   UNIP vote share

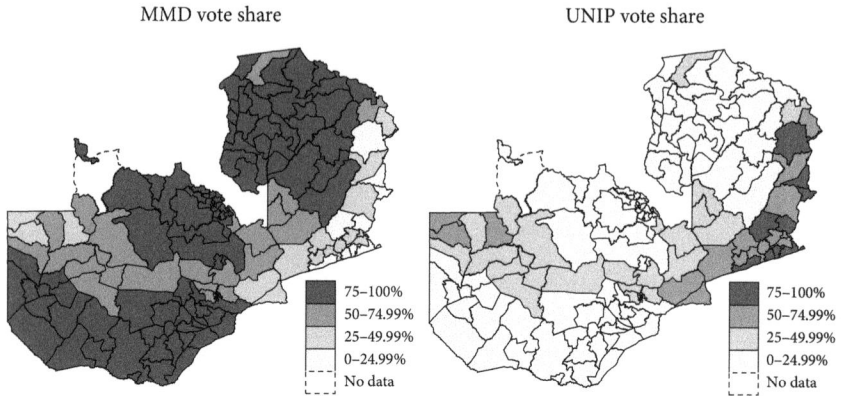

	75–100%
	50–74.99%
	25–49.99%
	0–24.99%
	No data

	75–100%
	50–74.99%
	25–49.99%
	0–24.99%
	No data

Figure 3.2 Presidential Electoral Map 1991.

Note: Election data from Electoral Commission of Zambia (ECZ).

The 1996 election was contested without much competition not at least because the most formidable challenger, former President Kenneth Kaunda, was barred from participating. MMD had also embarked on increasingly authoritarian measures to curb any meaningful opposition, and most critical local elites stayed within the realm of the dominant party (Rakner and Svåsand 2005; Helle 2016). The limited opposition participating in the 1996 election deployed various strategies. Some parties tried to compete with the hegemonic party using more nationalized strategies. Others concentrated their electoral efforts spatially, attempting to win limited support by activating regional political grievances. Rakner and Svåsand (2004: 55) conclude that the total dominance of MMD made it beneficial for opposition parties to pursue a more regionalized strategy. For example, although the more nationalized Alternative for Zambia (AZ) polled almost twice as many votes as the smaller National Party (NP), NP still won more parliamentary seats than AZ (5 vs. 2). While AZ spread their support across space, NP concentrated their following in Northwestern Province, a small province with pronounced economic grievances.

The full potential of the regionalized approach to electoral mobilization became apparent with the gradual demise of MMD's hegemonic position, starting in the early 2000s. MMD started to fracture at the end of Chiluba's second term in office. While the constitution limited the president to two terms in office, Chiluba had initiated debates about a potential constitutional amendment that would allow him to run for a third term. In reaction to the planned amendment, opposition grew not only from civil society but also from within MMD itself (VonDoepp 2005: 70). As a consequence, the ruling party fractured. Several new parties chaired by former MMD officials were created, including Christon Tembo's Forum for Democracy and Development (FDD), Godfrey Miyanda's Heritage Party, Benjamin Mwila's Zambia Republican Party (ZRP), and Michael Sata's Patriotic Front (PF) (Rakner and Svåsand 2004). Most of these MMD offshoots came to make a rather limited impact in the 2001 election, again largely because they were unable to create a strong regional base. Although FDD, Heritage, ZRP, and PF amassed 31.5% of the parliamentary vote combined, they only secured 18 seats in parliament (11% of the parliamentary seats).

Compared to FDD, Heritage, and ZRP, another new challenger, the United Party for National Development (UPND), made a much stronger impact. Led by a Tonga-speaking affluent businessman from Southern Province, Anderson Mazoka, the UPND claimed to be a continuation of the ANC, the party that successfully represented the Southern Province in the 1960s. Until 2001, Southern Province had reluctantly remained loyal to the MMD. However, growing discontent over the political and economic marginalization of the province made the province fertile ground for territorial opposition. Unlike Northwestern, which had previously been mobilized against the MMD, Southern Province was a populous province with serious national clout. To further strengthen its national appeal, UPND incorporated powerful political elites from Western Province, another aggrieved province looking to overturn the dominance of the MMD (Beardsworth 2018).

In the end, Chiluba's successor, Lewi Mwanawasa, narrowly won the 2001 election with 29% of the vote compared to Mazoka's 27%.[1] While UPND ultimately lost the election, the campaign still showed the viability of an approach focusing on winning large majorities in a limited geographical area. If UPND had won the same majorities in Western as they did in Southern, they would ultimately have carried the day.

Since the 2001 election, Zambia has seen a gradual movement toward a more geographically polarized electoral system. The most critical shift in the 2006 election was the serious rise of the PF. Much has been written about the ascent of PF.[2] Most of this writing has focused on the dual appeal that made the party successful, combing an ethnic Bemba appeal in the Bemba heartland with a populist appeal to the growing and increasingly dissatisfied urban

---

[1] The election results were, however, not credible as they were subjected to centrally organized rigging in favor of the incumbent party (Larmer and Faser 2007: 620).

[2] For particularly useful accounts, see Larmer and Fraser 2007; Cheeseman and Hinfelaar 2010; Resnick 2014; Skage 2016; Fraser 2017; Sishuwa 2018.

population of Lusaka and the Copperbelt. PF's rise led to MMD losing ground in Bemba areas and the ruling party losing its role as the perceived representation of northern interest. For instance, PF successfully painted Mwanawasa's anticorruption campaign as a witch hunt against Bemba elites (Sishuwa 2016).

However, the Bemba areas were not enough to win a national majority. Originally, a predominantly urban party, MMD was falling out of favor with the urban electorate. Urban unemployment, low housing standards, stagnating wages, and inflation had left many urban voters discontent with the country's political trajectory. The party was no longer regarded as advancing the interests of a hard-struggling urban population. Michael Sata, on the other hand, offered populist policies as a solution to urban poverty, promising lower taxes, better housing, more jobs, and universal education and healthcare (Larmer and Fraser 2007). PF also engaged the urban poor in marketplaces and bus stations and created a physical presence in Lusaka's and the Copperbelt's urban spaces (Skage 2016). Such physical presence created a sense of momentum and advocacy (Larmer and Fraser 2007). Ultimately, PF lost the 2006 election. Nevertheless, the election was a huge success for the party, increasing its vote to 29% from a very modest 3% in 2001. It also confirmed that the days of MMD dominance were most certainly over.

PF was given a second chance to win the presidency in 2008 after Mwanawasa's death in office triggered a by-election. Mwanawasa's successor, Rupiah Banda, hailed from Eastern Province. The ascent of Banda to the top of MMD perfectly illustrates the ever-changing character of regional mobilization among Zambian parties. In 1991, Eastern Province was the only province not carried by MMD, by 2008 the same province had become arguably the party's most important stronghold. The choice of Banda as Mwanawasa's successor, however, alienated MMD even more from its roots as a party representing the ethnic Bemba. Again, Sata was unsuccessful in the 2008 election but reduced the gap to MMD further. The election turned out extremely close, with Sata winning 38% of the vote compared to 40% for Banda. In an analysis of voting patterns, Cheeseman and Hinfelaar (2010) find that PF mobilized two distinct types of consistencies: diverse densely populated urban areas and sparely populated Bemba areas.

In 2011, PF finally manages to win the presidential election and put an end to 20 years of MMD rule. What were the strategies that finally tipped the balance in favor of Sata? How did the party go from 29% of the vote in 2006 to 42% of the vote in 2011? The eventual victory of the PF can be understood as a victory for the regional mobilization strategy. Figure 3.3 shows the share of the vote that the PF received in each province for the

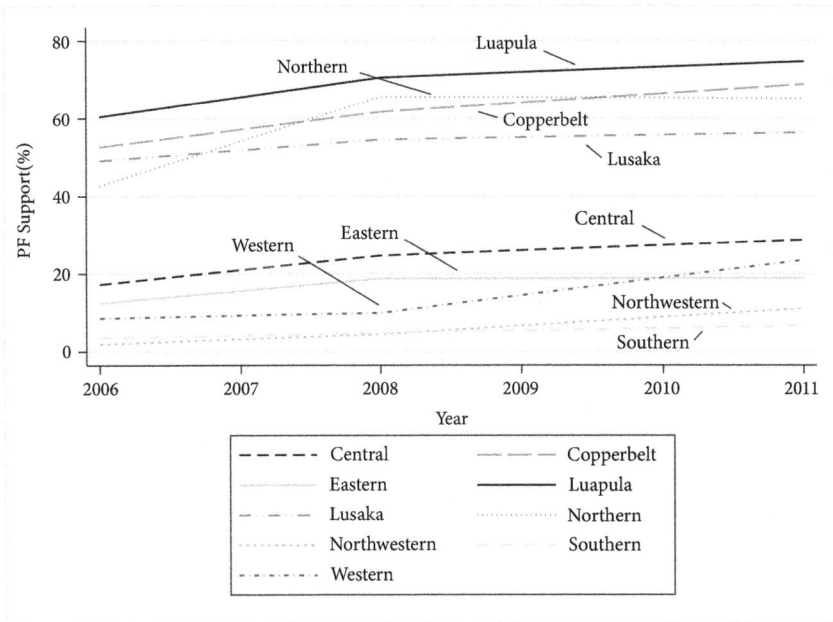

Figure 3.3 PF Support by Province 2006–2011.

Source: Electoral Commission of Zambia.

2006, 2008, and 2011 elections. In the 2006–2011 period, PF made very little gain in Eastern (strong MMD stronghold) and Southern (strong UPND stronghold) Province. They gained some ground in the relatively ethnically heterogeneous Central Province. More importantly, PF had some success in Western Province in the 2011 election. Sishuwa (2018) attributed this success partly to their promise to restore the historic privileges to Barotseland and devolve power to the formerly autonomous region. Similarly, Kim (2017: 29) notes how the PF used its campaign in Western Province to promote itself as the regional champion and criticize the track record of MMD in delivering agricultural development to the province. Nevertheless, Sata finished third in the province, behind both Banda and Hichilema of the UPND.

The main explanation for PF's 2011 victory is not its ability to make inroads in new provinces, but its increased vote margins, registration numbers, and turnout rates in its existing strongholds. In Northern Province alone (where 372,000 voters voted), PF won more votes than they did in Central, Eastern, Northwestern, Southern, and Western provinces combined (where 1,260,000 voters voted). Although PF made some improvements in their election results in Central and Western provinces, these improvements did not add much to their vote totals. Comparing 2011 to 2008, PF added more votes in the small rural Luapula Province by increasing their vote share from 70% to 75% of the vote (69,000 more votes in 2011 compared to 2008) than they did by becoming more viable in Central and Western Province (in these two provinces combined PF added 58,000 more votes compared to 2008).

Figure 3.4 shows the distribution of the vote in the 2011 election. It shows the overwhelming victories that PF secured in many constituencies in the more rural parts of Copperbelt, Luapula, and Northern Province. The vote patterns show the power of the geographically polarized approach to politics for insurgent parties. Whereas long-standing dominant parties like MMD were able to remain nationalized for an extended period, PF eventually defeated them on a strategy of winning large margins in restricted geographical areas. It is also worth noting that the third party, UPND, can also be described as regionalized, winning most of its votes in Southern Province.

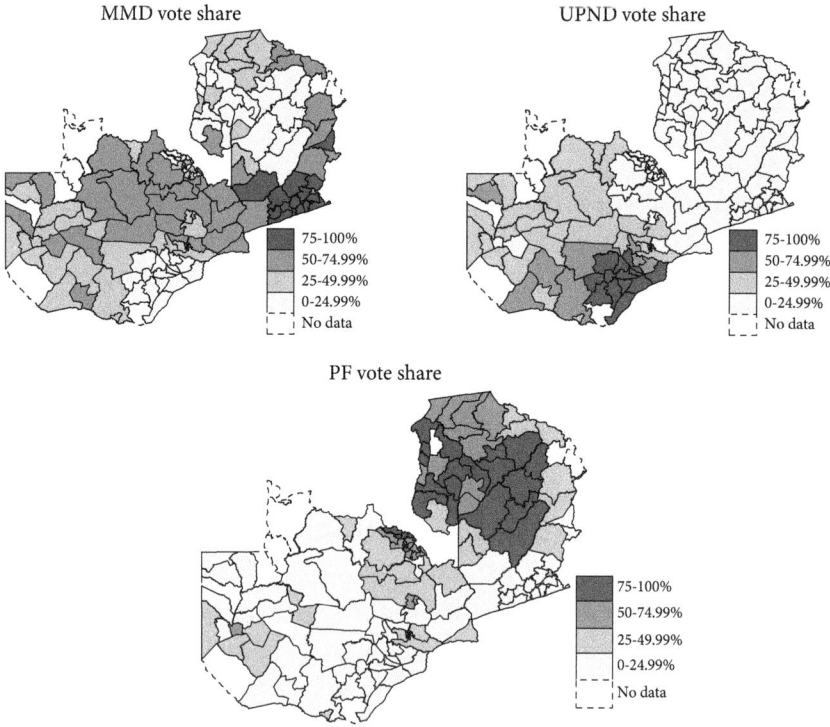

Figure 3.4 Presidential Electoral Map 2011.

Note: Election data from Electoral Commission of Zambia (ECZ).

3.4 Electoral Competition in the PF Regime

The previous section showed the ultimate success of regionalized political mobilization. It also shows how strong regional identities have been mobilized on an election-by-election basis and how regional alignments have shifted as parties have competed over regional mobilization. The PF finally won the 2011 election by becoming the uncontested and unequivocal promoter of Northern, Copperbelt, and Lusaka interests. Chapter 4 will study the subnational variations in campaign violence in the 2016 election and discuss how such violence relates to territoriality. For this reason, it is particularly important to under-stand how territorial politics shifted in the PF era. Chapter 4 will also discuss the use of centralized repressive capacity in the 2016 election. For this reason, it is also worth discussing how central capacity developed in the years between 2011 and 2016. In particular, this section will show that with MMD finally defeated the Zambian political landscape was fundamentally redrawn. The consequence was that Zambia emerged as more geographically polarized.

Sata's rule proved to be short-lived. Just three years after taking power, Sata died in office, triggering a by-election in 2015. The procedures for selecting a successor to Sata were unclear. The PF had been a highly personalized party and had never had a convention to elect a leader. The acting president Guy Scott, a veteran white politician, was constitutionally prevented from serving as president as his parents were not native Zambians. The succession bat-tle turned into a hugely controversial affair, with the incumbent Minister of Defense, Edgar Lungu, emerging as the new president of PF. Lungu's victory was enabled by serious intraparty violence, manipulation of institutions, and legal wrangles (Fraser 2017).

After its defeat, MMD had started to disintegrate with factional battles between Rupiah Banda and his mostly Eastern group of supporting MPs and his challenger, Nevers Mumba. In a long legal battle, Mumba was eventually declared the leader of the party. It was understood that Mumba would support the candidacy of UPND's Hakainde Hichilema, but instead moved to register himself as a presidential candidate in his own right. Banda and his Eastern faction on the other hand moved to support Lungu's candidacy (Beardsworth 2018). Lungu himself hailed from Eastern Province, and the consolidation of Eastern elites within PF was an important shift in both the PF's party identity and the political identification of Eastern Province.

With MMD decimated, there were essentially only two serious contenders in the 2015 election: Hichilema and his UPND and Lungu and his PF.

The election campaign was contested in an unusual environment by Zambian standard. Historically, Zambian incumbent parties have enjoyed huge incumbent advantages using the resources of the state for partisan causes (Helle 2016; Bwalya and Maharaj 2018). However, the fact that the transition government was run by an acting president with a problematic relationship to the official government party's candidate, limited the incumbent's access to resources. The final by-election results were extremely close, with Lungu defeating Hichilema with only 30,000 votes. The election was highly geographically polarized and a new electoral geography had emerged with the country divided neatly down the middle. UPND carried Western, Northwestern, and Southern provinces, and PF dominated the Copperbelt, Lusaka, Eastern, Muchinga, Luapula, and Northern. Only Central Province was more competitive.

In retrospect, UPND's strength in Western and Northwestern Provinces is often seen as more or less structurally determined. However, such arguments rest on feeble grounds. There is no particular ethnic logic to why these regions would fall in line behind the UPND, especially after 2016 when PF enlisted a vice-presidential candidate from Western Province. Moreover, as late as 2011, UPND finished second in both Northwestern and Western Province, winning only 36% and 29% of the vote respectively. UPND's growth in Western and Northwestern Zambia illustrates the active mobilization of regional cleavages.

The closeness of the 2015 by-election increased the stakes for the regularly scheduled elections planned only 19 months later. The 2015 election had given a strong indication of the strength of the major players, but the changing nature of the governing party had also led to further realignments. In preparation for the election, several PF heavyweights, including Guy Scott and former minister of defense Geoffrey Bwalya Mwamba (popularly referred to as simply "GBM") had defected from the party and joined UPND. Hichilema had even picked GBM, a northern Bemba businessman, as his running mate, possibly strengthening the opposition party's credentials in the PF-dominated north. Meanwhile, PF had strengthened its ties in Eastern Province (Beardsworth 2018).

More than that, the Zambian 2016 election was also contested under a new amended constitution that had preserved the tremendous executive powers of the old constitution but had also introduced some important changes to the electoral system. Most importantly, the constitution introduced a new 50 + 1 electoral system for the presidential election. As a consequence, the new system enables a second round of voting in the case that no candidate was able to win an outright majority in the first round (Hinfelaar et al. 2021).

It was clear to everyone involved that the 2016 election was set to be an extremely tight two-horse race between Lungu and Hichilema. However, it was not clear that any one candidate could win the election in the first round of voting. This uncertainty further pushed the contestants to maximize their votes to reduce the probability of a second round. The electoral geography of the 2015 election suggested that most subnational locations would be highly uncompetitive. A party that could safeguard its strength in its strongholds and increase turnout, while simultaneously disturbing the territorial control of the competition in its strongholds, would win the election.

The 2016 campaign was highly dependent on groundwork campaigning, with both the PF and UPND rolling out impressive presidential tours around the country. According to data from the Afrobarometer, 63% of rural Zambians attended campaign rallies in 2016. These campaigns were designed to create local report and a sense of local advocacy. In other words, they attempted to mobilize strong regional cleavages. For instance, talking about UPND presidential rallies, Beardsworth notes (2020: 53):

In each ward where he campaigned, Hichilema tailored the message to local concerns, addressing issues that animated local politics and tying it into a consistent narrative of government failure and maladministration. He always appeared on stage flanked by local elites who had fallen afoul of the PF administration, and each was called upon to denounce the PF and to extol the virtues of Hichilema's UPND.

Beardsworth (2018) finds that contrary to what has been argued in some other cases like Ghana (Rauschenbach 2015) and Kenya (Horowitz 2016), UPND spent a significant amount of time campaigning in government party strongholds.

The geographically polarized nature of the election is reflected in the electoral results displayed in Figure 3.5. Almost 60% of all constituencies had one presidential candidate winning over 75% of the vote. The country was entirely split between a PF-dominated east and a UPND-dominated west. The level of competition was particularly low in Eastern (79% PF), Luapula (82% PF), Muchinga (83% PF), Northwestern (87% UPND), Southern (92% UPND), and Western (82% UPND). The final election results gave Lungu an outright victory in the first round of voting. However, as in 2015, the election was extremely close. Hichilema captured 47.6% of the vote, compared to 50.4% for Lungu. Lungu managed to avoid a second round of voting by a margin of only 13,000 votes.

PF vote share   UPND vote share

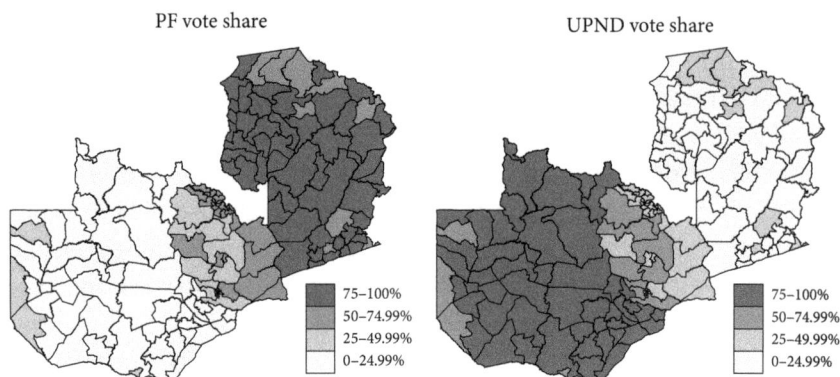

	75–100%
	50–74.99%
	25–49.99%
	0–24.99%

Figure 3.5 Presidential Electoral Map 2016.

Note: Election data from the Electoral Commission of Zambia (ECZ).

The electoral results were, however, not accepted by the opposition. The campaign period was hugely controversial, with violence, prevention of campaigning, media bias, and restrictions on media freedom (Goldring and Wahman 2016). State resources were also frequently used in the campaign. For instance, government ministers continued to enjoy their ministerial resources throughout the campaign in violation of the electoral code. The opposition also leveraged accusations against the government for rigging the actual vote. Although the merit of these accusations remains unknown, how the election and the aftermath of the election played out showed significant institutional bias in favor of the government. The opposition ended up challenging the presidential election in the constitutional court, a court that had been packed with Lungu loyalists. The court never seriously handled the petition but instead threw out the petition based on a technicality (Ndulo 2016a; Kerr and Wahman 2021).[3]

3.5 Analyzing the History of Geographic Polarization in Zambia

The previous sections have illustrated the power of the regionalized approach through an analysis of electoral history in Zambia since independence. This point can also be made using province-level election data. Analyzing such data,

---

[3] The constitution prescribes that presidential petitions have to be heard within 14 days after the release of the election results. The constitutional court hence threw out the petition, but prominent Zambian law scholar Muna Ndulo has argued that the constitution does not preclude that petitions need to be settled within 14 days and that petitioners have the right to have their petitions heard by the court (Ndulo 2016).

we find that national elections in Zambia can be won by stronghold mobilization. Turning out the party's regional base and winning it with great margin
has been more important for national success than competing for swing areas.

Figure 3.6 shows the number of total votes by province for each election.
The figure shows that three provinces dominate Zambian elections numerically: Copperbelt, Lusaka, and Southern.[4] Another noteworthy feature is that
the number of votes in these three regions has changed drastically over time.[5]
Most tellingly, the vote in Southern Province shows how parties with a strong
regional identity are better equipped to mobilize voters. The total number
of votes in the region has increased significantly especially since the birth of
UPND. In the last election before the creation of UPND (1996), voter turnout
(as a share of registered voters) was 57.9% in Southern Province, this was
below the national turnout at 58.6%. The province ranked seventh out of the
country's nine provinces in turnout. In 2016, Southern Province had a significantly higher turnout than any other Zambian province at 72.3% compared to

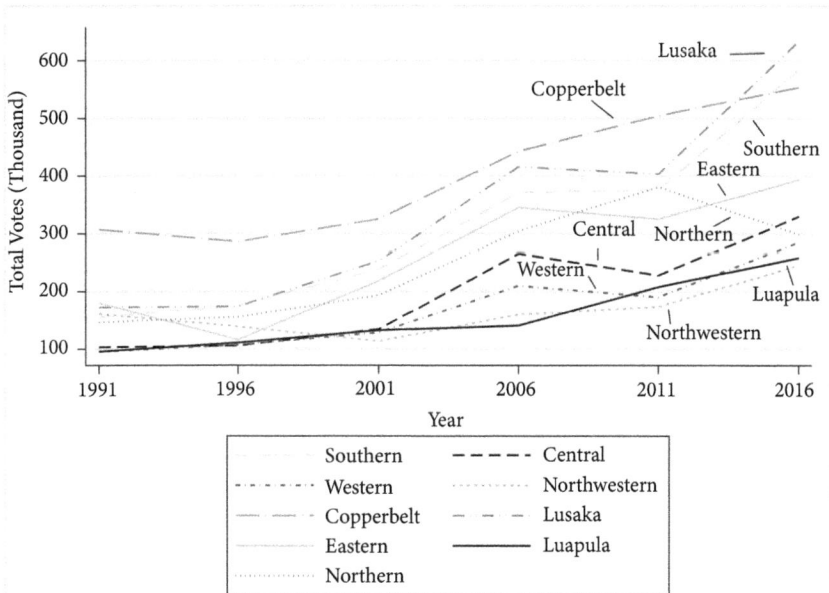

Figure 3.6 Total Votes Cast by Province 1991–2016.

Note: Muchinga Province is excluded as this province was only created in October 2011.

---

[4] One might argue that the importance of the Copperbelt is underestimated in this graph as the
smaller, mostly rural, provinces Luapula and Northern (and also the newly created province of
Muchinga) tend to vote together as one bloc with the Copperbelt (Boone et al. 2022).

[5] The number of votes in Lusaka has been steadily increasing, partly due to urbanization.

the national turnout of 53.6% (the province with the second highest turnout was Northwestern at 61.3% turnout).

Figure 3.7 shows the share of all votes won by the party that won the most votes in each province. On aggregate, the winner vote share started high in MMD's landslide 1991 election and steadily declined until 2001 when MMD was almost voted out of power. Since 2001, the vote share of the regional winner has increased steadily for almost every region, apart from Northwestern, Western, and Lusaka where the winning vote share decreased in 2011 but rebounded again for the 2016 election. Importantly, the 2016 election was more nationally competitive than any other election, but still the average province-winner won 75.8% of the vote.

There is some variation over time in what provinces that have overwhelmingly voted as a bloc and what provinces that have been more split. For instance, provinces like Northern, Luapula, Western, and Northwestern have varied considerably not only in the level of bloc-voting but also how they compare to other provinces in the same election. This is important, as it illustrates that the level of bloc-voting is not demographically or economically

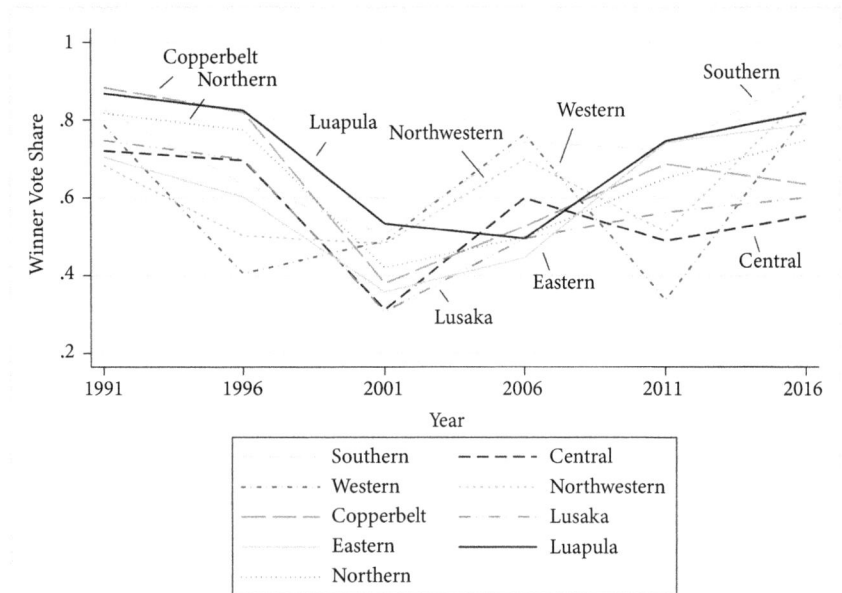

Figure 3.7 Share of Votes Won by the Most Popular Presidential Candidate by Province, 1991–2016.

Note: Muchinga Province is excluded as this province was only created in October 2011.

determined. Instead, this simple descriptive analysis reaffirms that high levels of regional cohesion in voting is contingent on effective political mobilization. Other provinces like Southern and Eastern (with the exception of the 2001 election) have consistently voted homogeneously compared to other provinces, whereas provinces like Central and Lusaka have consistently been more competitive.

While most regions grew less competitive between 2011 and 2016, the Copperbelt is the only region where this is not the case. Also, the other urban region, Lusaka (with its surrounding Central province), did not see the same sort of decreased competition as other more rural regions. PF won the 2011 election with significant support from Copperbelt and Lusaka, but ruling parties in Zambia have tended to lose support in urban areas (Wahman and Boone 2018). As described above, UPND tried hard to win over the urban vote, knowing that it had historically been prone to volatility due to dissatisfaction with government performance (Bates and Block 2013).

The combination of Figure 3.6 and Figure 3.7 is displayed in Figure 3.8. This figure shows the total number of votes added to the provincial winner's

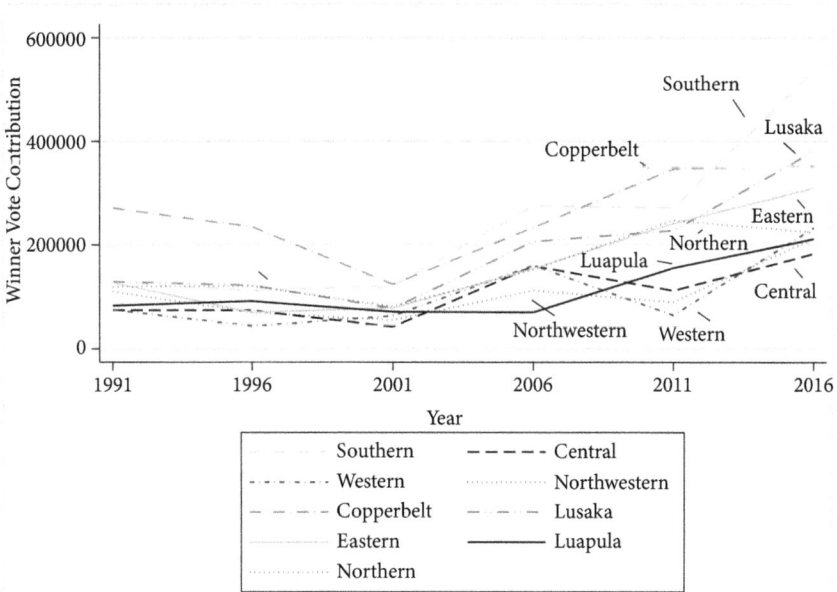

Figure 3.8 Number of Votes Won in Each Province for the Province's Most Popular Presidential Candidate, 1991–2016.

Note: Muchinga Province is excluded as this province was only created in October 2011.

national vote total from a given province. Four provinces stand out: Southern, Lusaka, Copperbelt, and Eastern. The province that added the greatest number of votes to the vote total of its provincial winner is Southern Province. In 2016, the UPND won 537,000 votes in Southern Province alone. This corresponds to 31% of all the votes the party won in this election. This is remarkable given that Southern Province is only the third largest province in terms of registered voters. The relatively large population of Southern Province in combination with extraordinarily high levels of bloc-voting has made the province an ideal base for opposition politics. This also means that a national victory for the UPND is absolutely contingent on an impressive showing in Southern Province. In the event of low turnout or smaller than expected victory margins for the opposition party, the UPND is almost certain to lose the national vote. Another noteworthy takeaway from Figure 3.8 is that Eastern Province delivered almost as many votes for the PF as the Copperbelt (88% as many) and Lusaka (81% as many) respectively. This is despite the province only having 75% as many registered voters as the Copperbelt and 69% as many registered voters as Lusaka.

Generally, both PF and UPND were highly reliant on large margins in key provinces. Looking at the UPND, the party won 55% of all its votes in Northwestern, Western, and Southern Province, despite these provinces only accounting for 29.5% of the registered voters. PF, on the other hand derived 49.5% of all its votes from Eastern, Luapula, Muchinga, and Northern Province. These provinces accounted for only 30% of the country's registered voters.

3.5.1 Local Party Volatility

The theory chapter argued that while basic regional cleavages create regional identities, the mobilization of those cleavages are contested in African poorly institutionalized party systems. It is often the case that parties do not have the sort of long-lasting ties to a particular region that would give them a monopoly on the position as regional advocates. The historical overview showed how provinces such as the Copperbelt, Western, Northwestern, and Northern have shifted their political allegiances over time.

To reiterate this point, I calculated province-level party volatility scores. First, I calculated overall volatility using the standard Pedersen Index (Pedersen 1979) at the province level, indicating the share of votes that change from one party to another in a given province between one election and the previous election.[6] I also calculate two different types of volatility, what has been referred to as type-A volatility and type-B volatility (Powell and Tucker 2014). Type-A volatility refers to "extra-system volatility," i.e., volatility caused by the entry of new political parties. Type-B volatility, on the other hand, refers to volatility of the vote between already existing parties (Mainwaring et al. 2017). In Africa, the distinction may be crucial (Weghorst and Bernhard 2014; Kuenzi et al. 2019). It may be hard to interpret the real meaning of volatility scores if volatility is mostly an effect of the instability of the organizational basis of parties (Elischer 2013). While elites may shift parties, some may argue that newly created parties are effectively continuations of old parties and mostly an expression of a slight change in inter-regional (or, if you want, inter-ethnic) coalition building. However, if we find high levels of province-level type-B volatility, this would strongly indicate regions re-evaluating their electoral loyalty between elections.

In practice, type-A volatility is calculated by subtracting the volatility caused by changes in the vote choice among parties that existed in both the current and the previous election. Type-B volatility is calculated by subtracting the volatility caused by new parties entering or old parties exiting. Together, type-A and type-B volatility make up the overall Pedersen volatility score. Figure 3.9 shows the average province-level volatility for each election. Figure 3.9 shows average province-level volatility for different provinces across elections.

As illustrated in Figure 3.9, province-level volatility has been extremely high in Zambia. The average overall volatility across provinces and elections is 0.43. As a point of reference, Weghorst and Bernhard (2014) find the average national-level volatility score for a sample of 41 African countries in the period 1950–2008 to be 0.28. There are also important variations over time, particularly with the elections of 2001 characterized by a high level of type-A volatility.[7] This is the election when Chiluba's unsuccessful third-term bid led to severe fractionalization of the previously dominant MMD.

Interestingly, in three out of five elections, type-B volatility has been higher than type-A volatility, meaning that volatility cannot simply be explained by elites creating new party outfits. Indeed, many of the important shifts in Zambian politics have happened through type-B volatility. For instance,

---

[6] Pedersen = $\frac{\sum_{i=1}^{n} |p_{it} - p_{i(t-1)}|}{2}$ where n is the number of presidential parties and p_i represents the share received by that party at time periods t and $t-1$. The index ranges between 0 and 1, with 0 indicating that all parties in a given province receive the exact same share of the vote at the election at point t as that they did at the election at point $t-1$, and 1 showing that all parties that received any share of the vote at point t did not exist at point $t-1$.

[7] Type-A volatility in 1996 was also high, but this was mainly caused by the UNIP presidential boycott.

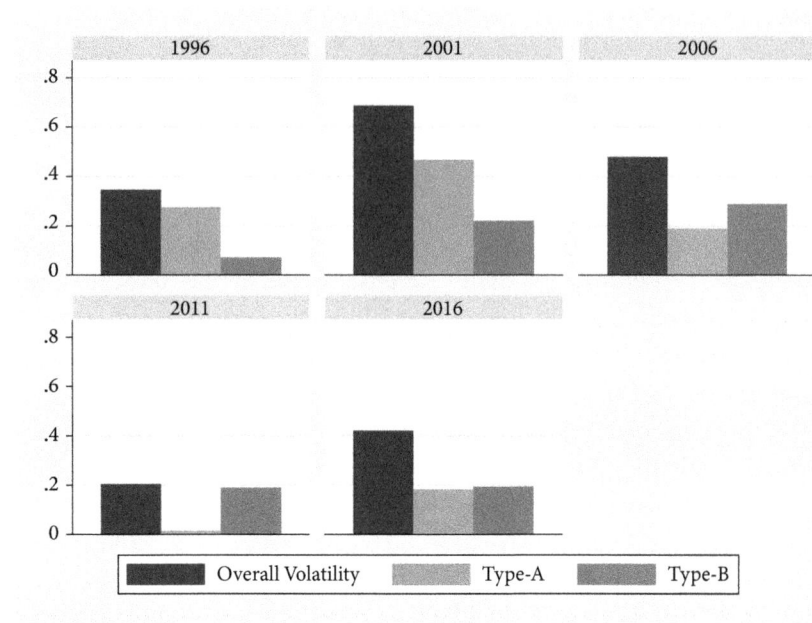

Figure 3.9 Average Province-Level Presidential Party Volatility, by Election.

Note: Across province average presidential party volatility by election.

PF gradually overtaking MMD in Northern, Luapula, and the Copperbelt, UPND growing to become the dominant party in Western and Northwestern or PF becoming the dominant party in Eastern Province. All these examples illustrate that regional mobilization is contested and that interpretations of regional advocacy can change. Looking at Figure 3.10, we see that all provinces have had a relatively high level of volatility. The provinces with the historically highest level of volatility are Eastern, Northwestern, and Western.[8]

3.5.2   Local Dominance and Turnout

Lastly, the theory section argued that parties will try to control area and create a strong sense of local viability. I have also argued that such momentum should translate to better mobilization (such as Southern Province since the creation

---

[8] Muchinga Province was created for the 2016 election and included parts of Eastern and Northern Province. I am, however, comparing Eastern and Northern in 2011 (with the old boundaries) with Eastern and Northern in 2016 (with the new boundaries) for the purpose of this analysis.

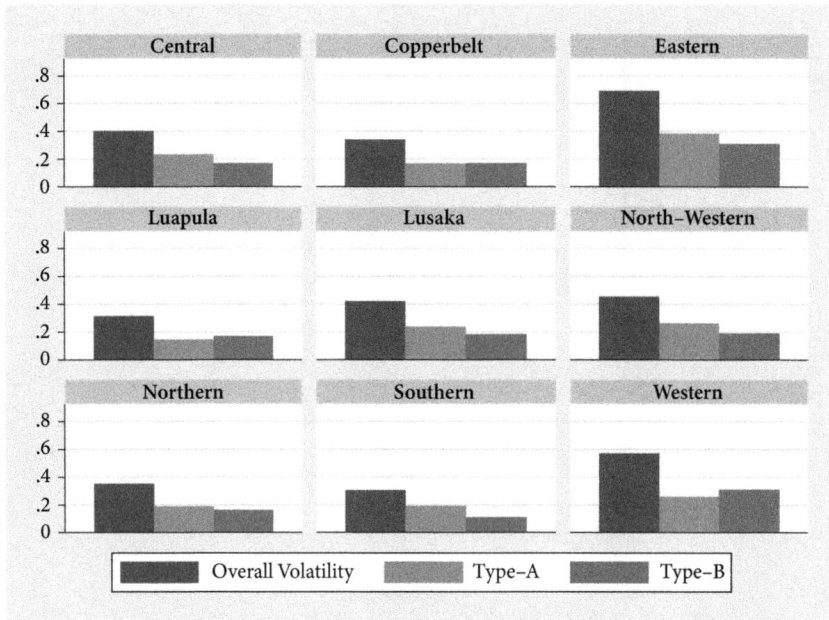

Figure 3.10 Average Presidential Party Volatility by Province, 1996–2016.

Note: Provincial average volatility for elections 1996–2016.

of UPND). One potential counterargument to this claim is that a strong sense of an inevitable victory may reduce the willingness of voters to turnout. However, there is little empirical evidence to support this argument. Using the 7th round of the geocoded Afrobarometer data (presented in Chapter 4), I modeled the probability that a respondent stated that he/she voted in the last election based on the level of constituency-level electoral competition and whether the voter supported the local minority or local majority party (i.e. whether the voter voted for the party that won or lost the election in the voter's constituency in the last election).[9] The full regression results are available in Table A3.1 in the Appendix.

The main results are plotted in Figure 3.11. The results show that while local minority supporters remain equally likely to vote regardless of level of

---

[9] Using lagged election returns from 2015 and the ratio between the constituency runner-up and the constituency winner's number of votes to measure competition. In the models, I also control for constituency population density (logged), the respondent's lived poverty index (Mattes 2020), and constituency-level nightlight. The full regression results are available in the appendix. The modeling approach used here mirrors the approach used in Chapter 5.

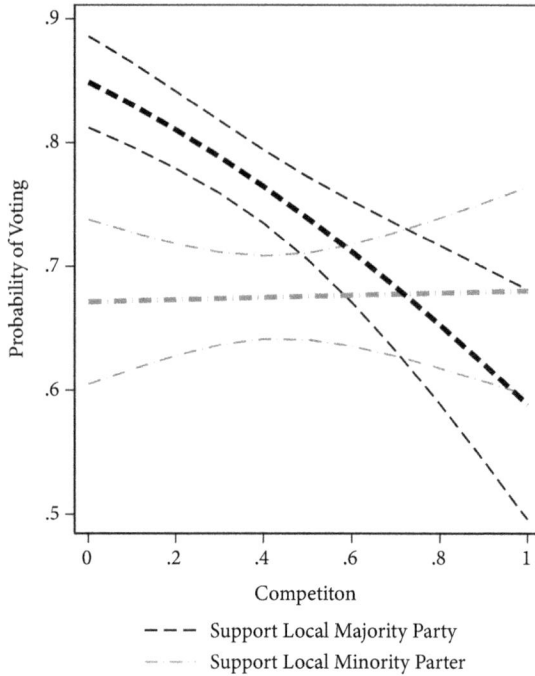

Figure 3.11 Reported Turnout among Local Majority and Minority Party Supporters Depending on Level of Competition.

Note: Postestimations based on Model 1 in Table A3.1 of the Appendix. Outer regions show 90% confidence intervals.

competition, local majority supporters are significantly more likely to vote in constituencies where the level of competition is low.[10] At the lowest level of competition, respondents supporting the local majority party had an 84% probability that they voted in the last election, compared to a 60% probability at the highest level of competition.

These findings suggest multiple reasons for parties to project local strength. First, such attempts will limit rival parties' abilities to make effective inroads and mobilize the regional cleavage. Second, stronger local dominance will also energize the base and enhance turnout within strongholds.

[10] This finding is also interesting in light of the findings in Chapter 6, showing that local minority supporters are not more afraid of violence when voting than local majority supporters. These two analyses seem to reiterate the same basic point of argument.

3.6 Conclusion

This chapter has outlined the main regional cleavages in Zambian politics and the nature of the political coalitions in the 2016 election. What does this imply more specifically for the electoral environment in which campaign violence occurred in 2016? There are a number of important conclusions which will help us interpret the findings about subnational patterns of electoral violence in next chapter.

First, political institutions in Zambia have rewarded political parties with a strong regional identity, particularly those that create multiregional coalitions. Political parties that have mobilized effectively within their strongholds have generally performed better in national elections. This has been particularly true for opposition parties. However, given the ethnic demography, where no group is large enough to win an election on a mono-ethnic appeal, parties need to create broader coalitions and make an appeal to multiple ethnic and regional constituencies.

Second, and relatedly, in the 2016 election political, parties (particularly the opposition) were highly dependent on turning out voters in great numbers within their regional strongholds. Southern Province, in particular, was important for the UPND's prospects of winning national majorities. The opposition party needed to have almost complete control of the province and create a sense of electoral momentum to mobilize voters. On the flip side, disturbing territoriality for the opposition in Southern Province was a potentially rewarding strategy for the government party. The next chapter will show how Southern Province became a hotbed for campaign violence orchestrated both by the UPND and the PF.

Third, some provinces like Northwestern and Western have been historically volatile. Although UPND was banking on mobilizing these provinces, the historical ties between the party and the regions were nowhere as established as the link between Southern Province and the UPND. This could also be said about Eastern Province and the PF. There are no long-reaching ethnic ties between these provinces and the main political parties. Instead, parties need to actively mobilize these regional cleavages and create credible claims of regional advocacy. Local campaigns are a key part of this process.

Fourth, the regional political identity of the major cities was contested. The cities had been historically mobilized by the PF, but UPND was increasingly trying to make a case as the party mobilizing urban interests. PF ultimately managed to maintain control over these areas and, as the next chapter will show, territorial violence was very much part of the PF's strategy to maintain control over urban areas.

Lastly, the government party maintained extraordinary levels of incumbency advantages. The government's access to state resources was unmistakable, providing the resources necessary for campaign violence. The government also controlled the legal system and the security apparatus and, as will be discussed in more detail in next chapter, the police were used to repress the opposition with impunity. All in all, the incumbent party's superior position increased its capacity for violence inside and outside its traditional strongholds.

4

Campaign Violence in Zambia

The previous chapter showed the importance of regionalism in Zambian political mobilization; Zambian political parties have increasingly relied on the mobilization of narrow and clearly defined regional bases for winning national majorities. Such trends have been exacerbated by the emergence of the post-2011 Zambian two-party system. Nevertheless, parties still lack deep-rooted attachments to the regions they mobilize and despite high levels of regionalism, regional mobilization remains contested.

This chapter will show how violence and intimidation has become an integral part of electoral competition under Zambian geographic electoral polarization. Zambian elections are more competitive than ever, but at the local level parties struggle to maintain and contest territorial control. In the chapter, I present two forms of data. First, I present different forms of qualitative data from focus groups with election observers, newspaper articles, parliamentary debates, and electoral petitions to describe patterns of violence in the 2016 election. Second, I present quantitative data from the Zambian Election Monitor Survey (ZEMS) to map election violence across space. I use data from ZEMS to statistically model constituency-level variations in violence in the 2016 election across Zambia's 156 constituencies.

The results presented here correspond with the central theoretical claim of this book: violence in the Zambian 2016 election was mostly used to enforce and contest territoriality in party strongholds. Parties frequently used violence to monopolize space, reduce visible opposition, and curtail rival parties' campaigns inside vital strongholds. Both the incumbent and opposition used violence inside their own strongholds in an attempt to enforce territoriality. I also show how the government Patriotic Front (PF) frequently used violence in opposition strongholds, taking advantage of their centralized coercive capacity. Such violence can be understood as an attempt to contest territoriality.

Controlling Territory, Controlling Voters. Michael Wahman, Oxford University Press.
© Michael Wahman (2023). DOI: 10.1093/oso/9780198872825.003.0004

4.1 Background to Election Violence in Zambia

Zambia is not a country historically known for high levels of electoral violence, particularly not the deadly kind (Brosché et al. 2020). It is just recently that the case has started to feature more prominently in the academic literature on this topic. Nevertheless, the absence of deadly violence should not be construed to imply that election violence has historically played no part in political competition. A reason that election violence in Zambia has been underemphasized is the general tendency to downplay and underreport incidents of low-scale violence. While international monitoring reports have alluded to instance of violence, they have commonly described election violence in Zambia before the rule of the PF as "isolated" or "sporadic." Nevertheless, even international monitors have acknowledged possible problems of under-reporting. For instance, in its report on the 2008 presidential by-election, the EU election observation mission admits (EU 2008: 19): "Interlocutors stated that violent clashes were not always reported to the police or journalists, leading the EU EEM to assume that the number of incidents could be higher than reported."

A review of election violence before 2016 reveals a pattern of escalating and increasingly organized violence, driven in no small part by the regionalization of Zambian politics in combination with an entrenched competitive two-party system. Using both V-Dem data (Coppedge et al. 2020) and Afrobarometer public opinion data (Afrobarometer 2017), the trend of increasing violence is clear. Levels of recorded election violence in the expert-coded V-Dem data were relatively stable in the period 1991–2011.[1] Smaller spikes in violence (in the 2001 and 2006 elections) are likely the product of coders reacting to post-election riots rather than significantly different levels of campaign violence. The sharp increase, however, occurred in 2016 (Figure 4.1).

More drastically, Zambians have become significantly more afraid of violence over time. Figure 4.2 shows the share of Zambians stating that they fear violence "a lot" during election times. While the time-series is short,[2] there is

---

[1] The exact question for government violence is: "In this national election, were opposition candidates/parties/campaign workers subjected to repression, intimidation, violence or harassment by the government, the ruling party or their agents?" The question for non-government violence is: "In this national election, was the campaign period, election-day, and post-election process free from other types (not by the government, the ruling party or their agents) of violence related to the conduct of the election or the campaign?"

[2] Earlier rounds of the Afrobarometer did not ask about fear of election violence.

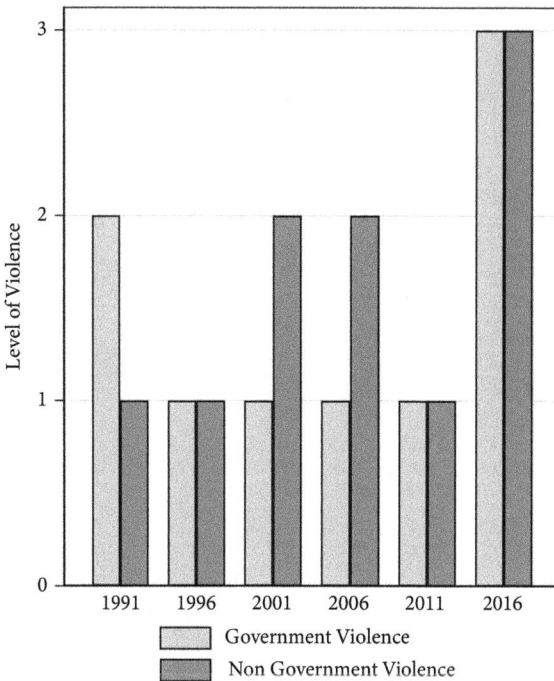

Figure 4.1 V-Dem Government and Non-government Violence in Zambia 1991–2016.

Source: V-Dem v 7.1, reported reversed versions of v2elintim_ord (government election violence) and v2epleace_ord (non-government election violence).
Note: Government violence: 0=None, 1= Restrained, 2= Some, 3=Frequent, 4=Strong.
Non-government violence: 0=None, 1=Almost no violence, 2=Limited violence, 3=Significant violence 4=Widespread violence.

a drastic increase from 17% in 2009 to 35% in 2016. An additional 15% of survey respondents stated that they fear election violence "somewhat" in the 2016 Afrobarometer. With half of the population expressing fear of violence in elections, violence must be assumed to be an important component of electoral campaigns in contemporary Zambia.

The territorial nature of violence has been a constant in Zambian political competition, but reported hotspots for violence have shifted as political parties have built varying regional coalitions. Territorial election violence was very much present in the highly regionalized electoral politics of the first Zambian multiparty state shortly after independence. The United National Independence Party (UNIP) employed violence strategically both in relation to the mostly Southern opposition from the African National Congress (ANC) and

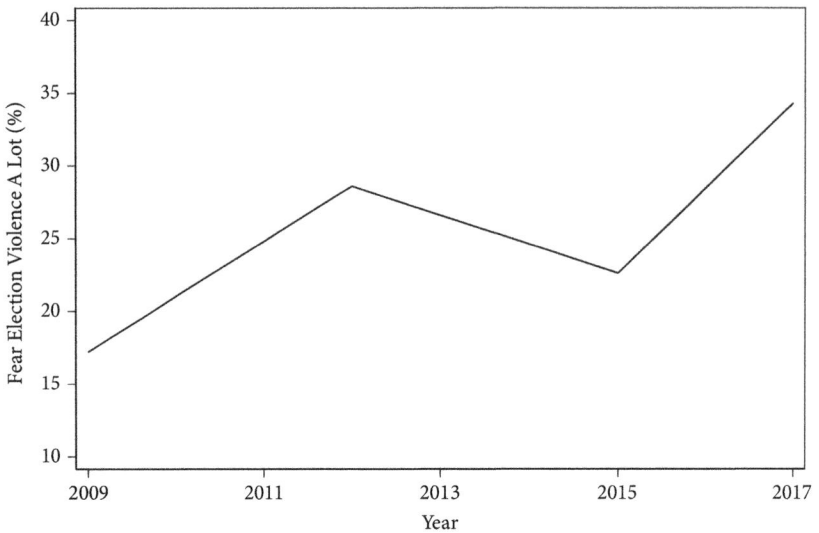

Figure 4.2 Fear of Election Violence, Zambia 2009–2017.

Source: Afrobarometer rounds 4, 5, 6, and 7. Question: "During election campaigns in this country, how much do you personally fear becoming the victim of political violence or intimidation?"

the mostly Copperbelt-dominated opposition from the United Progressive Party (UPP) (Larmer 2008). Macola (2008:39) describes a direct link between the regional character of the party-system and the strategic use of violence:

> [t]he regionalization of the ANC influenced the pattern on interparty warfare. If UNIP was responsible for the bulk of the violence in the Copperbelt and other Bemba-speaking areas [...] the ANC made sure that in their Southern and Central strongholds Kaunda's party [UNIP] was "treated with the same medicine that [it] treat[ed] others within other parts of the territory."

The turn to one-partyism in 1972 inevitably shifted the focus from inter-party to intra-party election violence. Violence in the one-party state was often an expression of vertical conflict between national-level party elites and local-level interest in connection to UNIP internal primary elections. In particular, violence was known to transpire in events where national-level elites ignored local preferences in favor of nationally favored candidates (Baylies and Szeftel 1992; Goldring and Wahman 2018).

While violence was certainly part of the strategy for upholding the Zambian one-party state, the Zambian government still allowed more pluralism—not at least within the labor movement—than the authoritarian regime in neighboring Malawi (Lebas 2011). Moreover, UNIP did not develop robust organization for violence. Such lack of violent infrastructure meant that UNIP had limited repressive capacity across the territory in the 1991 founding election.

In 1991, UNIP had been reduced to a regional party, maintaining only Eastern province as its stronghold. The opposition challenger, the Movement for Multiparty Democracy (MMD), on the other hand, was a broad nationalized coalition. Facing such a formidable challenger, UNIP used its limited repressive resources to instigate violence particularly in two areas: their own stronghold in Eastern Province and in pockets of urban Zambia, where the opposition was set to mobilize a great number of voters. In Eastern Province, in and around Chipata, there were frequent reports of UNIP supporters setting houses, crops, and granaries belonging to MMD affiliates on fire (Andreassen et al. 1992; Chan 1992). There were also frequent threats against MMD candidates. Chiefs were reported to have expelled alleged MMD supporters from their homes (NDI/Carter Center 1992). In Lusaka, the government deployed paramilitary forces in several townships in an effort to increase government presence and curb opposition campaigning and organizing. In townships like Kalingalinga, residents were reportedly picked up at night, arrested, and beaten. In markets, youth groups harassed traders lacking UNIP party cards (Andreassen et al. 1992; Lebas 2011). Nevertheless, UNIP was far too absent from most of the country and their central capacity was too weak to effectively use territorial electoral strategies effectively.

The early MMD rule saw moderate levels of violence, perhaps to a large extent due to the ruling party's ability to completely control the electoral scene using a combination of patronage politics and institutional meddling (e.g. prohibiting the candidacy of Kaunda in 1996). Weak opposition and strong government control reduced the need for campaign violence. Nevertheless, van Donge (1998) concluded that "Violence was always close to the surface." Some incidents were, however, recorded. These incidents were mostly clashes between MMD cadres and the opposition in Lusaka. One particularly serious clash between MMD and UNIP resulted in 16 injuries in 1996 (Human Rights Watch 1996).

When Zambian elections became more nationally competitive in 2001, violence did intensify, without appropriate intervention from law enforcement. The police also further complicated opposition campaigning under the guise of the Public Order Act (POA), a piece of colonial legislation designed to frustrate anti-colonial political mobilization. Using the POA, the police could deny opposition the opportunity to campaign, particularly inside government-party strongholds (Burnell 2001). Still, electoral politics in 2001 was nowhere near as regionalized as it would eventually become ten years later. Most of the reported violence in the 2001 election was concentrated in the Copperbelt, Luapula, and Northern Provinces. In 2001, these were still the MMD's most important strongholds, but MMD territoriality was threatened by the creation of parties such as the Patriotic Front (PF) and the Zambian Republican Party (ZRP) headed by charismatic Bemba politicians (Burnell 2001). In Luapula, ZRP rallies were frequently disrupted by MMD cadres (FODEP 2002). The situation became so bad that the ZRP's presidential candidate, Ben Mwila, had to fire several shots in self-defense during a rally in Chienge constituency (Bwalya 2002). In Kitwe (the Copperbelt), Michael Sata was beaten up twice while appearing on local radio. At one point, MMD cadres ended up destroying the radio station in an attempt to discourage opposition coverage in local media (Bwalya 2002; Carter Center 2002). In other words, campaign violence in 2001 was primarily used by the government to enforce territoriality. Much less violence was directed towards areas such as Southern Province, the primary site for mobilization by the main opposition party, UPND. There was also less violence observed in more competitive provinces such as Eastern, Western, and Northwestern.

The face of the Zambian opposition changed dramatically after the 2001 election, not at least due to the rise of the PF and the strong re-orientation of the MMD from a party mostly mobilizing the North and the Copperbelt to a party with a stronger focus on mobilizing rural Zambia (Resnick 2014). The change of political alignments and regionalization also incrementally changed the nature and use of violence as an electoral strategy.

The 2006 election saw clashes between the United Democratic Alliance (UDA), the electoral alliance spearheaded by the UPND, and MMD in Southern Province. The most serious incident occurred in relation to one of President Mwanawasa's rallies in Mazabuka. Mwanawasa's choice of a cite for the rally, right next to a UDA base was seen as a willful provocation against the opposition party (Commonwealth 2006; FODEP 2006).

The most important transformation after 2001 was, however, increased territorial competition in Lusaka between MMD and PF. As PF was enhancing its position in the capital, they also radically enhanced their organizational capacity for violence through an increased emphasis on caderism. More frequent clashes between the MMD and PF were enabled by more strongly entrenched economic interests of cadres associated with the two different parties. Owning space in Lusaka was integral to PF's original success. The way in which violence underpinned territoriality for PF in Lusaka was described by Larmer and Fraser (2007: 626):

> The commuter minibuses that dominate city streets were overwhelmingly and visibly supportive, playing pro-Sata songs and displaying PF slogans, flyers, and posters. At times when they carried PF supporters to events, they represented a threatening, lawless presence, with cadres singing, dancing, and riding on the roofs of the buses. When MMD cadres attempted to increase their visibility in cities they were soundly chased from the streets. Indeed, on one occasion the President was unable to travel through the capital as PF cadres blocked various routes with minibuses and threatened to stone his motorcade.

Competition between MMD and PF was also increasing in market places around Lusaka, not at least after PF won the control of the Lusaka City Council in 2006 (Hansen and Nchito 2013). In the 2006 election, PF had "taken control" of several markets in Lusaka and attempted to throw out "MMD traders." By 2011, MMD had enlisted veteran politician, William Banda, to hire so-called "call-boys" to ensure continued MMD control in the markets. PF did, however, not remain idle but created its own gangs of organized violent cadres. The battle between PF and MMD cadres became especially tense in Bauleni, a high-density area of Lusaka (Fraser 2017). Several clashes were recorded between cadres of MMD and PF in places like Lusaka City Market and Soweto Market as cadres were tearing down campaign posters to demarcate space (Lusaka Times 2011).

The real turn to violence, however, happened after the PF victory in 2011. The turnover meant the end of MMD-rule, but also the creation of a strongly regional, highly polarized, two-party system. With the death of Sata in 2014, the PF lost much of its ideological legitimacy and violence became a more important strategy for stabilizing the regime (Fraser 2017; Hinfelaar et al. 2020). The accession of Edgar Lungu to the party presidency was in itself enabled by violence. Deploying thugs to the party convention, Lungu was able to prevent delegates supporting alternative candidates from entering. The infighting that ensued within the PF around the time of party conventions even earned the PF the nickname "the Panga Family" after party members had attacked each other with *pangas* (machetes) (EISA 2016).

The 2015 presidential by-election was in many ways a dress rehearsal for the imminent general election in 2016. While the PF was somewhat constrained in its capacity for violence and in its access to state institutions due to the caretaker government of Guy Scott (who was still a PF member, but certainly not a Lungu supporter), there are still important forewarnings of some of the violence to come in 2016. PF used violence in 2015 both to contest and enforce territoriality. UPND also increasingly used violence to defend territory. Importantly, violence appeared in 2015 inside opposition strongholds that had not previously been hotspots for violence. These new hotspots were predominantly locations that had previously been more competitive. For instance, in Mongu (Western Province) a serious incident occurred between PF and UPND supporters as UPND tried to block the access to an airport where the presidential helicopter had landed in preparation for a campaign rally. The incident ended up with one UPND supporter being killed by PF cadres. Violence was also noted in Northwestern Province as outside PF cadres were ferried to the province (EISA 2016). In an incident in Shiwang'andu constituency (Muchinga Province), UPND were prevented from holding a rally after PF supporters had attacked a helicopter carrying some of UPND's most famous campaigners (including MMD MP Felix Mutati and former first lady Maureen Mwanawasa). When asked about the incident Shiwang'andu MP Stephen Kampyongo uses an explicitly territorial rationale: "Even you, do you think I can come and enter your house, address your wife and children without notifying you? This is anarchy they were asking for and they got it." (Lusaka Times 2015).[3]

While an exhaustive analysis of subnational patterns in violence is impossible without appropriate data, the discussion above shows escalating levels of violence before the 2016 election. Escalation of violence has coincided with increased levels of national competition and an increasingly geographically polarized electoral system. Moreover, key to understanding the enhanced levels of violence that will follow in the 2016 election is the willful investment in repressive capacity by political parties, especially the PF. This development is most notably connected to the political economy of cadreism that evolved from territorial competition in urban markets. Moving to the 2016 election, the organizational capacity derived from cadre networks in Lusaka

---

[3] This incident is almost identical one in which Hakainde Hichilema's helicopter was attacked in the same constituency in 2016 (described below).

and the Copperbelt also enriched the ruling party with significant capacity to perpetrate violence outside PF strongholds. Such violence to contest opposition territoriality outside major cities was historically fairly rare, but certainly led to much of the escalation of violence in 2016.

4.2 The Electoral Geography of Violence in the Zambian 2016 Election

Earlier chapters in this book provide empirical implications of the electoral geography theory of election violence. I particularly hypothesized that in geographically polarized electoral systems, such as Zambia, election violence will be particularly common in non-competetive constituencies. However, beyond observing such quantitative correlations, I also set out to explain such correlations with the concept of territoriality. That is, parties use violence in noncompetitive constituencies to enforce and contest territoriality in an attempt to shape local electoral environments. Before turning to quantitative evidence from the ZEMS survey, I will outline the general characteristics of violence and explore the mechanisms of violence using qualitative data.

4.2.1 Qualitative Data

In this chapter, I use a wealth of qualitative data. First and foremost, I conducted three different focus groups with local election observers in Lusaka, Southern, and Northwestern provinces. These provinces were all highly affected by election violence in the 2016 election but varied in terms of levels of urbanization and political leanings. While Southern and Northwestern provinces were UPND strongholds, PF dominated the Lusaka Province. In each of these focus groups, I invited constituency coordinators from the Foundation for Democratic Process (FODEP) domestic election observation network. Each focus group consisted of between five and ten participants and lasted for approximately two hours. All participants represented different constituencies within the same province, making it possible to discuss within-province variations in experiences. The focus groups were conducted in the respective provinces' capitals (Choma, Lusaka, and Solwezi) in the period December 2016–January 2017. The purpose of the focus groups was to obtain a local perspective on the electoral campaign, not available from aggregate narratives of election violence. I also complemented the information received from these focus groups with narratives from the ZEMS survey. These narratives helped to better understand the context of each violent event. Additionally, I use various secondary sources. A particularly important secondary source used here is a report commissioned by President Lungu after the 2016 election: the report of the commission of Inquiry into Voting Patterns and Electoral Violence (CIVPEV 2019). The commission held meetings in all ten provinces and accepted petitions on alleged instances of violence. Besides the report, I have also made use of newspaper articles, electoral petitions to the High Court and Constitutional Court, election monitor reports, and parliamentary debates.

4.2.2 General Characteristics and Spatial Distribution of Violence

Before turning to the mechanisms that may explain the purpose of election violence and the role that such violence filled in shaping local electoral environments, it is useful to provide a descriptive account of the extent, spatial distribution, and general characteristics of election violence in the Zambian 2016 election. Figure 4.3 shows the geographical patterns of violence observed through the ZEMS survey in both the pre- and post-electoral period.

First, it is important to note that violence in the 2016 Zambian election was mostly low scale, particularly in the pre-electoral period. There were, however, two incidents of deadly violence recorded in the ZEMS data. One case in Lusaka where an opposition supporter was shot by police and one case in Magoye (Southern Province) where a voter was stabbed. Most violence involved fights between supporters, sometimes—but not always—resulting in injuries or destruction of property. It would be easy to dismiss violence as a marginal feature of Zambian electoral politics. However, such an assertion is not at all supported by main political stakeholders, particularly not among those operating in local electoral environments. For instance, the presidential inquiry into election violence established that "intimidation of opponents and the general populace by party cadres has become a common feature in the political landscape in Zambia" (CIVPEV 2019:103). Domestic election observers in focus groups in Northwestern, Lusaka, and Southern Province describes local electoral environments entrenched in violence. Parties were unable to campaign and move around freely and voters were at risk of victimization for engaging in the campaign.

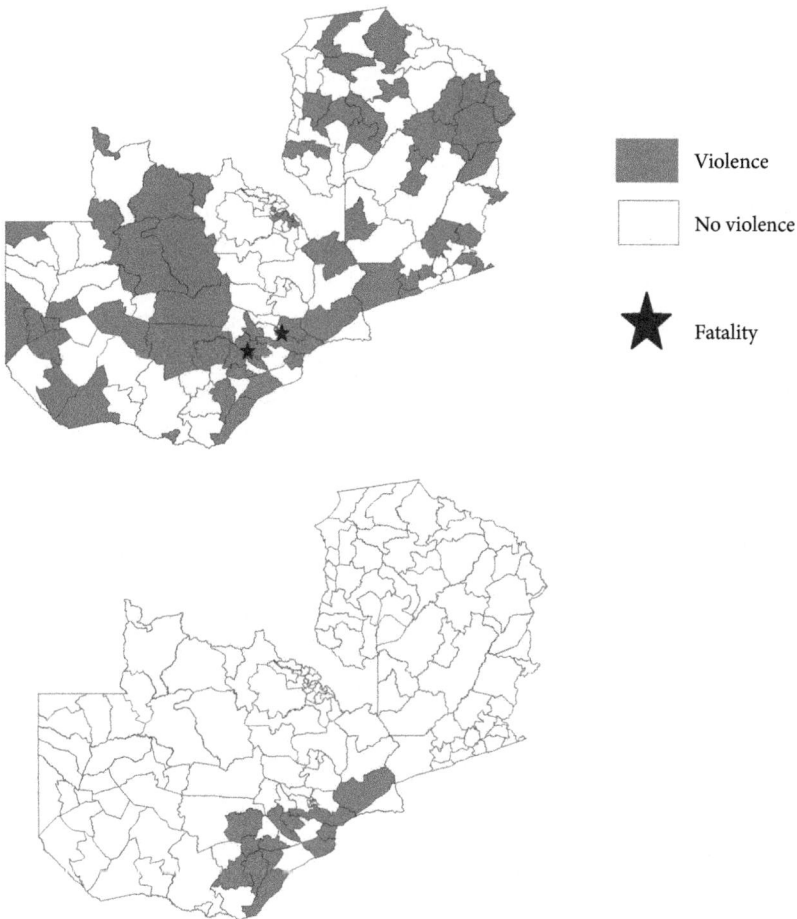

Figure 4.3 Pre- and Post-election Violence, Zambia 2016.

Note: The figure is a reprint of Inken von Borzyskowski and Michael Wahman, "Systematic Measurement Error in Election Violence Data," British Journal of Political Science 51(1): 230–252. Reproduced with permission. Data are from ZEMS.

The extent of violence was, however, not evenly spread across the territory. This is true for both pre- and post-election violence. Post-election violence was particularly concentrated in Lusaka and most importantly the opposition-leaning Southern Province. Although more disbursed, there are also geographic patterns in campaign violence. Much of the reporting on campaign violence in the news media concentrated on violence in urban areas such as Lusaka and the Copperbelt, but Figure 4.3 also shows significant violence in semi-urban and rural areas such as Southern Province, Northwestern, and Luapula. These data show a first indication that looking beyond media reports when mapping election violence is important for obtaining a comprehensive understanding of spatial patterns of election violence (von Borzyskowski and Wahman 2021).

While Southern Province has been known as an opposition stronghold for decades and appeared frequently in the reporting on election violence, high levels of violence in areas such as the PF stronghold in Luapula and the UPND stronghold in Northwestern and Western may be more surprising. Participants in the Northwestern focus group explained increased levels of violence in the province with the fact that they are now considered an opposition stronghold, while they had previously been more competitive. Territoriality in Northwestern was, however, still "up for grabs" and parties were competing over regional mobilization. As one member of the Northwestern focus group expressed: "We were a UPND stronghold, but for Northwestern Province our voting is not tribal. It's purely a matter of why we have been sidelined in terms of development."[4]

Is it possible to attribute any meaning to these patterns of violence? Countries like Zambia are often describes as having "isolated events of election violence." In particular narratives, violent events are described as spontaneous and the manifestation of a generally heated electoral environment, rather than a systematic electoral strategy (Murunga 2011). The media and political elites are usually quick to place the blame for violence on individuals with little power or influence, the sort of people that are expected to act impulsively and with little self-constraint. Commonly, blame is attributed to the young and marginalized that execute the violence, while individual politicians are rarely held directly accountable. Lack of personal accountability on behalf of political elites may be partly explained by the fact that it is hard to prove any direct links between perpetrators of violence and individual politicians, especially in a legal sense.[5] Nevertheless, a central tenant to this book is that violence is

---

[4] For instance, although we need to take the ACLED data with a grain of salt (due to the biases discussed in Chapter 1), it is noteworthy that there is no record of election violence in the dataset for the Northwestern Province before the 2016 election. However, 2016 was the first regular election where Northwestern was truly dominated by one single party. In 2011, the province was split three ways between UPND, MMD, and PF. In 2006, MMD won the province with 70% of the vote, but UPND still won 30%. In 1996, the province was only surpassed by Western in competitiveness, and in 2001 the province was a fairly close race between MMD and UPND.

[5] For instance, in relation to a parliamentary election petition in Lusaka Central constituency, the Lusaka High Court found evidence of two serious election violence events conducted towards the campaign of UPND parliamentary candidate Charlotte Scott. At both these events, UPND campaign workers were attacked by young men dressed in PF regalia. At one event, one of the UPND campaigners was stabbed by one of the perpetrators. However, in the appeal to the Constitutional Court, the incumbent PF MP, Margaret Mwanakatwe, withheld that she had no role in the organization of the violence or familiarity with the young men involved (Kerr and Wahman 2021). The Constitutional Court ruled in favor of Mwanakatwe, establishing that the violence was not attributable to the incumbent MP (*Mwanakatwe vs. Scott and Others*).

strategic and indicative of willful electoral manipulation. While "spontaneous" violence, in the sense that the specific act was not sanctioned by political elites, may occur, such violence is commonly the effect of signals sent by political elites, organizations set up by the same elites or the tacit acceptance of such strategies. The Zambian case shows how political parties and elites played a central role in organizing, encouraging, sanctioning, and enabling election violence both through their own semi-formal organizations and, in the case of the government party, through their control of the state coercive apparatus.

A majority of election violence events described in the narratives of the ZEMS survey was perpetrated by so-called party cadres. The term party cadre is frequently used in the Zambian public discourse but is loosely defined. Party cadres are not necessarily on party payrolls or even card-bearing members of political parties, instead the term has been evoked to describe youth associated with party campaigns. Such youth are predominantly men and recruited for their apparent ability to engage in violence and intimidation. Party cadres are often paid by political elites and employed as security details to powerful politicians during campaigns (Mukuntu 2019; Beardsworth et al. 2021). In the 2016 campaign, both the PF and UPND accentuated the violent role of their cadres by supplying them with weapons and military-style paraphernalia. Their physical presence in an area was designed to create an air of intimidation and physical control. Party cadres would often control entire areas, setting up headquarters in key localities with the expectation that cadres from other parties would not operate within the parameters of "their territory."

With the silent approval of the PF government, party cadres had been allowed to virtually occupy public spaces, such as marketplaces, taxi stands, and bus stops, extracting small rents from vendors and drivers. Such criminal gangs were allowed to operate with impunity, while the government party increased its coercive capacity and territorial control. The top-levels of PF cadres were able to amass significant wealth and became highly invested in the *status quo* (Lusaka Times 2021). For instance, as one participant in the Lusaka focus group explained:

> One observation I made about the violence in the town areas is that we have bus stations, we have the markets. You know these bus stations are run by cadres. If these cadres would relax and give the chance for the opposition to come in, they are definitely guaranteed that they would not be in those stations. They will not be in the bus stations. They will not be in the market. Sometimes there might not even be a leader there to incite violence. There could just be a single cadre who wants to defend that bus stop that belongs to

him. He collects K1 here and there, in the end of the day he goes home with
K100. That's enough for that person.

(Focus Group, Lusaka)

PF was certainly the party with the most developed organization of cadres,
but UPND also employed their own legions. Like PF, UPND encouraged
cadres to reinforce the opposition campaign through the use of violence.
For instance, UPND Vice-presidential candidate, Geoffrey Bwalya Mwamba,
instructed cadres in UPND to "hit back" when attacked by the PF (Lusaka
Times 2016c). "Hitting back" would often entail retaliating in areas where the
opposition had violent capacity, i.e. within opposition strongholds.

Besides party cadres, the police were also involved in several incidents of
violence. Such violence was almost always directed towards the opposition
while they attempted to campaign. A particularly controversial feature of the
2016 campaign was the frequent prevention of opposition campaigns with
reference to the POA. While the contemporary interpretation of the POA is
highly controversial, the police has often cited the law to deny the opposition the ability to campaign (Goldring and Wahman 2016). The president and
the vice president are not required to apply for a permit to hold campaign
meetings, but other public campaign rallies require such permits. In the 2016
election, the UPND was denied a permit at 23 occasions and had their rallies
cancelled at 10 occasions after having first been granted a permit. The PF was
only denied a permit at two occasions and had no rallies cancelled (CIVPEV
2019: 72).

The most noteworthy incident of police perpetrated violence occurred in
Lusaka after the police had cancelled a UPND rally in Chawama constituency.
UPND supporters initiated protest against the cancellation, but were met by
bullets from the Lusaka police. Police ended up shooting two UPND supporters, one of the supporters, a woman named Mpenzi Chibulu, tragically
lost her life due to the horrific display of police brutality. Although the incident in Chawama was the one that came to represent police repression in the
2016 election, a number of other incidents also took place. For instance, the
police used teargas against UPND supporters during campaigning in Lusaka's
Kabwata constituency (*Sata v. Lubinda and others*). Similarly, police in Luan-
shya district on the Copperbelt used teargas to disburse a group of UPND
supporters after having cancelled an election rally (CIVPEV 2019: 132).

The high levels of election violence in Zambia was observed by important
government institutions in Zambia, including the Electoral Commission of

Zambia (ECZ). However, the interventions from these institutions seem to have overwhelmingly favored the ruling party and appeared inconsistent at best (Kaaba and Haang'andu 2020). In light of the shooting of the protester in Chawama, the ECZ suspended the campaign in Lusaka for ten days. In the same decision, they also suspended campaigns in Namwala constituency (Southern Province) for the same period of time, citing a violent episode where a candidate for the Forum for Democratic Development (FDD) had been brutally attacked by UPND cadres. For the opposition, the decision seemed suspicious. Why suspend the campaign in Namwala, long after the violent episode in question? Why react to these violent events and not others? The suspicion was that the ECZ tried to hinder opposition mobilization in the south, while reducing the chances of the opposition making any inroads in the capital. In a press statement, the UPND Secretary General, Stephen Katutka, concludes: "UPND implores the ECZ to act in the best interest of Zambia and her young democracy and to desist from taking unlawful, biased and unfair actions such as the issuance of the directive in issue" (Zambia Reports 2016). Similarly, while the High Court of Lusaka decided to annul elections in Lusaka Central and Kabwata constituencies, partly because of serious violence, this ruling was later overturned by the Constitutional Court. The Constitutional Court in Zambia has been widely criticized for its pro-government bias, stemming from the system of presidential appointment (Ndulo 2016b; Kerr and Wahman 2021).

4.2.3 No-Go Zones and Watermelons: Election Violence to Enforce Territoriality

Violence to enforce territoriality was systemic in the Zambian election, it happened in both PF strongholds such as Lusaka, Copperbelt, Northern, and Muchinga and in UPND stronghold such as Southern, Western, and North-western. Both PF and UPND used violence to shrink the democratic space in their respective strongholds and reduce the rival party's ability to campaign. While most of this violence was low scale in nature, it served to create a sense of dominance for the regionally strong party and often severely restricted the way that local partisan minorities could engage in the campaign. In fact, territorial violence in some parts of the country was so widespread that no meaningful local democracy existed. As concluded by the presidential inquiry on election violence: "the creation of 'no-go' areas during election campaigns deprived other parties of the opportunity to present their manifestos and deprived voters of the necessary information upon which they could base their vote choice" (CIVPEV 2019: 53).

Many incidents of violence in the 2016 campaign clearly converge to the idea of violence to enforce territoriality or what can be labeled as "no go-zone politics." In some cases, central actors even explicitly identified the violence as territorial. For instance, one such famous incident occurred in relation to a planned Hichilema rally in Shiwang'andu constituency (Muchinga Province). In this incident (that was almost identical to a similar incident in 2015, described in the section above), PF cadres blocked the roads to the rally, lit fires around the venue, and threw stones at the UPND president's helicopter in an attempt to make it impossible for the opposition leader to land. In the end, the rally had to be aborted due to security concerns. When asked about the incident, UPND Secretary General, Stephen Katuka, stated: "There should be no such thing as a 'no-go' area during an open, free, and fair campaign." (Lusaka Times 2016d).[6] Similar episodes of PF-orchestrated violence against opposition campaigns in PF strongholds were also noted by our observers in places like Chinsali (Muchinga Province), Chipili (Luapula Province), Malambo (Eastern Province), Kasama Central (Northern Province), and Mpulungu (Northern Province) (ZEMS).

Incidents of territorial violence go beyond what can be described as "isolated events" in many parts of the country. Indeed, violence completely shaped the electoral environment in several key geographical areas. One useful illustration of the way in which territorial violence shaped the electoral environment was the systemically violent campaign orchestrated by the PF in Lusaka. As in earlier elections (Fraser 2017), PF tried to control the urban spaces through the use of cadres who operated in the markets and in the bus depots. The capital was visibly dominated by the ruling party with posters, party flags, and voters wearing the green PF-branded T-shirts, hats, and chitenge (cloth). Any attempt by the opposition to make inroads was met with violence: opposition billboards were burned, posters were torn, and people wearing the opposition's signature color, red, were assaulted. Opposition rallies were frequently blocked by PF cadres.

High levels of victimization meant that the opposition in Lusaka had to redesign their campaign and rely on less outward facing campaign strategies. As a response to violence, opposition supporters were asked not to wear the

---

[6] The PF ended up winning 91% of the presidential vote in Shiwang'andu.

party's red regalia, but instead disguise themselves as PF supporters wearing the government party's green attire. This strategy was famously dubbed the "watermelon strategy."[7] By using the watermelon strategy, opposition voters did not have to be victimized for their support of the opposition, but could still vote for UPND on election day. Nevertheless, the absence of physical UPND presence in the capital made a tremendous impact on the electoral environment. For instance, as one participant in our Lusaka focus group relied: "One thing I witnessed in town was that the regalia during the time of the campaigns were all PF. If you wear anything red you were in danger of being beaten up."

Lusaka provides an interesting case in point why territorial violence may ultimately be effective, despite no direct effect on actual vote choice or perhaps even turnout. The PF was able to effectively reduce political participation in a broad sense, through the use of violence and the culture of intimidation that was created in the capital. PF came to dominate the electoral environment and appeared to be the only locally viable and present party. As the judge in the High Court petition on Lusaka Central concludes in the judgment on *Scott vs. Mwanakatwe*, the number of voters directly affected by violence was limited, violence nevertheless changed the entire campaign environment and effectively tilted the playing field to the incumbent party's advantage. Commenting on the violence, the judge concludes that it "affected the petitioner's ability to reach out to voters in that part of the constituency. The act created a hostile atmosphere against the petitioner" (*Scott vs. Mwanakatwe*:J41).

Importantly, PF was not alone in using violence to enforce territoriality. The Zambian case shows that it is a mistake to assume that all violence perpetrated in opposition strongholds is perpetrated by the government to reduce opposition turnout. Indeed, a great deal of the violence perpetrated in opposition areas such Southern, Northwestern, and Western was perpetrated by the opposition itself in an attempt to enforce territoriality. Such violence is logically inconsistent with many previous understandings of election violence (e.g. Collier and Vicente 2012; Rauschenbach and Paula 2019) but was frequent in the Zambian example. For instance, one participant in our focus group in Northwestern Province explained, "For Solwezi Central, during the campaigns, there were fights when both parties organized rallies. The PF will follow them and when they meet they will fight and vice versa. It was not just one party that caused noise, but both were involved." Similarly, one participant

---

[7] The metaphor "watermelon" refers to wearing green on top of red.

in the Southern Province focus group noted that the idea of no-go zones was widespread: "Especially in areas like Monze, where Hichilema comes from, other parties are not welcome." Speaking of election violence in the 2016 election, Kapesa et al. (2020: 217) note that "Most notable were attacks on PF supporters by suspected UPND supporters, in Southern, Northwestern and Western Provinces, the party's heartland."

Much of the violence by UPND against PF affiliates was motivated by a desire to monopolize the electoral environment in its strongholds and prevent the PF from threatening their territoriality. ZEMS note several attacks orchestrated by UPND inside their strongholds against cadres and supporters at PF rallies in constituencies such as Solwezi Central (Northwestern), Magoye (Southern), Livingstone (Southern), Gwembe (Southern), Mazabuka (Southern), Kalabo Central (Western), and Luampa (Western). For instance, UPND cadres blocked roads leading to a presidential rally addressed by President Lungu in Bweengwa (Southern Province) on February 13, 2016. Cadres proceeded to throw stones at the presidential motorcade and attack voters, police officers and journalists. Several police officers and journalists were injured in the incident. When discussed in parliament, UPND member of parliament from Mapatizya constituency (Southern Province), Clive Miyanda, suggested that the president should "slow down" his campaigning to avoid violence in areas such as Bweengwa. Upon this suggestion, PF Minister of Home Affairs, Davies Mwila, responded: "His Excellency the President of the Republic of Zambia has the right to visit any province, including Southern Province." (National Assembly of Zambia, 2016). In a similar remark, Chief Government Spokesperson Chishimba Kambwili concluded "Southern Province is not only for one political party. The province is part of the whole Zambia, and as such, everyone should be free to visit the area." (Lusaka Times 2020).

4.2.4   Teargas and Busses of Cadres: Campaign Violence to Contest Territoriality

Violence in the case of Zambia was not only used to enforce territoriality, but also to contest it. In particular the PF, with its superior resources, frequently used violence as a tool to disturb UPND territoriality in its strongholds. An important conclusion in focus groups in provinces such as Southern and Northwestern Province was that violence in these provinces was mainly a consequence of clashes between local UPND cadres and outsider PF cadres.

These clashes often coincided with government party rallies in places like Choma (Southern Province), Mazabuka (Southern Province), and Solwezi (Northwestern Province). Government party rallies became important tests of strength for the two major parties. For the PF, the party needed to show strength in the opposition stronghold and could not afford to organize failed rallies with little attendance. The government party needed to show that despite locally prevailing narratives, they did indeed have local following and were seriously concerned with local development challenges. Violent capacity was important to clear the opposition strongholds of hostile elements and diffuse any possible attempts by UPND cadres to interrupt PF rallies. Moreover, while the UPND was keen to outperform the PF in visibility by flooding the streets with red T-shits, billboards, and party cadres in preparation for crucial PF rallies, PF was equally ready to challenge such territoriality with the use of intimidation and violence. Several incidents were reported when the government party sent cadres to intimidate supporters wearing UPND regalia close to the venue of PF rallies.

As a way to artificially inflate the sense of local viability in opposition areas, the PF systematically used a strategy of "bussing." Rallies would be accompanied by large busloads of PF supporters and cadres, especially when the president or vice president were addressing crowds in opposition areas. While an expensive strategy, such strategies could, at least temporarily, change the sense of territoriality inside opposition strongholds. One focus group participant in Northwestern Province noted that, "PF in this province had no support, as a result they hired people to boost the morale in the campaign."

The practice to import followers from one area to another was particularly conducive to violence. On the one hand, local party cadres seemed less reluctant to use violence against outsiders who may belong to other ethnic groups and who are not part of their own communities. On the other hand, outsiders were also more enabled to engage in violence knowing that they are largely shielded from repercussions outside their own communities. As one focus group participant in Southern Province noted: "They were going to a zone where they were not wanted. People were imported from one place to another to cover their parties, this fueled violence. You see, when you are in another world you can act in a violent way." The Inquiry on Election Violence Report found that imported cadres was one of the major drivers of campaign violence: "The commission observes that the political party campaigns are based on mass mobilization strategy whereby political parties strive to portray their popularity in the area by their number of followers. Moreover, the commission observes that when a party is not popular in a certain area, it supplements this deficit by importing cadres from other areas" (CIVPEV 2019: 95).

Both Northwestern and Southern Province experienced significant violence in relation to PF rallies. Most of this violence occurred between locals and imported PF cadres. The noteworthy feature of both Northwestern and Southern Province is that these locations were in easy access for the PF. In Northwestern, election observers noted a great influx of cadres from the nearby Copperbelt during the campaign. Upon arrival in Northwestern Province cadres were often intoxicated from alcohol and cannabis consumption and arrived "ready to fight" (Northwestern Focus Group). In Sothern Province, locations such as Mazabuka, Choma, and Monze, were just a few hours' drive south of Lusaka along the T1 highway and became main targets for PF violence.

Police was also involved in violence in relation to political campaigns in opposition strongholds. With the help of the police, the PF could extend its territorial reach and complicate the opposition's ability to mobilize its base. Focus groups in both Northwestern and Southern Province described frequent altercations between the police and UPND supporters. For instance, one participant in the Southern Province focus group explained: "Then the other thing is the police. You find that people are just in town singing their songs and the police just come with their teargas." In Northwestern, participants noted similar incidents and concluded that the UPND often organized their meeting in "bush areas" in fear of either being denied a permit to campaign or being victimized by the police. The participants also noted lopsided access to security during campaigns: "Another challenge was that when the PF had a rally and UPND comes to fight, police would come and arrest UPND supporters. But if it is a UPND meeting and the PF comes in, no matter how often you call the police, they will come after the meeting is over."

The data contains many examples of PF instigated violence in UPND strongholds, but there are many fewer examples of the opposite. The narratives show the asymmetry between the opposition and government. The point is not that the opposition is uncapable of perpetrating violence, but that they are more geographically restricted in doing so. In other words, while the opposition and government party were both able to use violence to enforce territoriality, the government party was more able to use it to contest it.

4.3 Statistical Analysis of Subnational Variations in Election Violence

In this section, I will provide statistical analysis of subnational variations in campaign violence. According to the theoretical discussion, I expect to find most violence in non-competetive constituencies both government and opposition strongholds where parties attempt to enforce territoriality. However, I expect to see particularly high levels of violence in opposition constituencies where the opposition is attempting to enforce territoriality and the government is trying to contest the same.

4.3.1 Using ZEMS to Measure Constituency-Level Campaign Violence

The introduction chapter introduces the book's general approach to measuring election violence at the constituency level. Rather than relying on media-based event data, like most earlier work on subnational variations in election violence (e.g. Reeder and Seeberg 2018; Daxecker 2020; Choi and Raleigh 2021; Oyewole and Omotola 2021; Müller-Crepon 2021), I make use of surveys with domestic election observers (see also von Borzyskowski and Wahman 2021). In Zambia, the name of this survey is the Zambia Election Monitor Survey (ZEMS). I conducted ZEMS in collaboration with two Zambian monitoring networks: the Foundation for Democratic Process (FODEP) and the Southern Africa Center for Constructive Resolution of Disputes (SACCORD). FODEP and SACCORD had joined forces in the 2016 election to cover all 156 Zambian constituencies. The collaborating organizations were chosen as partners due to their long history of election monitoring, their reputation for impartiality, and their great reach throughout the country. Fieldwork was initiated two weeks after the announcement of results and after post-election violence had settled. Surveys were concluded within five weeks after the results of the elections were announced and were carried out by phone by seven trained enumerators based in Lusaka.[8] The interviews were conducted in Bemba, Nyanja, Tonga, and English.

---

[8] I am grateful to Edward Goldring and Josefine Chanda for managing the group of enumerators.

For each constituency, we selected three observers with intimate knowledge of the whole election cycle for the entire constituency. In total, we collected data from 464 domestic election observers. The sample of observers was deliberately not a random sample. Observers were purposely selected as those with the deepest knowledge of the constituency and with no known partisan biases. For each constituency we selected the constituency coordinator (which would normally be the one with the most knowledge) together with two other observers. The observers were selected in consultation with the regional and national offices of the collaborating observer organizations. The benefit with surveying multiple observers from each constituency is that it reduces the potential of recall bias from individual monitors. Looking at the ability to note or not to note campaign violence, intercoder reliability was relatively high.[9] However, I would not expect perfect intercoder reliability since the respondents varied in terms of their position in constituency hierarchies. I would especially expect that the constituency organizer (coder 1) would observe more violence than the other respondents. Indeed, this is also the case.

In ZEMS each respondent was asked the question "Thinking *only* about the election in your constituency. To what extent have you personally experienced or received *credible* reports of pre-electoral violence during the general election campaign (i.e. physical violence targeted at voters, party officials, candidates, monitors, election officials, or property)." In the event that the monitor did indeed note such violence, they were asked a follow-up questions: "How many violent events occurred in your constituency," we also asked for a qualitative narrative of event(s) in the constituency: "Please describe for each event: What happened? When did it happen? Who were involved (perpetrator/victim)? Was anyone injured or killed (how many)? Where in the constituency did this happen?"

The narrative question was crucial for coding the data as it allowed us to do many things. First, we could use it to eliminate incidents that did not live up to our definition of violence (as described in Chapter 1 of this book). For instance, in some cases the respondents described events of non-physical violence. We could also eliminate incidents that were described in vague terms without specificity and could be disregarded as speculative rumors. Moreover, we could use the descriptions to figure out whether respondents were

---

[9] I Use Kuder-Richardson (1937) to measure intercoder reliability. Kuder-Richardson scores range from 0 to 1, with higher scores indicating higher reliability. Scores above 0.5 are usually regarded as reasonable. Pooling surveys from Zambia and Malawi, the intercoder reliability (ICR) score for pre-election violence is 0.56.

referring to the same or different events. In some cases, different respondents may have indicated only one incident of violence each, but they were referring to different events, indicating that, in fact, there were multiple events.

In the analysis of Zambian constituency-level violence, I use the narratives to code several dependent variables. First, I will use a binary measure of election violence. This measure will record whether any pre-electoral violence happened in the constituency as reported by anyone of the coders. However, for a better and more nuanced understanding of the violence in a constituency, I will code two additional dependent variables:

Severity of Violence: For each constituency, I record the severity-level of election violence. I distinguish between constituencies with no violence, low-intensity violence, and high-intensity violence. I record constituencies as having high intensity violence if respondents note that in at least one incident at least one person was killed or injured or property was completely destroyed. Low-intensity violence are incidents without reports of injuries or cases where property was targeted but not completely destroyed. For instance, a case where a house is burned to the ground would be recorded as high-intensity but a case where a rock is thrown at a car, smashing the windshield, is recorded as low-intensity violence.

Frequency of Violence: For each constituency, I also record whether it had none, one, or several events. I opted to code this variable on an ordinal scale rather than a count variable to reduce measurement error, particularly as it is often difficult to delineate events in cases where violence is connected but temporally separated. Moreover, since most constituencies that recorded incidents of violence only had a single episode (80% of all consistencies with violence in Zambia) this simpler distinction captures the variation rather well and does not seriously truncate the dependent variable.

I have not attempted to code the perpetrator and victim of each episode, simply as I believe that such coding would introduce serious reliability concerns. In many incidents of election violence, it is unclear who the provoking party was, especially if violence occurs between supporters of different parties. Moreover, even when observers get credible reports of violence, different actors will provide different information of who the provoking party is. My skepticism about assigning perpetrators of violence also extends to media-based event data and any attempt of doing so most likely lead to considerable measurement error. Instead, the qualitative accounts above provide a better understanding of general tendencies in terms of violent perpetrators.

4.3.2 Independent Variables and Controls

The main independent variable in the analysis is *competitiveness*. To measure competition, I use election results from the previous election i.e. the constituency-level presidential results from the 2015 presidential by-election. I would argue that these results are a very reliable prediction for expected competition in the 2016 election for two reasons: (i) the two elections were temporally extremely close, only 18 months apart (ii) the main presidential rivals were the same (Lungu and the PF vs. Hichilema and the UPND) in both elections.[10] It is also not possible to use 2016 election results to measure election competition as the 2016 results may in themselves be caused by the campaign violence.[11] Election results are provided at the constituency level by the ECZ. Competition is measured by the runner-up's number of votes divided by the winner's votes. Higher values indicate that a constituency was more competitive. In separate models, I will also study whether the number of *UPND votes* is related to a higher probability of violence. I will use the number of UPND votes in the 2015 election as the main independent variable. Some readers may have expected opposition strength to be measured by UPND vote share. However, as explained in the theory chapter, the main motive for perpetrating violence to disrupt territoriality is to affect the level of mobilization in national elections. Many of the constituencies with the highest UPND vote share are extremely rural constituencies with a sparse population and a small number of registered voters. The constituencies where the government party would be best served by disrupting territoriality are those where UPND win a large share of the vote, but also those that are numerically important.

The models also require controls for a number of possible confounders that may be related both to constituency-level propensity for election violence and competition. Most importantly, research on African elections in general and Zambia in particular, has suggested that competition is highly related to levels of wealth, population density, and modernization (Cheeseman and Hinfelaar 2010; Wahman and Boone 2018). For this reason, I will include controls for *population density*, which measures the number of people/km². These data are extracted from the 2012 Zambian census. I will also include a control for

---

[10] Vote shares for PF in 2015 and 2016 correlate at 0.96, while for the UPND the figure is 0.97.

[11] Some earlier election violence research has used opinion surveys to measure perceptions of closeness, but such surveys are not available at the constituency level in Zambia or most other African democracies (Hafner Burton et al. 2014).

constituency-level *night-light density*.[12] I use the log of population density and night light to account for the heavily skewed distribution of both variables. As an additional indicator of modernization, I include a control for *literacy rates* among citizens over the age of 16. These data are also extracted from the 2012 census. I also control for *history of election violence*. For this control, I record whether a violent event had been recorded in previous elections in either the Armed Conflict Location and Event Data Project (ACLED) (Raleigh et al. 2010) or Social Conflict Analysis Database (SCAD) (Salehyan et al. 2012) datasets. Although an imperfect measurement (due to the reporting biases in these measures), the control mitigates the possible problem that violence is related to other underlying political conflicts that are not related to the level of competition in this election. Lastly, I control for ethnic composition as *ethnic fractionalization* has been associated with violence in earlier research and is also related to level of competition (Wilkinson 2004). The ethnicity data are extracted from the 2012 census and used to calculate a constituency-level Herfindahl index of ethnic fractionalization.[13]

4.3.3 Model Specification

This chapter will present the results from a number of regression analyses estimating the probability of election violence of various intensity and severity across electoral constituencies. Throughout the analysis, I will present two different types of models. First, I will present results from an ordered probit model with standard errors clustered on province, to account for the lack of independence between constituencies in the same province. The ordered probit model is used to account for the ordinal nature of my two dependent variables, severity, and intensity. Ordinal regression is commonly used when the distance between the categories is unknown, as this violates an important assumption of the linear regression model (King 1998). However, since ordinal probit increases the complexity of the model, especially given the relatively small number of observations, I also present the results from a logistic regression (with standard errors again clustered on province). In this model, I dichotomize the dependent variable (violence or no violence). To interpret the substantive effects of competition on probability of violence, I will present

---

[12] Data are extracted from Boone (2016)

[13] Herfindahl index is calculated as $HI = 1 - \sum_{i=1}^{n} s_i^2$ where s_i is the share of ethnic group I out of a total of n ethnic groups. The ethnic groups recorded in the data include Barotse, Bemba, Lozi. Mambwe, Nyanja, Tonga, Tumbuka, and Other.

simulations using the same logistic regression. In all simulations, I will keep other covariates at their means. It has also become increasingly common to use Ordinary Least Squares (OLS) regressions with ordinal scale dependent variables, especially in models with many categories on the dependent variable, few degrees of freedom, and several dummy variables on the right-hand side of the equation. Such conditions may lead to separation issues. While none of these issues are acute for the models estimated here,[14] I have also included robustness checks using OLS regression in the Appendix.

4.3.4 Results

Table 4.1 below shows the results of the ordered probit models, Table 4.2 displays the results from the same analysis using a dichotomized dependent variable and a logistic regression. The results in Table 4.1 distinguishes between severity and intensity in violence, while no such distinction is made in Table 4.2. Model 1 (Table 4.1) displays the results when using the severity of election violence as dependent variable and Model 2 shows the results from the model using frequency as the dependent variable. Looking at the results of Model 1 (Table 4.1), I find a statistically significant and negative effect of competition on the severity of violence. Higher levels of competition are associated with a lower probability of more severe categories of violence. In Figure A4.1 of the Appendix, I estimate the probability of different severities of violence dependent on levels of competition. The estimation shows that the probability of no violence (as opposed to low severity and high severity) increases steeply as competition increases. Interestingly, no other covariate is associated with higher severity violence. More ethnically diverse constituencies do not have more severe violence, nor do more connected or densely populated constituencies. In the Appendix, I rerun the model using a simpler OLS regression and find substantively similar results.

Model 2 (Table 4.1) estimates the probability of different categories of violence frequency. The results are very similar to those of Model 1 (Table 4.1). Higher levels of competition are significantly associated with less frequent violence. The predicted probabilities of the various categories are plotted in the Appendix, Figure A4.2. As with severity, I also find no statistically significant relationships with any other covariates (other than competition)

---

[14] The dependent variables only have two categories, and I have no dummy variables on the right-hand side of the equation.

Table 4.1 Analysis of relationship between competition and constituency-level campaign violence (Ordered Probit).

	Model 1 Severity	Model 2 Frequency
Competition	−1.022***	−.827**
	(.395)	(.412)
History EV	.019	.040
	(.340)	(.398)
Population Density (log)	.028	.044
	(.150)	(.138)
Nightlight (log)	.841	.122
	(.980)	(1.029)
Literacy	−.254	.342
	(1.223)	(1.157)
Ethnic Fractionalization	.715	.549
	(.600)	(.577)
N	156	156
Pseudo R^2	.03	.02

Notes: ***≤p.01 **≤p.05 *≤p.1. Entries are ordered probit coefficients with standard errors in parentheses. Standard errors clustered by province.

and the results are robust for running the models using OLS regression (Table A4.1 in the Appendix).

I re-run the model using a logistic regression and a dichotomous dependent variable in Table 4.2 below. When running the model with a dichotomous dependent variable, I do lose some of the information from the ordinal dependent variable (i.e. I am unable to separate between different levels of severity and frequency) and the coefficient for competition does not reach conventional levels of significance. However, plotting the relationship between competition and probability of violence, I do find statistically significant differences in predicted probabilities of violence along substantially important levels of competition (i.e. there is a statistically significant difference in the probability of violence between constituencies with low and high levels of competition).

Figure 4.4 shows the predicted probability of violence in the 2016 Zambian election along different levels of competition. The estimations are based on the results from Model 3 (Table 4.2). As competition increases, the predicted probability of having violence decreases substantially. At the highest level

Table 4.2 Analysis of relationship between competition and constituency-level campaign violence (Logistic Regression).

	Model 3 Election Violence
Competition	−.929
	(.730)
History EV	−.320
	(.706)
Population Density (log)	.050
	(.223)
Nightlight (log)	.870
	(1.324)
Literacy	.533
	(1.692)
Ethnic Fractionalization	.686
	(1.019)
N	156
Pseudo R^2	.02

Notes: ***≤p.01 **≤p.05 *≤p.1. Entries are logistic coefficients with standard errors in parentheses. Standard errors clustered by province.

of competition observed (Kapiri Mposhi constituency in Central Province), the predicted probability of violence is 46%. At the lowest level of competition observed (Dundumwezi constituency in Southern Province), the predicted probability of violence is 56% (the differences in predicted probabilities are even more dramatic when estimated as an ordered logit in the Appendix). These results confirm that constituencies within party strongholds are particularly affected by election violence.

I theorized that although all constituencies within party strongholds would be particularly prone to election violence, we would see particularly high levels of violence within constituencies controlled by the opposition. This expectation is also brought out by qualitative observations in the focus groups interviews. Table 4.3 models the relationship between UPND votes (in the previous, 2015, election) and violence severity and violence frequency in the 2016 election. Indeed, I find a strong and statistically significant relationship between the number of votes for UPND and probability for more severe and more frequent violence. The predicted probability for different levels of

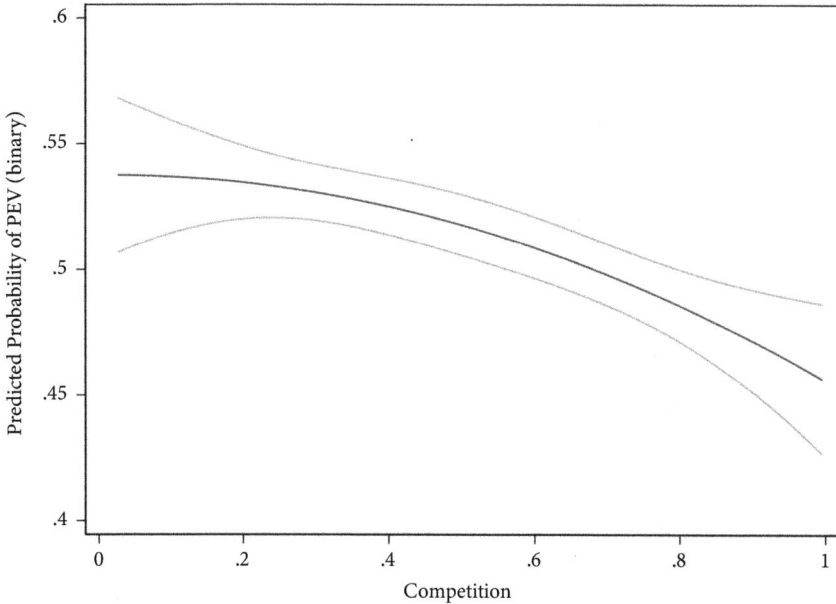

Figure 4.4 Relationship between Predicted Probability of Violence and Competition.

Note: Predicted Probabilities based on Model 3 in Table 4.2. Figure displays 95% confidence interval displayed.

severity and frequency along different levels of UPND vote are plotted in the Appendix (Figure A4.3).

Looking at the severity of violence Model 4 (Table 4.3), I find that more UPND votes are significantly associated with more severe violence. The same is true for frequency of violence. The coefficient for competition is statistically significant and positive in Model 5 (Table 4.4). The results are robust for both severity and frequency when rerunning the model using OLS regression in the Appendix (Table A4.3).

Table 4.4 re-runs the model using a logistic regression. Again, I find a positive and strongly significant relationship between the number of votes for UPND and the probability of violence. The results from Model 6 are plotted in Figure 4.5 and show a substantially very strong effect of UPND votes on the probability of violence. The lowest number of votes for UPND in 2015 was observed in Mfuwe constituency in Muchinga Province (166 votes) and the highest number was observed in Choma Central in Southern Province

Table 4.3 Analysis of relationship between
opposition vote and constituency-level
campaign violence (Ordered Probit).

	Model 4 Severity	Model 5 Frequency
UPND Votes 2015	.062***	.050***
(Thousand)	(.016)	(.012)
History EV	−.046	−.009
	(.335)	(.388)
Population Density (log)	−.037	−.009
	(.135)	(.128)
Nightlight (log)	.837	.111
	(.790)	(.924)
Literacy	.346	.829
	(1.096)	(1.057)
Ethnic Fractionalization	.085	.040
	(.583)	(.602)
N	156	156
Pseudo R^2	.05	.03

Notes: ***$\leq$p.01 **$\leq$p.05 *$\leq$p.1. Entries are ordered probit
coefficients with standard errors in parentheses. Standard
errors clustered by province.

(21,900 votes). At the lowest observed value of UPND votes, the predicted probability of violence is 40%. At the highest number of UPND votes, the predicted probability of violence is 76%. In Figure A4.4 of the Appendix, I estimate the probability of different severities of violence dependent on opposition votes. The results are robust for running the models using OLS regression (Table A4.2 in the Appendix).

While Table 4.2 reaffirms the hypothesis that election violence is particularly common in opposition party strongholds, this finding questions whether the findings in Table 4.2 are completely driven by violence in opposition party strongholds and not related to competition per se. The visual display of the data in Figure 4.3 suggests that this is most likely not the case, as it notes high levels of violence also in government party strongholds such as Northern and Luapula. Moreover, the qualitative accounts made clear that the PF frequently used violence in its own strongholds to regulate space and curb opposition campaigning.

As a further test, I introduced a model with the share of PF votes in the 2015 election and also a quadratic term. The motivation behind this model

Table 4.4 Analysis of relationship between opposition vote and constituency-level campaign violence (Logistic Regression).

	Model 6 Election Violence
UPND Votes 2015	.069***
(Thousand)	(.023)
History EV	.259
	(.690)
Population Density (log)	.003
	(.221)
Nightlight (log)	.744
	(1.255)
Literacy	.945
	(1.640)
Ethnic Fractionalization	.096
	(1.077)
N	156
Pseudo R^2	.03

Notes: ***≤p.01 **≤p.05 *≤p.1. Entries are logistic coefficients with standard errors in parentheses. Standard errors clustered by province.

is to investigate whether there is a curvilinear relationship between PF vote and election violence. The hypotheses suggest that the highest level of election violence would be observed in opposition strongholds (where the PF vote is low), but that there would be more election violence in government party strongholds than in competitive constituencies. The results of the quadratic term are illustrated in Figure 4.6 below.[15] The results show an inverse J-shaped relationship between PF vote and election violence. The highest probability of violence is observed in opposition strongholds, but PF strongholds have higher probability of violence than competitive constituencies. These findings suggest that the correlation between competition and election violence is not only driven by higher propensity of violence in opposition strongholds. Indeed, the sort of violence designed to maintain territorial control in government party strongholds also adds to the relationship between competition and election violence.

---

[15] Table A4.3 of the Appendix.

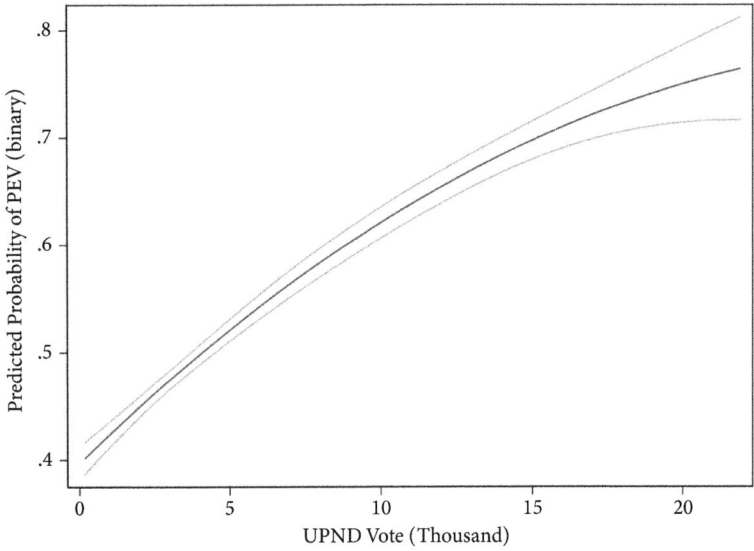

Figure 4.5 Relationship between Predicted Probability of Violence and Competition.

Note: Predicted probabilities based on Model 6 in Table 4.4. Figure displays 95% confidence interval.

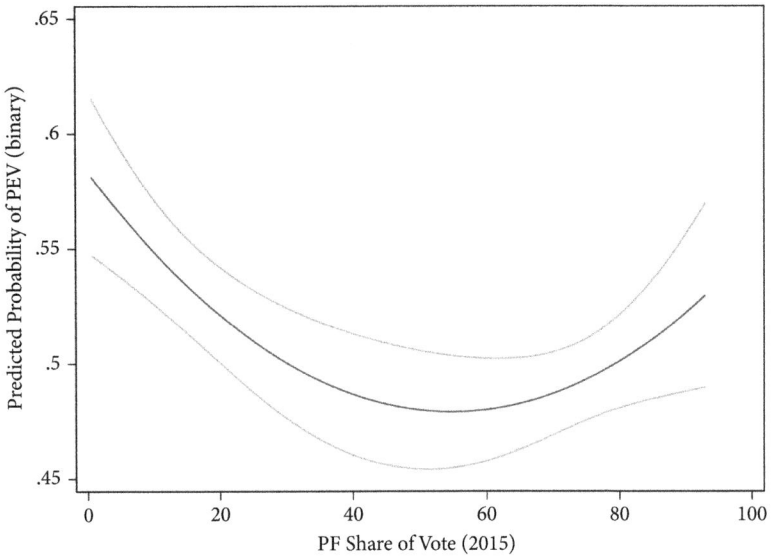

Figure 4.6 Post-estimation of Relationship between PF Vote Share and Pre-election Violence.

Note: Regression table displayed in Table A4.3 of the Appendix. Figure displays 95% confidence interval.

4.4 Conclusion

This chapter showed how territorial violence has been a constant in Zambian electoral competition since independence. The way that varying parties throughout Zambian history have used campaign violence can be understood in the context of regional politics discussed in Chapter 3. Nevertheless, election violence has become increasingly serious as Zambian politics has become more competitive nationally and increasingly regionalized (i.e. increasingly geographically polarized).

The qualitative and quantitative evidence provided in this chapter shows the territorial nature of campaign violence in the 2016 election. Both PF and UPND used violence to enforce their territoriality within their respective stronghold. The qualitative narratives describe how violence was commonly used as a tool for de-campaigning of rival parties. The statistical analysis shows how violence was particularly common in stronghold constituencies and particularly those controlled by the opposition. Whereas some earlier research has suggested that the concentration of violence in opposition strongholds could be attributed mainly to the government party's attempts to reduce turnout within such areas, this interpretation is not fully supported by the data from Zambia (Rauschenbach and Paula 2019). Indeed, campaign violence in regions such as Southern and Northwestern Province was perpetrated both by the opposition and the incumbent party. Existing behavioral theories of campaign violence would disallow such patterns as it would be highly counterproductive for parties to perpetrate violence within their own strongholds as it may depress voter turnout. However, thinking about campaign violence as a territorial tool meant to shape the electoral environment, such violence makes more sense. One additional takeaway from the analysis here is that PF's central coercive capacity made opposition strongholds particularly prone to election violence. In Chapter 7, I will replicate the analysis of this chapter for the case of Malawi. The Malawian case will show that geographic patterns of election violence may look rather different in cases where the incumbent government lacks the capacity to organize much violence from the center.

The findings in this chapter support the assertion that electoral violence in Zambia needs to be understood in light of regional politics. This interpretation is shared by election observers on the ground and supported quantitively by showing a strong relationship between local level competition and campaign violence. In the next chapter, I will focus on the micro-level experiences of violence to better understand the ways in which violence affects fear of different forms of electoral participation in Zambia. This analysis will lend further credence to the argument that election violence affects mainly local electoral environments rather than individual-level turnout.

5

Individual-Level Fear, Electoral Geography, and Political Participation in Zambia

Chapter 4 mapped the occurrences of violence in the Zambian 2016 election, showing that violence was particularly common in party strongholds. Opposition party strongholds were most affected, but also to a lesser extent government party strongholds. The findings in Chapter 4 might appear slightly at odds with some earlier micro-level work in the electoral violence literature, showing that voters residing in competitive constituencies are *particularly* fearful of violence (Rauschenbach and Paula 2019). How do we square this finding with the fact that most violence happens in non-competitive constituencies? Furthermore, narratives from focus groups and other qualitative sources presented in Chapter 4 showed that the locally dominant party often perpetrated the violence against "outside" parties. This finding seems counterintuitive given earlier work's pre-occupation with understanding violence as mainly a way to deter turnout among rival party voters (Collier and Vicente 2012; Burchard 2015). If parties want to use violence to deter turnout, surely perpetrating violence inside one's own party strongholds could be counterproductive.

The electoral geography theory of campaign violence presented in Chapter 2 provides some tools to understand the geographic patterns of violence presented in Chapter 4. The theory highlights how locally dominant parties use violence as a territorial tool to shrink the local democratic space. This means that we cannot understand micro-level spatial variation in fear without reference to a voter's local minority or majority status. The electoral geography theory of campaign violence also highlights the importance of localism. When electoral narratives are created locally, parties can affect local electoral environments through violence. It would therefore be a mistake to assume that violence is used only to restrict participation in a narrow sense, by restricting turnout. Indeed, violence may be used to affect a much broader repertoire of political behavior. Chapter 4 illustrated this point with evidence from the Zambian campaign. Political actors seem to have used violence to regulate

Controlling Territory, Controlling Voters. Michael Wahman, Oxford University Press.
© Michael Wahman (2023). DOI: 10.1093/oso/9780198872825.003.0005

and restrict campaigns, manufacture local dominance, and alter local electoral narratives. For instance, violence can be used to limit ordinary citizens' willingness to attend rallies, discuss politics in public, or wear party regalia. Such electoral activities have been attributed marginal or no significance in most of the earlier work on election violence. However, the concept of localism clarifies why such activities are crucial in geographically polarized electoral systems. If voters are afraid to participate in political campaigns, this will effectively disable the electoral campaign of the affected party. In geographically polarized electoral systems such campaigns are not organized at the national level through national modes of communication, they are organized at the local level and require local participation to activate regional political cleavages, create local momentum, and a sense of local advocacy.

This chapter has two main empirical tasks. First, I want to determine whether Zambians living in competitive or non-competitive constituencies are more fearful of violence. However, contrary to most existing research, I will distinguish between voters supporting the local minority and majority party. I hypothesize that local minorities living in non-competitive constituencies will be particularly fearful of violence. To study this question, I will use geo-coded Afrobarometer data, merged with constituency-level election data.

Second, I want to find out *what* electoral activities are associated with most fear among Zambian voters. This is a question that has so far attracted very little attention. Most of the earlier work has assumed that fear of electoral participation is particularly related to the act of voting itself. However, I hypothesize that fear of election violence is associated with fear of a much broader repertoire of political participation. Such forms of participation are not *directly* related to electoral outcomes but can have immense indirect effects by affecting local electoral environments. I use new survey data from the 2021 Zambia Election Panel Survey (ZEPS) (Lust et al. 2021). To my knowledge, this is the first survey that asks Zambian voters directly what activities they are fearful of participating in.

The results presented in this chapter show that the voters most fearful of violence support a party with little local support. In other words, the ones most restricted in their political participation are those that live in areas where rival parties try to enforce territoriality. I also show that Zambian voters are particularly afraid of election violence in relation to political activities such as rally attendance, wearing party regalia, and publicly discussing politics. Voters are, however, not particularly fearful of violence while voting. As a consequence, we may expect that parties are more likely to use violence to shape the campaign environment than to deter turnout.

5.1 Fear of Violence among Local Minority and Majority Voters

Who was afraid of election violence in the Zambian 2016 election, and how can we assume that such violence affects political participation? To gauge how individual-level factors interreact with local electoral geography in predicting fear of election violence, I rely on the geo-coded Afrobarometer data presented in Chapter 3. Earlier research has used this Afrobarometer data to suggest that violence is particularly common in competitive constituencies (Rauschenbach and Paula 2019). However, such research has neglected the electoral environment that voters reside in. If election violence is used as a tool to maintain territorial control, as suggested in this book, violence is likely to be targeted particularly at local partisan minorities. While numerically, there will be few local minority supporters in highly uncompetitive constituencies, these rare minority supporters may be more fearful of violence than voters living in the most competitive constituencies.

I introduce several logistic regressions to find out how the level of fear varies between local minority and majority supporters depending on the level of competition. I here dichotomize the Afrobarometer fear indicator and particularly study the correlates of fearing election violence "a lot" (felt by 35% of the sample in the Afrobarometer 7th round sample) or "somewhat" (felt by 11% of the sample in the Afrobarometer 7th round sample). I will divide the sample into two sub-samples, voters residing in UPND (opposition) constituencies and voters living in Patriotic Front (government) constituencies. I will then interact partisanship with level of competition. Is it the case that local minority voters will feel more or less safe as competition increases? Whereas those arguing that local competition drives violence would expect that both local minority and majority supporters become more fearful as competition increases, I would expect that voters are more fearful when living in constituencies that heavily support the opposing party.

The models include several control variables at the individual level. I control first for gender, as recent research has stressed the often gendered nature of election violence (Bjarnegård 2018). I also control for the lived poverty index[1] as socioeconomic factors have been related to fear of violence in earlier research (von Borzyskowski and Kuhn 2020). At the constituency level, I control for population density (logged) and also constituency-level wealth, proxied by night light (Weidemann and Schutte 2016). Most importantly, I

---

[1] The lived poverty index is an experiential measure of poverty, capturing how often respondents go without access to basic necessities, including cash income, medical care, water, food, and cooking fuel (Mattes 2020).

introduce a control for competition. As in the models presented in Chapter 4, I use levels of competition from the 2015 Zambian presidential by-election to ensure that the electoral competition was temporally prior to incidents of violence in the 2016 election. Competition is again measured by the runner-up's number of votes divided by the winner's votes.[2] Higher values indicate that a constituency was more competitive.

Model 1 (Table 5.1) shows that voters in more competitive constituencies are more afraid of violence. This finding is line with most of the current literature. I also find that women are more afraid of violence than men. Keeping all other variables at their means, the predicted probability of fearing election violence is 43% for a male PF supporter and 48% for a female PF supporter. The predicted probability of fearing election violence for a male UPND voter

Table 5.1 Correlates of fear of election violence.

Dependent variable	Model 1 *All voters, all constituencies*	Model 2 *PF Constituencies*	Model 3 *UPND Constituencies*
Competition	.677*	.225	1.531***
	(.3369)	(.706)	(.455)
UPND Voter	212	.834**	–
	(.153)	(.366)	
PF Voter	–	–	–1.263
UPND Voter*Competition	–	–1.486**	–
		(.728)	
PF Voter*Competition	–	–	1.263
			(.974)
Female	–.241***	.360***	.034
	(.084)	(.102)	(.156)
Lived Poverty Index	–.008	.104	–.221
	(.077)	(.087)	(.153)
Constituency Population Density (logged)	.054	.078	.127
	(.089)	(.087)	(.260)
Constituency Nightlight	.009	.011	–.087
	(.009)	(.009)	(.128)
Pseudo R^2	.03	.04	.03
N	1176	766	410

Notes: ***≤p.01 **≤p.05 *≤p.1. Logistic regressions with standard errors clustered on constituency

[2] All electoral data are sourced from the official results gazette by the Electoral Commission of Zambia (ECZ).

is 48%, compared to 54% for a female UPND voter. These results are an important reminder that the consequences of election violence are not felt equally among voters. Violence tends to exacerbate political inequalities.

Looking at models 2 and 3 (Table 5.1), we can say more about the relationship between electoral geography and fear of violence. Model 2 looks particularly at constituencies where PF won more votes than UPND. The model includes an interaction effect between level of competition and being a UPND voter. Looking at the standalone variable for UPND supporter, I find that in PF constituencies UPND supporters are significantly more afraid of violence than PF supporters when competition is zero.[3] Looking at the interaction effect, I find that UPND voters become significantly less afraid of violence as the level of competition increases. The relationship is plotted in Figure 5.1. While non-UPND voters (mostly PF voters and independents) feel slightly more afraid as competition increases, the opposite is true for UPND voters. In other words, it is not in competitive constituencies that opposition supporters are most afraid of violence. It is also not in their own

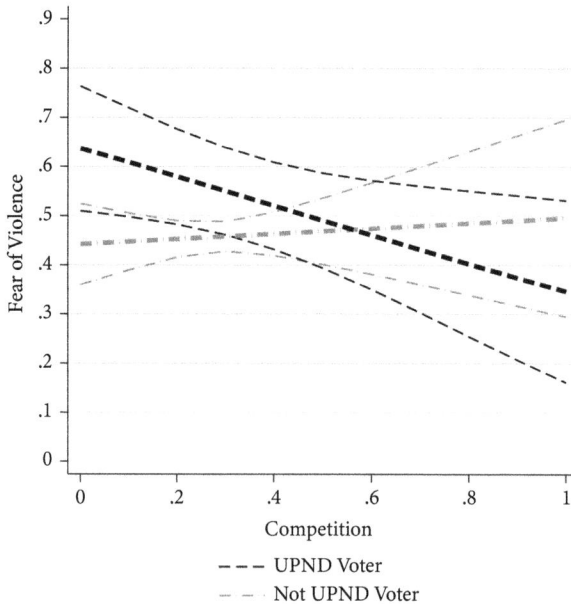

Figure 5.1 Predicted Level of Fear in PF Constituencies for UPND and Non-UPND Supporters Depending on Level of Competition.

Note: Post-estimation based on model 2. Predicted probability with 90% confidence interval.

---

[3] This is a theoretical value, the lowest observed value is 0.044 in PF constituencies.

strongholds where government parties are supposed to direct violence to reduce turnout. The highest level of fear for opposition supporters is in constituencies where the government party has a firm political grip. This finding adds important micro-level nuance to the meso-level findings in Chapter 4. Indeed, instilling fear in minority supporters is a key part of the no-go zone politics described in Zambia. It appears PF was successful in its attempt to use violence to enforce territoriality.

Model 3 and the corresponding Figure 5.2 shows the opposite relationship. In model 3 (Table 5.1), I look particularly at constituencies won by UPND to see whether PF supporters feel more afraid in constituencies with high UPND dominance than those with just a slight UPND advantage. For PF voters, I do not find a significant difference in fear between high and low competition UPND constituencies. The fear for PF supporters is constant across different levels of competition. While this finding is perhaps somewhat surprising, given that Chapter 4 discussed several cases where UPND supporters attacked PF supporters in UPND strongholds, it is also important to remember that many of these PF supporters were non-local. Indeed, as revealed in focus groups in Southern and Northwestern provinces (both PF strongholds), the opposition

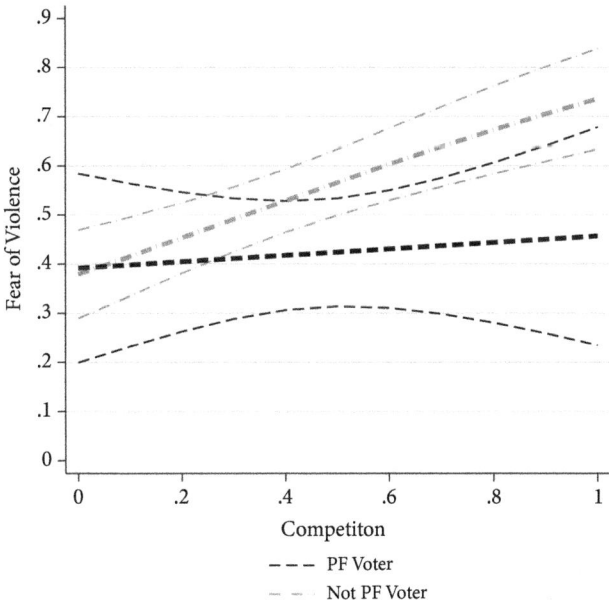

Figure 5.2 Predicted Level of Fear in UPND Constituencies for PF and Non-PF Supporters Depending on Level of Competition.

Note: Post-estimation based on model 3. Predicted probability with 90% confidence interval.

violence in opposition strongholds were often perpetrated against perceived outsiders as PF utilized their central capacity to organize campaign meetings and bus outside supporters into opposition strongholds.

I do, however, find that UPND voters feel significantly safer in constituencies that are strongly held by UPND. This finding is interesting as much of the earlier election violence literature has suggested that violence is mostly used in opposition strongholds to curb opposition turnout (e.g. Rauschenbach and Paula 2019). Following this logic, it appears that violence as a strategy was not particularly successful for the PF. However, the results displayed here suggest that violence was more successful in enforcing territoriality in PF strongholds than curbing participation in UPND strongholds. Indeed, this finding suggests that the numerical and local strength of the opposition inside their strongholds was enough to guarantee a higher sense of security. While the government tried to instill fear in the opposition inside the opposition strongholds, the opposition was far from defenseless in relation to this government violence. This finding might also explain why the opposition was able to mobilize their stronghold voters in great numbers throughout the election despite the government's attempt to quell the electoral campaign.

5.2 What Are Voters Afraid Of?

One noteworthy aspect of the violence in the 2016 election, described in Chapter 4 was that the vast majority of violence that happened in the campaign occurred long before election day. This violence was often directed toward election rallies or people in the streets wearing party regalia. Indeed, in the focus groups, many observers attested to the fact that it would be almost unthinkable to wear opposition party T-shirts in the cadre-controlled markets of Lusaka. Monitors frequently described how party cadres would block access to rallies or how police used teargas against opposition campaign meetings. All this violence seems to have been designed to curb political participation. However, none of the monitors in the focus groups mentioned violence as a tool to deter turnout. This is a curious finding given that the standard assumption in the literature is that election violence is mostly used exactly for this purpose (Bekoe and Burchard 2017; Collier and Vicente 2012; Gonzalez-Ocantos et al. 2020; Rauschenbach and Paula 2019).

The theory chapter suggested that violence can significantly impact political participation by altering local electoral environments. An example is UPND's "watermelon strategy" where violence changed the nature of the electoral environment. While UPND supporters refrained to wear party regalia, they could still vote with the protection of the secret ballot. However, in electoral systems characterized by localism, the lack of visual opposition presence will still affect the opposition's electoral performance. If campaigns are affected, the opposition's perceived viability in key areas will be decreased.

If the electoral geography theory is correct, we would see election violence being associated with political participation in many ways. If voters are more fearful of participating in activities such as attending rallies, wearing party regalia, and discussing politics in public, it would help to answer some puzzles presented in earlier micro-level research on election violence. For instance, Burchard (2020) shows that voters who fear violence are *more* likely to vote, while Berkoe and Burchard (2017) show no relationship between turnout and violence at the aggregate-level across Africa. Rosenzweig (2021) even suggested that violence can be counterproductive, as it is ineffective at deterring turnout but may provoke a backlash against those responsible. Previous research has rarely examined the relation between different forms of political participation and fear of election. I will here present unique data from the Zambian 2021 election. While I do not have such data from the 2016 election (the election analyzed in Chapter 4), 2021 featured very similar levels of violence and patterns of electoral competition (Resnick 2022; Siachiwena 2022).

5.2.1 New Data on Fear of Campaign Violence and Different Forms of Participation

One of the obstacles to understanding the role of violence in African election campaigns is the lack of detailed data on fear in relation to different forms of electoral participation. Most research on fear of election violence has used one specific question in the Afrobarometer: "During the last national election campaign, how much did you personally fear becoming a victim of political intimidation or violence?" While useful, the question does not help us understand what activities such fear is related to. For instance, it is possible that the respondent would feel no fear of voting but high levels of fear while participating in campaign meetings.

To better understand the extent to which Zambians felt fear in relation to different forms of political participation, I included specific questions on this issue in the 2021 Zambia Election Panel Survey (ZEPS) (Lust et al. 2021).

Here, I will present results from Round 1 of the survey, fielded before election day in the midst of the election campaign, June–July 2021 (the election was held in August 2021). The data contains 1692 respondents drawn from 74 districts in Zambia. Using data before the election is preferable as voters' perceptions of risks associated with voting will not have been affected by the general calm on election day. The survey was conducted over the telephone in Nyanja and English by Ubuntu Research in Lusaka. The sample for the survey is not nationally representative, the sampling for ZEPS builds on a previous survey conducted by University of Gothenburg's Governance and Local Development Institute (GLD) in 2019 (Lust et al. 2020). In the baseline survey, GLD collected telephone numbers for respondents living in two regions 1) a 50 km radius of Lusaka and 2) a 100 km radius from the Zambia–Malawi border.[4] Notably, both of these areas are previous PF strongholds. The respondents in ZEPS were randomly drawn from the Local Governance Performance Index (LGPI) number dataset, meaning that most of the respondents will be concentrated in the originally surveyed areas.[5] The nonrepresentativeness of ZEPS mean that we cannot infer national averages from the data. Nevertheless, they will give a strong indication of relative differences in fear of violence related to different forms of participation. Moreover, the sample is divided in relatively equal shares between urban (31%), peri-urban (29%), and rural (39%) respondents.

In the survey, respondents were asked the following question: "Do you fear being subject to violence or intimidation if you did the following?" The respondents were then asked about a list of common forms of electoral participation in Zambia, including "wore party regalia," "publicly discussed politics with others in your village or neighborhood," "Worked for a candidate or party," "Attended a campaign rally," and "voted." For each of these questions, respondents were asked to give a simple yes/no answer.

ZEPS also asked the standard Afrobarometer question about general fear of election violence in the election campaign. Figure 5.3 shows the levels of fear that respondents in ZEPS felt during the election campaign. The survey uses the same question wording as the 7th round of the Afrobarometer survey. In the ZEPS sample, 30% report that they fear election violence "a lot" during elections, and 68% state that they fear election violence at least "a little bit."

Figure 5.4 shows how fearful respondents were in relation to different forms of electoral participation. The findings are clear, contrary to what much of the

---

[4] See sampling map in the Appendix, Figure A5.1. Note that some respondents who have moved out of the initially surveyed regions are also included in the data.
[5] The original dataset contained 4226 numbers.

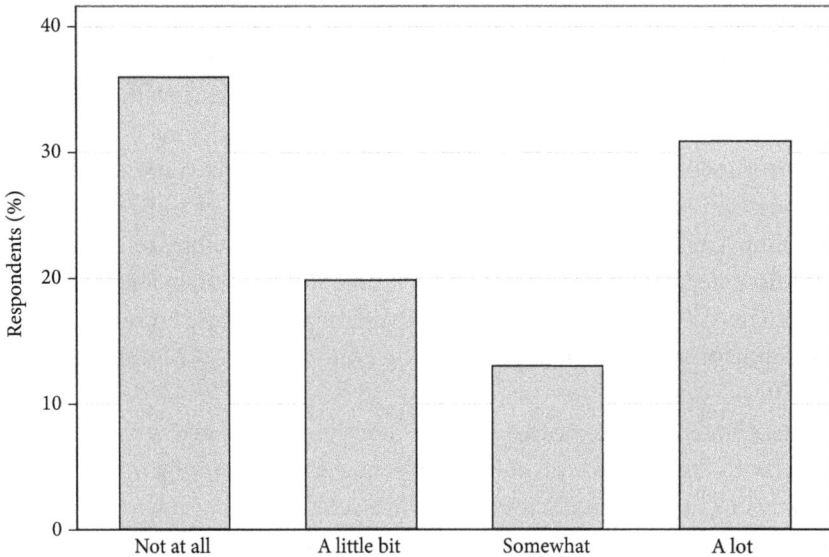

Figure 5.3 Fear of Election Violence, ZEPS.

Source: ZEPS

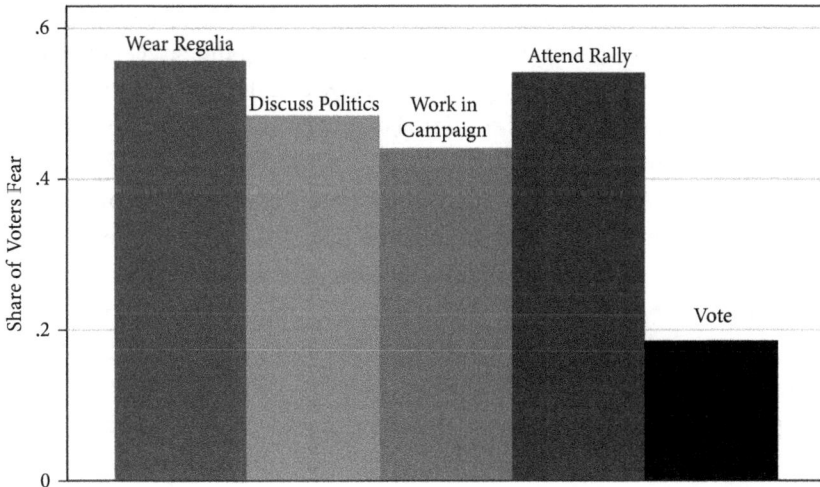

Figure 5.4 Fear of Election Violence Related to Different Forms of Electoral Participation.

Source: ZEPS

current literature suggests, the activity that voters are the least fearful of partaking in is voting. Only 18% of respondents state that they would be fearful of violence if they voted. Looking at other forms of participation, we find much higher levels of fear. In the sample, 54% of respondents stated that they would fear becoming the victims of election violence if they wore party regalia. 52% of respondents feared becoming the victims of election violence if they attended a rally and 44% of respondents feared becoming the victims of violence if they worked in a campaign. Even engaging in vital democratic deliberation is associated with a high level of fear: as much as 48% of respondents state that they would fear becoming the victims of electoral violence if they publicly discussed politics with members of their community. Obviously electoral campaigns will be severely affected in an environment where more than half of the population are fearful of participating even in the most common election activities.

These statistics indicate that voting is not the political activity that is associated with the highest level of fear. Consequently, when trying to understand the way in which political actors engage in electoral violence it would be a mistake to theorize such activities solely as a way to reduce turnout. Instead, we must think about participation in a much broader sense.

One possible objection to this argument might be that although certain activities are associated with more fear than voting, voting is still the most important act in terms of determining electoral outcomes. Even though only 18% of respondents claim that they would fear being the targets of election violence when voting, deterring as much as 18% of the population from voting could potentially swing an election. I do not have data to establish a causal link between fear of voting and actual voting. However, one way to, check the plausibility of this objection is to look into differences in planned voting. ZEPS also asked respondents whether they planned to vote in the upcoming election. Although crude, looking at the difference between voters that feared voting and did not fear voting gives a rough indication of the extent to which violence may deter turnout. The descriptives are presented in Figure 5.5. Among respondents stating that they do not fear violence when voting, 93.4% state that they plan to vote. Among respondents stating that they fear violence when voting, 89.6% state that they plan to vote. The difference in means between the two groups is not statistically significant at the 95% level using a two-tailed t-test. In other words, while some voters may refrain to vote due to fear of violence, this seems relatively rare.[6] The findings presented here also add to previous literature finding no negative relationship between fear of violence and voting (Berkoe and Burchard 2017; Burchard 2020). Previous null findings could

---

[6] Although measuring intention to vote in surveys is difficult due to problems of social desirability and respondents' desire to show a sense of civic duty, there is no particular reason to believe that voters afraid of voting due to violence would be particularly prone to overstate their intentions to vote.

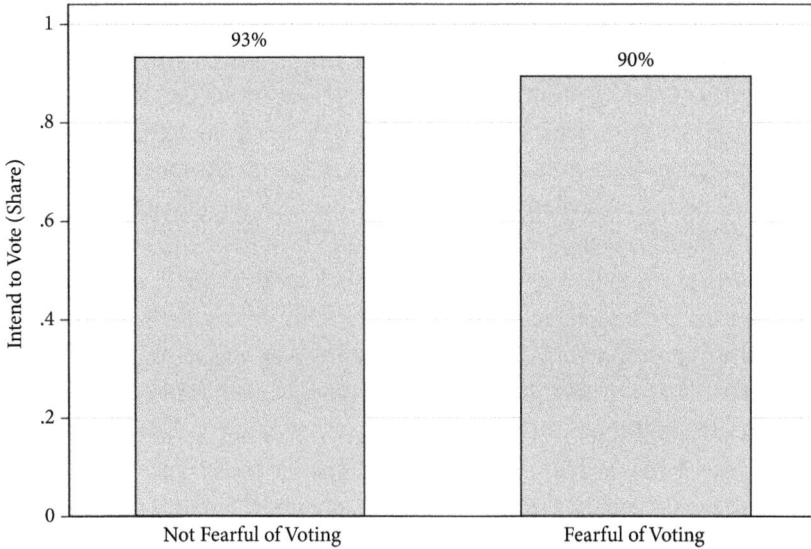

Figure 5.5 Intention to Vote among Voters Fearful of Election Violence While Voting.
Source: ZEPS

possibly be explained by the fact that some voters fearful of election violence may not have a particular fear of voting.

Another point of data to support the claim that violence has been generally ineffective in curbing turnout are overall levels of Zambian turnout. Although the 2021 Zambian election was arguably the most violent election experienced in Zambia and most of this violence was directed towards opposition supporters, the violence did not seem to have deterred opposition supporters coming out to vote in great numbers. The 2021 election had a voter turnout of 71%, the highest turnout of any election in Zambia's multiparty history.[7]

5.2.2 Local Political Context and Fear of Different Forms of Participation

How does fear of different forms of participation correlate with minority/majority status? To further study this question, I ran several logistic regressions using the ZEPS participation categories as dependent variables. I am particularly interested to see if local party minorities, i.e. those not supporting

---

[7] For instance, turnout in the previous 2016 election was 56%.

the party that won the election in a constituency feel more or less fear when participating in different forms of activities. Above, I showed that voters are more fearful of participating in other activities than voting, but it could still be the case that violence deter local partisan minorities from voting. Due to the geographic clustering of the ZEPS data, I do not specify the model in the same way as the models presented in Table 5.1. Rather than modeling the vote share at the constituency level, I simply note whether a voter belongs to the minority/majority partisan group (using a simple dichotomy).[8] To account for other individual-level characteristics, I also include controls for whether a voter supported the opposition UPND, whether the voter was female, and whether the voter was urban or rural.[9] The results of the models are presented in Table 5.2.

The results in Table 5.2 clarify how violence may affect different forms of participation and which groups of voters will be particularly reluctant to participate in various political activities. First of all, model 5 stands out compared to models 1–4. No group of voters is particularly fearful of voting. Women voters are not more fearful of voting than male voters, UPND voters are not more fearful of voting than other voters, urban voters are not more fearful of voting

Table 5.2 Correlates of election violence fear for different forms of electoral participation.

Dependent variable	Model 1	Model 2	Model 3	Model 4	Model 5
	Wear Regalia	Discuss Politics	Work in Campaign	Participate in Rally	Vote
Female	.095	.211*	.204	.468***	.206
	(.108)	(.109)	(.140)	(.109)	(.143)
UPND Voter	.449***	.496***	.643***	.580***	.159
	(.116)	(.104)	(.131)	(.100)	(.151)
Urban	.601***	.522***	.628***	.572***	.087
	(.134)	(.104)	(.123)	(.137)	(.198)
Partisan	−.421***	−.273**	−.046	−.244**	.031
Majority	(.100)	(.109)	(.148)	(.119)	(.154)
Pseudo R^2	.03	.03	.03	.04	.00
N	1568	1580	1561	1556	1565

Notes: *** ≤p.01 ** ≤p.05 * ≤p.1. Logistic Regression coefficients displayed with standard errors in parentheses. Standard errors clustered on constituency.

[8] Most voters are either in competitive Lusaka or dominant Eastern and Muchinga provinces.
[9] I use the blunt urban/rural categorization again due to less geographical variation in the sample.

than non-urban voters, and local partisan majorities are not less fearful of vot-ing than local partisan minorities. For instance, although a vast majority of the violence in 2021 was directed towards opposition supporters, the difference in the predicted probability of fear of voting among UPND and non-UPND sup-porters is negligible. For non-UPND supporters, the predicted probability of fear while voting is 18%, compared to 20% for UPND supporters.[10]

Models 1–4 reveal much more striking group differences in other forms of participation. I find that women voters are significantly more afraid to discuss politics in public and participate in campaign rallies. Whereas the predicted probability of men being fearful of attending campaign rallies is 49%, the pre-dicted probability for women is 60%. These are troubling findings that confirm how violence marginalizes women in electoral participation. I also find that UPND supporters are significantly more afraid of participating in all elec-toral activities other than voting. This finding reaffirms the argument from Chapter 4 and underscores how the incumbent party has leveraged its cen-tral repressive capacity to curb the opposition campaign. For instance, while the predicted probability for a non-UPND supporter of being fearful of vio-lence when attending a rally is 50%, the corresponding predicted probability for UPND supporters is 64%. Similarly, the predicted probability of fear when wearing party regalia for UPND supporters is 63%, compared to 53% for non-UPND supporters. All of these activities were also associated with higher levels of fear among urban compared to nonurban respondents. Then predicted probability for urban respondents to be fearful of violence when attending rallies is 63%, compared to 50% for rural respondents.

The results are particularly interesting regarding local partisan majorities. Partisan local majorities were significantly less fearful of wearing regalia, dis-cuss politics in public, and participate in campaign rallies. Keep in mind that these findings are in control for UPND partisanship. For instance, the pre-dicted probability of fear while wearing party regalia was 59% for local partisan minorities, compared to 49% for local partisan majorities. The predicted fear for participating in rallies was 56% for local partisan minorities, compared to 50% for local partisan majorities. In other words, territorial politics may have severely limited the electoral participation of partisan minorities in their local communities.

---

[10] All predicted probabilities are calculated when keeping other covariates in the model at their means.

5.3 Conclusion

This chapter has dealt empirically with some of the micro-foundations under-lying the electoral geography theory of election violence proposed in this book. Will voters feel free to engage broadly in the campaign without fear of becoming the victims of violence? Do voters feel equally safe to participate in campaigns regardless of their individual characteristics, their local political environment, and the interaction between the two? And what forms of elec-toral participation will be associated with fear for different voters in varying local contexts? I have focused particularly on the case of Zambia due to data availability. Although data on fear in relation to different forms of electoral par-ticipation do not exist for the Malawi case, it is likely that patterns in Malawi would be similar in many regards. Later chapters will show how violence in Malawi and Zambia are used in common ways. However, given the lower lev-els of violence in Malawi compared to Zambia, it is likely that we would find overall lower levels of fear when engaging in all forms of participation. It is also possible that the partisan difference would be less stark.

The findings presented here challenge some of the main assumptions in the electoral violence literature. First, it shows that Zambian voters living in competitive constituencies are less fearful of violence than voters who sup-port minority parties in government party strongholds. This is an important corrective and a finding that is easily obscured without taking local electoral context into account. This finding reinforces the theoretical proposition that election violence may be perceived as a territorial tool and a way to shrink democratic space by limiting participation among those that support local minority parties. All in all, showing high levels of fear among local minori-ties, women, and opposition supporters, this chapter shows how violence is a form of manipulation entrenching the role of the powerful at the expense of those more marginalized. Violence not only distorts political competition, but exacerbates political inequalities.

Second, I show that voting was not the activity most associated with fear. Moreover, there was no single group more fearful of voting than other groups. This is interesting given that opposition party supporters were disproportion-ately the victims of violence (CCMG 2021). Instead, there are other forms of political participation such as wearing party regalia, participating in cam-paign rallies, and discussing politics that are more associated with fear. Also, opposition supporters and local partisan majorities are particularly fearful of engaging in such activities. The extent to which fear was associated with political participation among local partisan majorities really illustrates how stifling violence can be for a functioning local electoral environment.

These results show territoriality at work. Election violence is designed to prevent active campaigning inside party strongholds. These findings also explain why parties perpetrate violence inside their own strongholds. While such violence has often been considered theoretically unlikely (Collier and Vicente 2012), we know it to be empirically common (Fielding 2018; Lewanika 2019). Violence in party strongholds can be used to limit campaign activities among partisan minorities and enforce territoriality.

6

Democracy, Elections, and Electoral Geography in Malawi

This chapter introduces Malawi's electoral history, institutions, and electoral geography. The purpose of the chapter is to anchor the analysis of subnational variations in campaign violence in a firm understanding of Malawian political mobilization. Given the book's argument that we cannot understand electoral violence as a tool of electoral manipulation without understanding electoral institutions, cleavages, and modes of mobilization, this chapter is crucial for interpreting the geographic patterns of violence displayed in the subsequent Chapter 7. The analysis of Malawian electoral geography will reveal important similarities with Zambia and underscore some general dynamics of elections in geographically polarized electoral systems. It will also show some important differences that help us understand variations in subnational patterns of campaign violence in the two countries.

As with Zambia, Malawian political competition has been strongly characterized by regionalism. This regionalism may not be reduced simply to ethnic voting. While regional voting has been significant, regions are multiethnic. Moreover, ethnic groups straddling regional divides have been known to develop different political allegiances. However, while Zambian national majorities were cobbled together by parties making multiregional appeals, Malawian majorities have generally been based on a strong presence in one region. In particular, this chapter will show the strong dominance of Southern Region in Malawian multiparty politics.

Another important similarity with Zambia is that parties have generally pursued a strategy of stronghold mobilization. This is particularly true for parties based in the powerful and populous Southern Region. The importance of Southern Region will help us understand the region's frequent violent clashes between the Democratic Progressive Party (DPP)—the traditional regional hegemon—and the insurgent People's Party (PP) in the 2014 election (Chapter 7).

Another similarity between Malawi and Zambia is the active mobilization of regional cleavages. This has been particularly true in Southern and Northern

Controlling Territory, Controlling Voters. Michael Wahman, Oxford University Press.
© Michael Wahman (2023). DOI: 10.1093/oso/9780198872825.003.0006

Region, while the less volatile Central Region has been more reliably mobilized by the more institutionalized Malawi Congress Party (MCP). The strong rivalry over regional mobilization was particularly pronounced in the 2014 election, where three parties—the DPP, the United Democratic Front (UDF), and the PP—all made realistic claims to be the regional advocate of the vital Southern Region. DPP and PP also competed over mobilizing the regional cleavage in Northern Malawi.

The chapter will also explain some important idiosyncrasies of the 2014 election. I will focus particularly on the central government's weakness and low repressive capacity. Here, I argue that the difference in the strength of the incumbent party in Malawi and Zambia will make for an interesting comparison of subnational patterns of campaign violence. While Chapters 3 and 4 discussed the considerable government advantages enjoyed by the PF and the Lungu government's frequent deployment of central repressive resources during the campaign, this chapter will illustrate that the PP government of Joyce Banda did not possess such centralized repressive resources.

6.1 The Origins of Regional Competition in Malawi

Malawi gained independence from British colonial rule in 1964 amid rising anti-colonial sentiment and public protest (Rotberg 1971). After independence, political power was quickly personalized around Malawi's first prime minister, Dr. Hastings Banda, an ethnic Chewa from the Central Region. The original personalization of power has often been traced to the 1964 cabinet crisis, where Banda successfully managed to survive the collapse of his initial cabinet and pack his administration with ideologically and politically aligned loyalists (McMaster 1974; Chirwa 2001). The 1964 crisis was the origin of political centralization and personalization in the postcolonial state, but also increased the concentration of political power in Malawi's Central Region. Hodder-Williams (1974) argued that the 1964 cabinet crisis was an expression of regionalism. The slow pace of Banda's Africanization reforms had infuriated both highly educated civil servants in the north and cash-crop-producing farmers in the south. Two years after the cabinet crisis, with the passing of the new 1966 constitution, Malawi became a presidential one-party state under the rule of Dr. Banda and his MCP.

Several scholars of Malawian political history have emphasized the regional favoritism that resulted from the Banda presidency. Favoritism was felt both culturally and economically. In 1968, President Banda changed national language policies to promote Chichewa (the language of the Chewa tribe) to become the symbolic national language next to English. In a multicultural country with a diversity of tribes, languages, and religions, Banda continued to hail the Chewa culture as culturally superior and a symbol of national unity (Moyo 2002). Banda also announced the plans to move the Malawian capital from Zomba in the Southern Region to Lilongwe in the Central Region in 1965. Lilongwe, at this time, was a fairly unremarkable city, far smaller than the bustling economic hub of Blantyre. It was, however, located close to Banda's home district of Kasungu and in the political heartland of his ruling party (Potts 1985). The relocation of the capital to Lilongwe contributed to an economic boom in the Central Region, but the economic favoritism of the Central Region was also evident in the implementation of economic development policies. Central policy initiatives aimed to increase the production of cash crops where heavily biased towards farmers in the Central Region. Chewa interests had also been favored in the building of the new Malawian economic elite (Kaspin 1995).

The Malawi one-party state was highly repressive and intolerant of any form of political dissent. A state that penetrated social affairs down to the village-level enabled high levels of repression. Malawians in the countryside and in the cities were linked to the central government through a network of local regional/district committees. In 1964, Dr. Banda founded the Malawi Young Pioneers (MYP), a paramilitary group of the MCP. The MYP, in Banda's own words, were there "to see for me, to hear for me, [and] to help the security forces when necessary." Members of the MYP stood above the law and the police could not be arrest them without prior permission from the commanding officer (Chirambo 2004). The MYP was systematically utilized to undermine civil society, spy on ordinary Malawians, and torture and kill dissidents. They offered a tool for centralized control by the authoritarian state, and the MYP's omnipresence was felt in the everyday lives of Malawians (Chirambo 2001).

The protest wave that hit Africa in the late 1980s and early 1990s was not instantaneously felt in Malawi, possibly due to high levels of repression (Bratton and van de Walle 1992). Still, as it turned out, Malawi was not immune to the wind of change that swept through the continent. By 1992, the one-party state was under immense pressure, not least from increased opposition from civil society and religious institutions. Riots and protests had spread and student organizations had increasingly mobilized against the regime.

In the wake of intensifying protests, two new pressure groups were formed: the Alliance for the Restoration of Democracy (AFORD) and the UDF. These groups were initially not known as political parties. MCP was still the sole legal political party, but eventually UDF and AFORD would transform into Malawi's first major opposition parties. In April 1992, the leader of AFORD, Chakufwa Chihana, publicly demanded a referendum on multipartyism with little immediate response from the Banda regime. However, by September the same year, internal and external pressure had mounted and the issue of a referendum was tabled at the MCP annual convention. Although the convention rejected the proposal, Dr. Banda nevertheless announced a referendum a few weeks later (van Donge 1995).

In a referendum on June 14, 1993, Malawians voted overwhelmingly for the introduction of multipartyism. The final results showed a 37% support for maintaining the one-party state against 67% in favor of the introduction of multipartyism. Although President Banda had tried to control the referendum process and stifle debate, the referendum was a major blow for the aging president. In the campaign, Dr. Banda tried to essentially make the referendum a presidential election: a choice between his allegedly cohesive national brand or the regionalist divisive brand of the two major opposition leaders, Muluzi and Chihana. This framing was supposed to evoke a sense of patriotism and loyalty among Malawians, but ultimately Banda only managed to rally support in his stronghold in Central Region (Dzimbiri 1994; van Donge 1995). The regional division in the referendum may be a first sign of the geographical polarization that would later come to characterize elections in multiparty Malawi.

6.2 Institutions Favoring Regional Politics

From the 1994 election onwards, elections in Malawi have been held under strongly disproportional rules. The institutions created after the defeat of Banda's MCP in 1994 served to lock in regional dominance of the South vis-à-vis its Central Region rival. The constitution heavily concentrated power in the executive and institutions favored disproportionality to enable regional mobilization without necessitating political nationalization.

The 1995 constitution creates a unitary presidential democracy with a bicameral legislature. Although the 1995 constitution created an upper house in parliament, this system was never implemented and later abandoned. The electoral system is described in the 1993 Presidential and Parliamentary Elections Act. First-past-the-post presidential elections are held nationally, and parliamentary elections are held in single member districts. The electoral commission determine parliamentary constituency boundaries but the executive has manipulated them for political purposes. Most strikingly, the Muluzi government used its sway over the electoral commission to create several new constituencies in its Southern stronghold in preparation for the 1999 election (Khembo 2004; Boone and Wahman 2015; Wahman and Chapman 2015).

Frequent calls for electoral system reforms have been heard in the Malawian political debate. Civil society has advocated for more proportional parliamentary elections and a 50+1 presidential electoral system, where a second round of voting would be called if no presidential candidate obtained an outright majority in the first round of voting. However, subsequent governments have been able to fend off any attempts to implement fundamental electoral reform (Chinsinga 2015; Patel 2015). The 50+1 presidential electoral system was only realized through a ruling by the Malawi Constitutional Court in 2020. In sum, Malawi embodies the archetype of a winner-takes-all system. Given the regionalization of voting patterns and high levels of fragmentation, certain regions of Malawi have been able to dominate electoral politics.

6.3 The 1994 Election: Regional (Not Ethnic) Cleavages Prevail

After losing the referendum, Banda was further undermined in the run-up to the decisive founding election in 1994. Most importantly, the repressive capacity of MCP was permanently damaged when the Malawi military finally decided to disarm the MYP and reassert the monopoly on violence (Chirambo 2004). Banda's last remaining hope to cling on to power was a divided opposition. Malawi's opposition had split into two major parties: UDF, drawing most of its support and political leadership from the Southern Region, and AFORD, with its regional base in the Northern Region. Northern Malawi, educationally advanced but economically marginalized, was fertile ground for opposition politics. Southern Region, on the other hand, had been economically relatively prosperous in the colonial era but had fallen behind during the MCP's economic prioritization of Central Malawi. Chewa-favoring cultural policies had also created grievances in the multiethnic South, where most did not identify as ethnic Chewas. UDF concentrated its campaigning in the South, while AFORD's presence was mostly felt in its northern stronghold.

The final results of the 1994 election showed an electorate split in three, evidently along regional lines (see Figure 6.1). Muluzi (UDF) won 78% of the presidential vote in the South, Banda (MCP) won 64% of the vote in Central, and Chihana (AFORD) won 88% of the vote in the North. Interestingly, UDF won very few votes in the North, and AFORD had almost no support outside

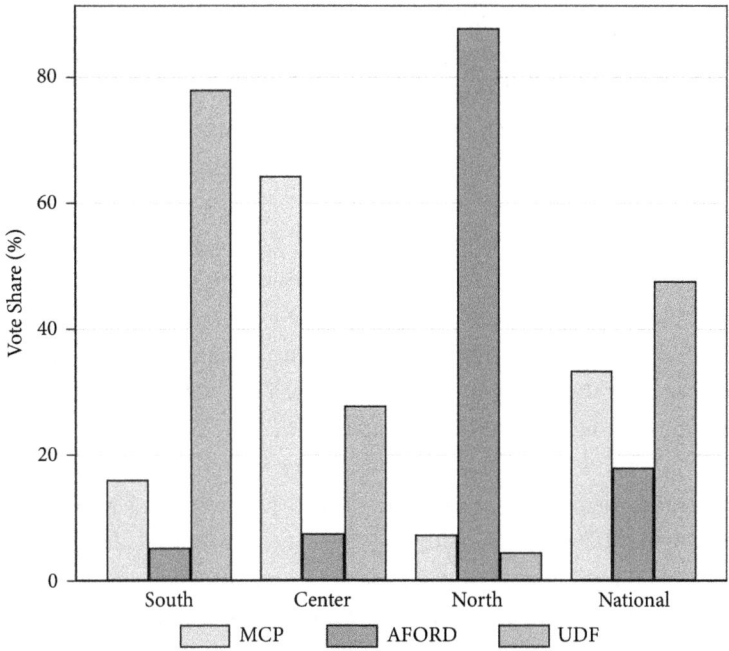

Figure 6.1 Regional Results Malawi 1994 Election.

Source: Kalipeni (1997a)

its Northern stronghold. MCP, which still had some patronage power among rural populations in the Southern Region (Kaspin 1995), finished second in both the Northern and Southern Region. Nevertheless, higher nationalization did not help the government party stay in power when faced with a main opposition rival with a stronger regional base in a more populous region. Riding the wave of overwhelming support in the Southern Region (which accounted for almost 50% of the Malawi population), Muluzi secured a historic victory.[1] The election put a definite end to the 30-year rule of MCP and Kamuzu Banda. It also marked the transfer of power from Central to Southern Region. Southern Region's political dominance would last for the next 25 years.

It is tempting to interpret the voting patterns in 1994 as a sign of an emerging ethnic party system. However, as several scholars of Malawian politics have emphasized, doing so would be reductionist (Kaspin 1995; Kalipeni 1997a). Regional identities in Malawi are often understood in ethnic terms.

[1] If MCP had been able to replicate UDF's performance in the Southern Region in the Central Region (i.e., if MCP had received the same share of the vote in the Central Region as UDF did in the Southern Region and UDF the same share of the vote in the Central Region as MCP did in the Southern Region), the gap in votes between UDF and MCP would have been reduced from 438,000 to 126,000.

As an analytical category, regional identities have been interpreted as a sort of "super-ethnic" identity of groups that are supposedly related due to their geographic proximity and political alliances. However, neither of the three main regions are ethnically homogeneous. In the Northern Region, the Banda regime attempted to build a unified "Tumbuka" identity based on a shared language. However, a significant share of northerners are actually not Tumbuka in ethnic terms (although often linguistically). The Northern Region is ethnically diverse and composed of culturally distinct groups such as the Ngoni, the Tumbuka, the Tonga, and the Ngonde. Nevertheless, a sense of collective regional identity has emerged from a sense of economic marginalization. Southern and Central Regions are similarly diverse, with the Central Region having large communities of Ngoni and Chewa and the Southern Region are primarily compromised of Lomwe, Sena, and Yao ethnic groups.[2] Kalipeni (1997b) argues that regional identities have been promoted as ethnic identities among politicians attempting to build larger coalitions of supporters.[3] It is important to note that most Malawians did not vote for a co-ethnic in the 1994 election. Out of the ten districts won by Bakili Muluzi, only three were co-ethnic majority Yao (and Muslim) districts.

The geographic patterns also showed that certain ethnic communities that stretch over different regions, like Tonga and Ngoni, split their votes along predictable regional lines. For instance, Ngoni in the South voted most for Muluzi, whereas Tonga in Central tended to vote for Banda. Taken together, this leads Kaspin (1995) to conclude that "Unfortunately regionalism tends to be conflated with ethnicity and to disappear as a category" (see also Chikadza 2021).

6.4 Malawian Elections 1999–2004: Regionalism is the Name of the Game

The regionalistic voting patterns born from the founding 1994 election have become a constant feature in most elections. As opposed to Zambia, where the geographically polarized electoral system developed over time, Malawian politics has more or less constantly converged to the pattern of high national-level

---

[2] The Southern Region is also religiously diverse, with the Lomwe and Sena being mostly Christian and the Yao being mostly Muslim.

[3] Similar arguments were developed in greater detail in the pathbreaking work of Posner (2005).

competition and low local-level competition. Figure 6.2 shows the level of geographic polarization in Malawi over time. The figure shows that both national and local-level competition has remained remarkably constant. The only slight outlier is the 2009 election, when the government party secured an unusually decisive victory on the back of impressive economic performance (Cammack 2010). Contrary to Zambia, Malawi did not develop a hegemonic government party after its founding election. Whereas Zambia featured a more nationalized hegemon against regionalized challengers, Malawi has more commonly pitted various regional parties against each other. Even the incumbent party has struggled to nationalize, but has maintained power through a combination of stronghold mobilization and electoral manipulation.

The 1999 election saw President Bakili Muluzi come under enhanced pressure as MCP and AFORD formed a joint alliance, nominating MCP's

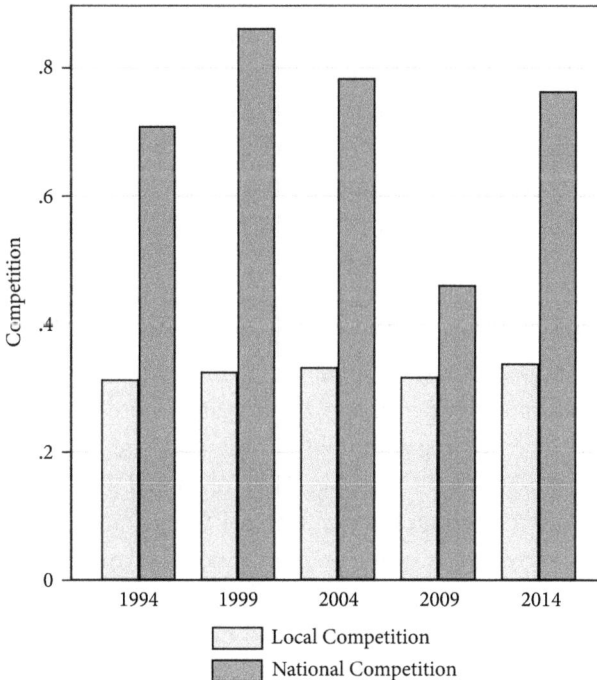

Figure 6.2 Local and National Competition in Malawi 1994–2014.

Note: Local Competition shows the number of votes won by the runner-up presidential candidate divided by the winner's number of votes as an average across all constituencies. National competition shows the national runner-up's number of votes divided by the national winner's number of votes. Constituency results are from parliamentary elections in 1994, 1999, and 2004.

Gwanda Chakuamba as their presidential candidate. The coalition drew regional divisions between the Southern Region and the rest of the country. However, despite opposition coordination, President Muluzi still won the presidential election, partly due to electoral manipulation. A biased electoral commission, media, and state machinery favored the incumbent (Khembo 2004).

Political realignments characterized Malawi's third multiparty election in 2004. President Muluzi's attempt to change the constitution to extend his stay in power and run for a third term dominated the debate prior to the 2004 election. The president's effort to change the constitution was defeated in parliament and created major splits in the ruling party, with several MPs defecting to new smaller splinters. The events that transpired around Muluzi's third-term bid are highly reminiscent of what happened in Zambia by the end of President Chiluba's second term (VonDoepp 2005). As in Zambia after the split of the MMD, the opposition was also deeply divided. MCP had split into several parties in 2003. Most importantly, divisions had pitted John Tembo and Gwanda Chakuamba against each other, two men who were both seen as possible heirs to Kamuzu Banda during the one-party state. The conflict ended with Tembo staying in MCP and Chakuamba defecting to build his own Republican Party (RP). AFORD entered into a coalition with UDF, but several dissatisfied AFORD MPs defected from the party as a consequence (Rakner et al. 2007).

As a result of these fundamental realignments, the regionalist character of the 2004 election was less stark than in the 1994 and 1999 elections, although it certainly did not disappear. RP won most of the votes in the Northern Region, carrying five out of six districts, and MCP again won most of the votes in the Central Region, winning seven out of nine districts. The most competitive region was the Southern. Although UDF remained the largest party, the RP and a smaller UDF splinter party, National Democratic Alliance (NDA), also won respectable shares of the Southern vote (Dulani 2006; Ferree and Horowitz 2010).

In the end, UDF's presidential candidate, Bingu Mutharika, emerged victorious, with only 36% of the vote. Mutharika's victory was largely enabled by his ability to win larger shares of the vote outside his own strongholds (Lemon 2007), but would most likely not have been possible with a more cohesive opposition with a strong Central Region base. The election victory was also enabled by an unleveled playing field created by strong executive control over the electoral commission and a staggering resource advantage enjoyed by the government party (Khembo 2004; Gloppen et al. 2006). The opposition did not recognize the final election results, and violent protests erupted in Blantyre, with Chakuamba alleging that the Malawi Electoral Commission (MEC) had rigged the election on behalf of UDF (Dulani 2006).

Major realignments occurred after Mutharika's election victory in 2004. Swiftly after winning the presidency, President Mutharika broke away from the UDF. By breaking with the UDF, Mutharika was able to rid himself of the informal influence of the retired president. Moreover, the new DPP party also attracted several MPs from opposition parties and extended its national representation beyond UDF's predominantly Southern stronghold (Hussein 2009).

Mutharika won re-election in 2009 more comfortably than any other Malawian president. The incumbent benefited from repeated years of unprecedented economic growth, significant improvements in food security, and high presidential approval ratings (Smiddy and Young 2009; Ferree and Horowitz 2010; Mpesi and Muriaas 2012). The final election results revealed Mutharika as the winner with 66% of the vote, compared to only 30% for MCP's John Tembo. Mutharika's impressive victory was achieved in a relatively open and transparent electoral environment. Perhaps because of the government's overwhelming popularity, MEC was allowed to operate with unusual independence, and levels of repression were low (Rakner 2010).

Another noteworthy aspect of the 2009 election, acknowledged by many scholars of Malawian politics, is DPP's relatively high level of nationalization (Tsoka 2009; Chinsinga 2010; Ferree and Horowitz 2010). Figure 6.3 shows the regional support of the two major political parties in the 2009 election. The figure shows how DPP managed to win both the South and the North. MCP, on the other hand, held on to most of its Central stronghold. The MCP had also created a coalition with the remaining parts of UDF. The UDF was, at this point, mostly loyal to Bakili Muluzi and his home area in the predominantly Muslim eastern part of the Southern Region (around Lake Malawi). Although the 2009 election was less regionalistic than previous elections, local competition was still just as limited as in other elections (see Figure 6.3). In the Northern and Southern constituencies won by DPP, the DPP, on average, received as much as 80% of the vote. Localism still seems to have prevailed, although the regional patterns were more complex than in earlier elections.

MCP vote share   DPP vote share

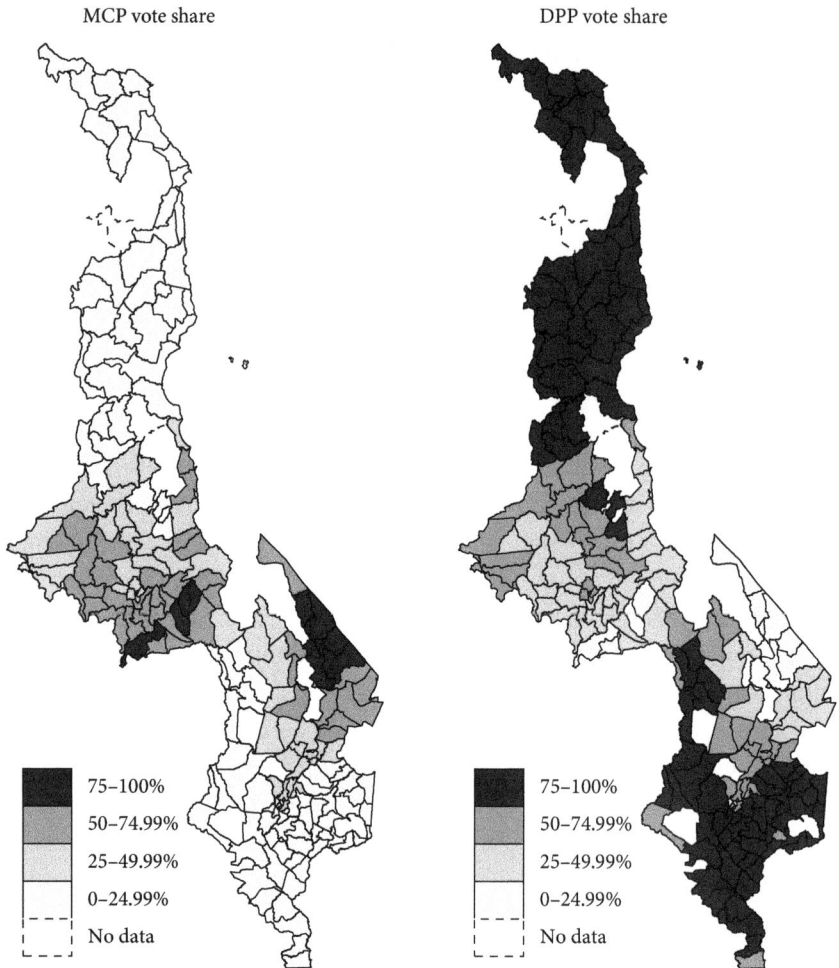

■	75–100%
▨	50–74.99%
░	25–49.99%
□	0–24.99%
⌐ ⌐	No data

■	75–100%
▨	50–74.99%
░	25–49.99%
□	0–24.99%
⌐ ⌐	No data

Figure 6.3 2009 Presidential Election, Malawi.

Note: Election data from Malawi Electoral Commission (MEC).

6.5 The 2014 Election: Political Turmoil and Executive Weakness

The 2014 election was held against a hugely dramatic presidential term. Malawi's economic fortunes had quickly turned shortly after Bingu's re-election, amid severely flawed monetary and fiscal policies. The country went from boosting some of the world's highest GDP growth figures to a severe economic crisis, spiraling national debt, inflation, currency devaluation, fuel shortage, and a foreign currency crisis (Chinsinga 2015). The economic crisis was combined with a democratic one. In the face of an economic melt-down, the Malawi government had enhanced levels of repression against civil society, intellectuals, and the organized opposition (Dionne and Dulani 2013). Relations with the donor community were also deteriorating. In April 2011, a communiqué from the British High Commissioner, Fergus Cochrane-Dyet, had been leaked in which he had communicated that Mutharika was "becoming even more autocratic and intolerant against criticism." President Mutharika responded to the leak by expelling the British diplomat, and the UK decided to stop all bilateral aid to Malawi. Other European donors soon followed suit (Wroe 2012).

In July 2011, national demonstrations against the country's deteriorating economy and democracy were called. Although the NGOs organizing the demonstrations had received permission from the Malawi police, a judge had banned the demonstrations the day before. The police responded by beating several protesters and the protests turned into riots. The police ended up firing against the protesters, and 20 people were killed. The episode led to the United States also suspending their bilateral aid. Fighting, protests, and tension continued to characterize Malawi's public space for the coming months (Cammack 2012).

The most acute phase of the crisis ended in April 2012 after President Mutharika unexpectedly passed away from a heart attack. Mutharika's death introduced a precarious constitutional situation. Mutharika had won the election with Joyce Banda as his vice-presidential running mate, and the constitution dictates that the presidency will pass from the president to the vice-president in the event that the president dies in office. However, at President Mutharika's passing, Joyce Banda had been estranged from DPP. Mutharika had clearly shown his intention to line up his brother, Peter Mutharika, as his successor, making him the party president rather than Banda. In frustration, Banda left the party and formed her own party, the People's Party (PP). She was able to bring a few MPs with her to her new party, but until Mutharika's death, PP remained a minor party in parliament (Patel and Wahman 2015).

However, the transition from the deceased Bingu Mutharika to Joyce Banda was not seamless. After Mutharika's death on the morning of April 5, private media companies started to report the news on the death of the president, but the Malawi Broadcasting Cooperation (MBC) remained silent, and the government issued no public statement. Later that evening, MBC released a statement saying that Mutharika was ill and was being transported to South Africa. The message was a deliberate attempt to conceal the fact that the president had died and that the process of a replacement should be activated. On April 6, six cabinet members[4] organized a press conference to declare that Banda could not succeed Mutharika since she had left the government party and was now heading an opposition party. The intentions of the cabinet members were clear: to pave the way for a Peter Mutharika presidency and to safeguard their own access to power and maintain the Southern Region's political dominance (Dulani and Dionne 2013).

The military ultimately had to settle the power struggle between Peter Mutharika and Banda. On April 6, Banda called the Commander of the Malawi Army, Henry Odillo, to request a public statement of support. Meanwhile, the Mutharika camp urged the military to seize power. The famously apolitical Malawi military decided to defend the constitution. General Odillo pledged his allegiance to Banda and sent army officers to defend her residency. Bingu Mutharika was officially declared dead on April 7 (two days after his actual death) and Joyce Banda—Malawi's first and Africa's second female president—took office (Wahman et al. 2021).

Although Banda was now the president, her position of power was remarkably weaker than previous presidents. Her party was shallow, lacking in organization and outreach. Although she had a few MPs in her fold, most PP MPs joined after Banda's accession to power. After the 2009 election, Banda's old party, DPP, was the strongest party that had ever been represented in the Malawi parliament. Although many DPP MPs defected to PP, many also stayed with their old party. Some that initially defected also returned to the DPP when the PP government encountered various crises (Svåsand 2015).[5]

Furthermore, the fact that President Banda had never been elected to power undoubtedly weakened her authority and created uncertainty about her electoral viability. Her position was further weakened by continued economic hardship. Despite having launched several vital reforms after assuming office, including a radical devaluation of the currency, an end to policies regulating fuel prices, important changes to fiscal policies, and normalization of Malawian donor relations, the economic crisis was still felt by many

---

[4] The six cabinet ministers have later been dubbed the "midnight six" and have been accused of treason.

[5] The exact number of MPs who defected is hard to estimate (Svåsand 2015: 90).

ordinary Malawians (Chinsinga 2015). Banda's normalization of donor relations brought aid back, at least temporarily, but also enhanced donor leverage over the Malawian administration and reduced Banda's discretionary power (Wahman and Drury 2018).[6]

Most importantly, the reputation of Banda's administration was deeply hit by the so-called "cashgate scandal." The scandal unfolded after an investigation into a failed attempted murder of a government budget director, Paul Mphwiyo. In the investigation, police uncovered evidence of gross corruption involving several government officials in several administrations (Riley and Chilanga 2018). Joyce Banda was the president when the scandal erupted, but by no means was the scandal restricted to officers and ministers in Banda's administration. The scandal spanned several administrations, not at least the Bingu Mutharika regime. Still, experimental work by Brigitte Zimmerman (2015) suggests that voters placed the blame for the cashgate scandal squarely at president Banda's feet. Nevertheless, many people directly benefiting from the cashgate scandal were competing the 2014 election on a DPP ticket and did not shy away from using stolen resources to run the opposition campaign (Mail and Guardian 2015).

Banda also did not have the same grip on government institutions as previous administrations. Her weak position vis-à-vis other parties and the international community increased the need for her to compromise. The MEC was appointed in the Banda presidency, but the process had been much more inclusive than in earlier elections. Banda had appointed the commissioners on recommendation from the party leaders, and the commission was for once not generally biased in favor of the incumbent (Patel 2015: 107). She also did not have much time in her presidency to appoint other important actors, such as High Court judges. Dulani and Chunga (2015), analyzing the defeat of Banda from the perspective of incumbent advantage, conclude that Banda lacked many of the typical advantages of African incumbents. The ruling party did not have the kind of centralized manipulating capacity that other Malawian governments have had or, indeed, as PF did in the Zambian 2016 election. As I will argue in Chapter 7, this also had repercussions on patterns of campaign violence.

---

[6] As a theoretical discussion on leverage and electoral authoritarianism, see the work by Levitsky and Way (2010).

6.5.1 The Results and Conduct of the 2014 Election

The 2014 election was a highly competitive race, not at least since the incumbent party was the weakest since Malawi's founding election in 1994. The election was widely perceived as a four-horse race between Joyce Banda and her PP, Peter Mutharika of the DPP, Lazarus Chakwera of the MCP, and Atupele Muluzi of the UDF.

Despite being born in the Southern Region, Banda could be considered a northerner by marriage. More importantly, with the Northern Region lacking a presidential candidate of their own, Banda had created strong ties with northern political elites during her presidency. For instance, she had selected Khumbu Kachali, a prominent Northern politician and businessman, as her vice president. Banda's campaign had a strong clientelistic appeal, and observers noted that the campaign blurred the line between government functions and party rallies. So-called "development rallies" were often used to promote the governing party's electoral campaign. In such rallies, voters were provided with all sorts of handouts, from cash, iron sheets, and maize to large ticket items like motorbikes, cows, and even houses (Chinsinga 2015: 25; Mbowela and Mwalubunju 2015: 121).[7]

Banda also tried to make inroads in other parties' strongholds, but ultimately failed. One key strategy in Banda's re-election campaign was to mobilize chiefs in her favor. In the run-up to the election, the Banda administration had promoted a record number of chiefs. As many as 40,000 new chiefs were elevated at different levels of the traditional authority hierarchy. Most of these chiefs were elevated in Central Region. Kayuni (2015) explains the geographical patterns of elevations in line with the expectations in a geographically polarized electoral system. Whereas three parties (UDF, PP, and DPP) all fielded presidential candidates from the South, and the North had no presidential candidate, the Central Region was dominated by only one party (MCP). In the words of Kayuni (2015: 209): "In summary, it was rational for the PP to focus on the Central Region considering the perceived threat that the MCP posed if it was to monopolize the region."

For the opposition DPP, the strategy was based primarily on dominating the non-eastern parts of Southern Region and also winning significant support from rural voters in other parts of the country who had benefited from some of the party's agricultural policies while in office (Andrews 2015). For the DPP, it

---

[7] The houses came from a controversial government scheme labeled the Mudzi Transformation Trust (MTT).

was particularly important to protect their strongholds from inroads by the PP. For the other main opposition challenger, MCP, the choice of Lazarus Chakwera as the frontrunner for MCP was an important break from the past for the former authoritarian ruling party. The previous party leader, John Tembo, was intimately associated with the Kamuzu Banda regime and had limited appeal outside the Central Region. With Chakwera, MCP was hoping to branch out of its Central stronghold. However, the party was criticized for failing to build a strong organization beyond its base and attract viable candidates for non–Central Region parliamentary seats. Similarly, UDF had little presence outside its stronghold of the predominantly Muslim Eastern region, the home region of its presidential candidate.

Figure 6.4 shows the regional voting patterns in the 2014 election. Again, Malawi exhibits geographically polarized voting patterns where a majority of constituencies were uncompetitive despite high levels of national competition. The DDP dominated the Southern Region, particularly in districts such as Mulanje, Thyolo, and Phalombe. MCP dominated the Central Region, particularly in districts such as Dedza, Dowa, and Lilongwe rural. UDF won overwhelmingly in the Eastern districts Mangochi and Balaka. PP found its stronghold in the Northern Region and won with great margins in districts like Nkhata Bay and Rumphi. The more competitive areas were generally cities like Blantyre and Lilongwe and diverse border districts like Kasungu and Mzimba.

On May 20, MEC released their preliminary results. With 30% of the votes counted, Banda was only in third place, lagging seriously behind opposition candidates Peter Mutharika (DPP) and Lazarus Chakwera (MCP). Banda, however, was not going down without a fight. On May 24, Joyce Banda issued a remarkable public radio announcement. Rather than acknowledging defeat, she claimed that the election was characterized by "serious irregularities" and announced that: "I am nullifying the elections, using the powers invested in me by the Malawian constitution." It did not take long before other government institutions weighed in, firmly establishing that President Banda had no legal authority to nullify the election. The MEC Chairman quickly communicated to the media that: "As far as I know, the President doesn't have any constitutional powers to nullify the election, only the electoral commission has the power to do so" (Al Jazeera 2014). A few hours later, the High Court issued an injunction preventing the president from nullifying the elections.

The episode was telling in many respects. First, government institutions showed a remarkable amount of independence vis-à-vis the executive. In a country where the constitution grants tremendous power to the executive in appointing judges and commissioners, Malawians have not at all come to

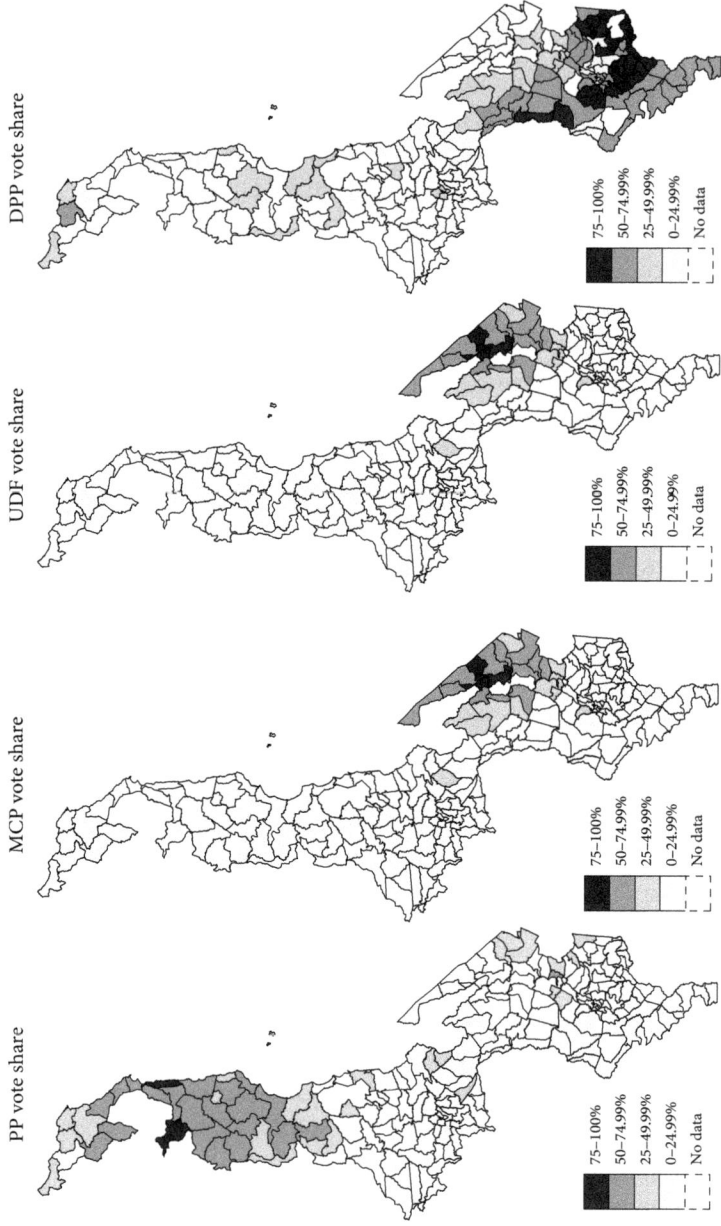

Figure 6.4 2014 Presidential Election, Malawi.

Note: Election data from Malawi Electoral Commission (MEC).

expect this kind of independence from their government institutions (Cam-mack 2012). Second, although defeated African parties have often criticized the quality of elections, it is rarely a sitting president that cries foul after an election. All in all, the episode again showed the unusual weakness of the incumbent regime in this election. With its support base in the sparsely populated North, far from the power bases in the major cities, the PP also had limited ability to stage any post-election protest.

6.6 Analyzing the History of Polarization in Malawi

The discussion about electoral politics in Malawi has shown that regional politics can be traced back to the pre-democratic era and has been rein-forced and reproduced through multiparty politics. Although often described as "ethno-regionalism" the ethnic geography and diversity of Malawi really question the extent to which "ethnic" and "regional" voting can be understood as interchangeable concepts. Having established the re-occurence of political regionalism in the case of Malawi throughout individual elections, it is finally worth taking stock of more aggregate trends using electoral data.

The institutional choices made early in key constitutional moments have reduced the necessity to build broad regional coalitions, especially in the face of elite fractionalization. Importantly, the winning presidential candidate won national elections in Malawi with less than 50% of the national vote in four out of six elections in the period 1994–2019. If we take the three main regions as a rough proxy for the key electoral blocs in Malawian politics,[8] we find that par-ties have often relied heavily on mobilization in one single region. Figure 6.5 graphs the share of a party's total national vote that was obtained in the region where they amassed the highest number of votes. The graph shows the share for both the winner and the runner-up in each election. On average, the win-ning party amassed 66% of its vote from only one region, and the runner-up gained 72% of all its votes from its main regional stronghold.

The stronghold strategy is particularly useful for parties with their strength in the Southern Region. Winning an overwhelming majority of the Southern Region has often meant that parties need very little support from other regions. Figure 6.6 shows two important statistics, the share of the regional vote won

---

[8] Although this is commonly done (see e.g., Kaspin 1995, Killepeni 1997a, and Ferree and Horowitz 2010), it is not entirely unproblematic as the main regions have also experienced some heterogeneity in electoral behavior. For instance, the eastern part of Southern Region has not always voted with the rest of the Southern Region and Ntcheu district often does not coalesce with the Chewa-dominated parts of the Central Region (Boone et al. 2022).

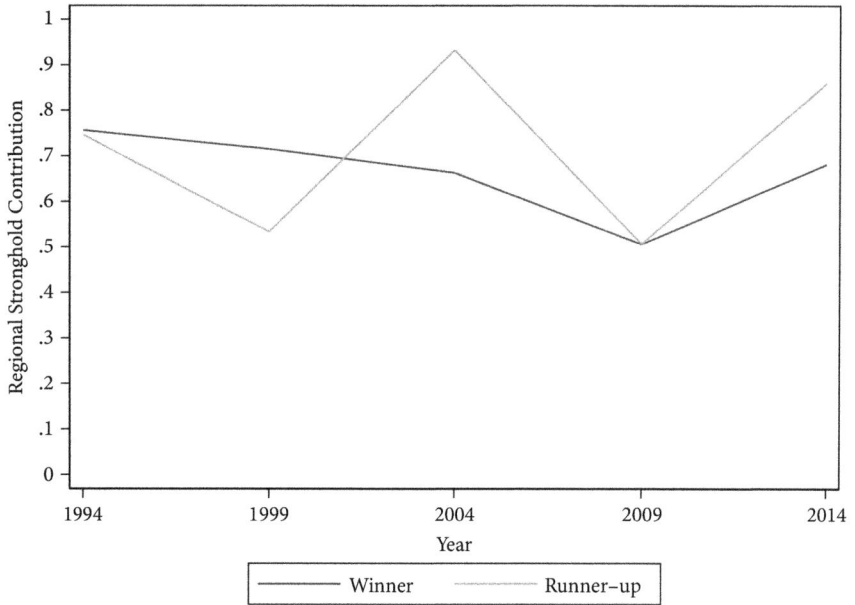

Figure 6.5 Share of Party's National Vote Derived from the Region Where it Won the Highest Number of Votes.

Note: Graph shows the share of a party's total national vote originating from the region where the party received its highest number of votes.

by the regionally most popular candidate and the number of valid votes across regions. The Southern Region's electoral advantage vis-à-vis Central is due to a combination of the numerical advantage of the South compared to Central (on average, 35% more valid votes were cast in the Southern Region compared to the Central Region) and a generally higher propensity for regional bloc-voting.

A possible alternative interpretation of the structure of Malawian politics is to regard Northern Region as the kingmaker. Southern and Central Regions have predictably competed for power in every election, but the allegiance of the Northern Region has varied across electoral contests. The region has typically also not had its own regional party (with the exception of AFORD in the 1994 election). It is true that in all but one election (1999), the winning candidate outperformed the runner-up in the Northern Region. However, this argument is not particularly persuasive when looking at the historical data for two primary reasons. First, even if we were to transfer every single vote won by the winning candidate in the Northern Region to the runner-up candidate, the national winner would still stay the same in every single election

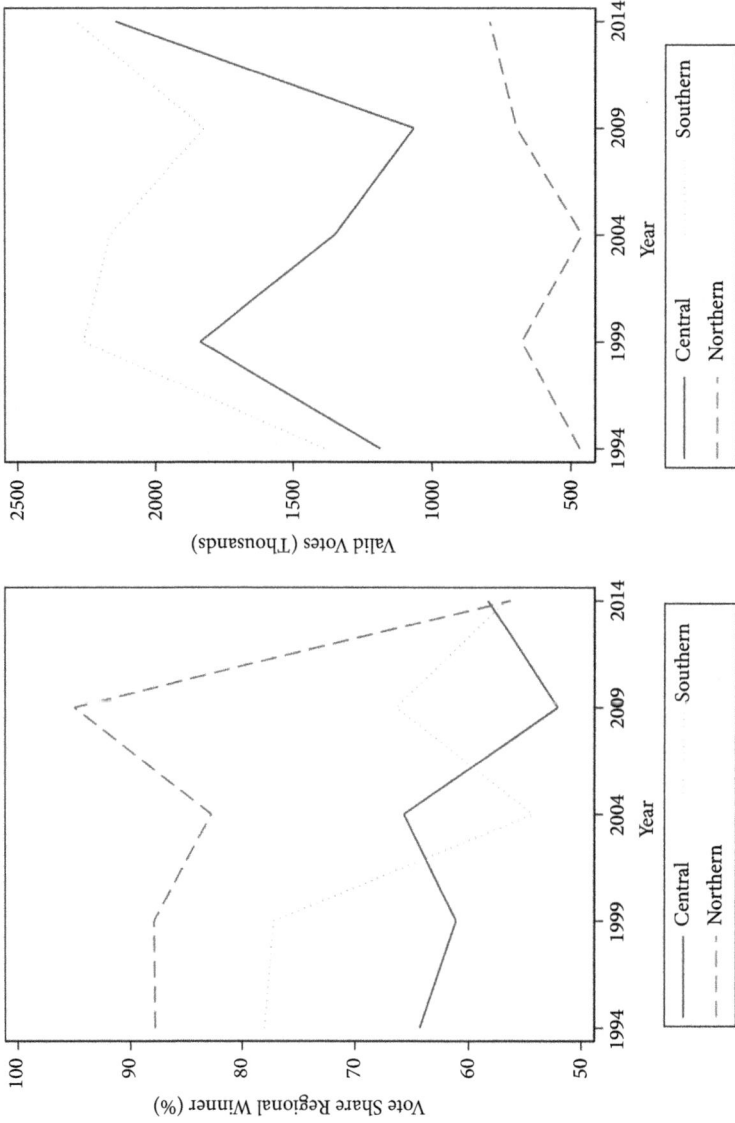

Figure 6.6 Regional Winner's Vote Share by Region and Valid Votes by Region.

apart from one.[9] Second, the Northern Region has shown voting patterns just as regionalized as the other two main regions. In fact, there has been more regional bloc-voting in the Northern Region than in Central and Southern Regions. On average, the regionally most popular candidate won 82% of the vote in the Northern Region, compared to 67% in Southern and 60% in Central. In other words, the logics of localism has applied in Northern Region despite the lack of stable regional representation and commonly without a co-ethnic candidate in the race.

6.6.1 Party Volatility and Mobilization of Regional Cleavages

High levels of regionalism do not imply that elections are predetermined and mobilization uncontested. On the contrary, fluidity in the party system and elite fractionalization has meant that election campaigns feature competing claims over regional representation and advocacy. As with the analysis of Zambia, I below provide regional-level data on party volatility in Malawi in the period 1999–2014. Figure 6.7 shows average region-level overall volatility, Type-A (extra-system volatility), and Type-B volatility (intra-system volatility)[10] by election, and Figure 6.8 shows this distinction for the three different regions.[11]

Figure 6.7 shows significant levels of party volatility at the regional level for every Malawian election. In fact, levels of volatility are even higher in Malawi than in Zambia. Also, for every election apart from 2009 (which was highly affected by the creation of DPP), levels of Type-B volatility have been similar or higher than the levels of Type-A volatility. This implies that changes in regional support are not only a product of new party entry but an active re-organization of regional support. The 2014 election had particularly high levels of Type-B volatility as regions earlier mobilized by DPP reoriented their support towards other parties (particularly PP).

---

[9] The only exception was 2009, when MCP would have just narrowly beaten DPP in this hypothetical scenario by some 10,000 votes. However, the 2009 election was unusual, with the Southern Region split between the Eastern part and the rest of the region. If DPP had won the Eastern part of Southern Region, they would not have needed the support of Northern Region to win a national majority.

[10] See Chapter 3 for more discussion on measurement and meaning of these different forms of volatility.

[11] Volatility in Malawi is not entirely easy to measure, as parties have sometimes formed short-lived electoral coalitions or created new party labels but maintained the bulk of the party organization of an old party. For this analysis, I code the MCP/AFORD alliance in 1999 as a continuation of MCP (as the presidential candidate represented MCP). I also coded the MCP/UDF alliance in 2009 as a continuation of MCP for the same reason. I treat DPP in 2009 as a new party, although Mutharika was the presidential candidate for UDF in the 2004 election.

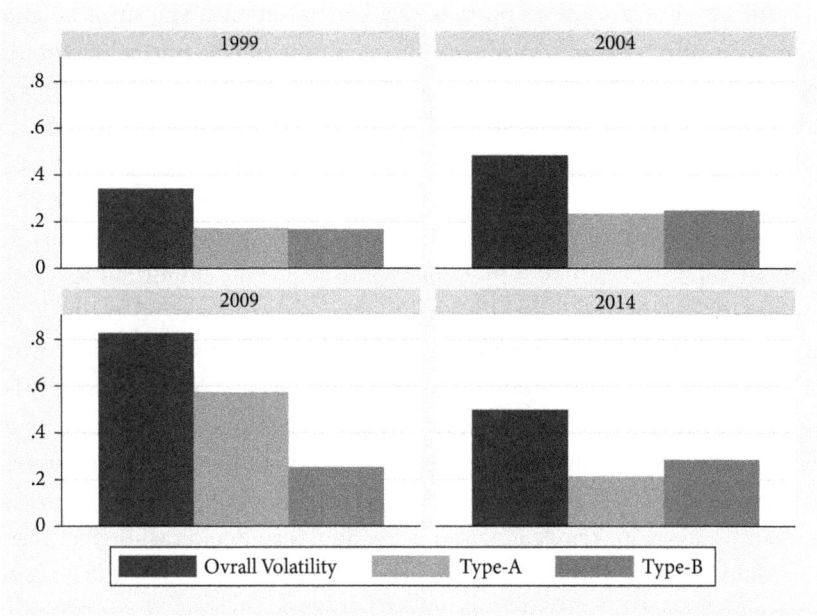

Figure 6.7 Average Region-Level Presidential Party Volatility, by Election.

Note: Across province average presidential party volatility by election

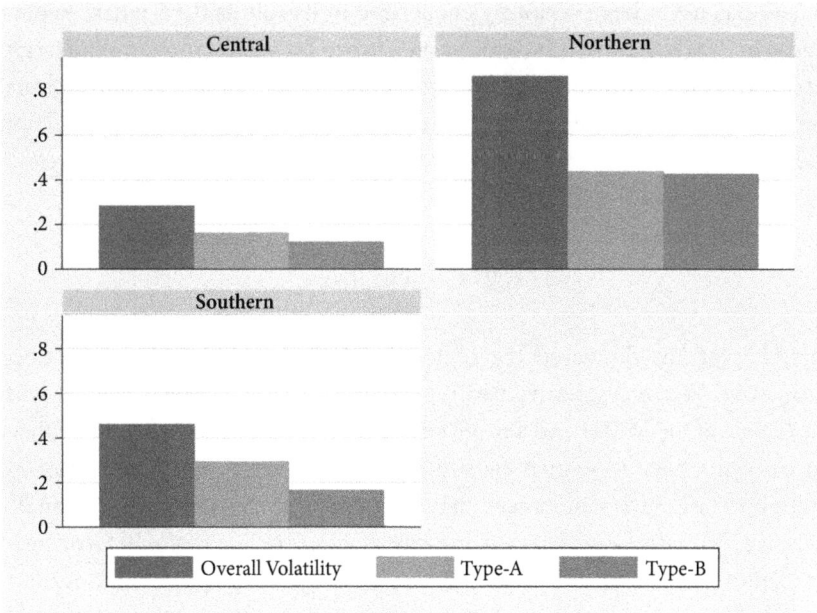

Figure 6.8 Average Presidential Party Volatility by Region, 1999–2014.

Note: Provincial average volatility for elections 1999–2014.

Figure 6.8 shows some important regional variations. The most volatile region is Northern Region. However, keep in mind that Northern Region has still been more prone to bloc-voting than any other region. Locally strong parties have been able to mobilize the region decisively, but there has always been important contestation over regional mobilization. In 1994 the region was won by AFORD, in 1999 it was won by MCP, in 2004 by RP, in 2009 by DPP, and in 2014 by PP. In 2014, DPP and PP competed intensely for the Northern support, often actively tapping into regionally important issues to create a sense of regional advocacy. One such policy often evoked in Northern Region is that of educational quotas, a hugely unpopular policy in the Northern Region widely understood as discriminatory against Northern students. Also, the Southern Region has seen remarkable volatility. In the 2014 election, there was significant competition over regional mobilization, with three presidential candidates born in the South (Mutharika, Banda, and Muluzi). Also, as the analysis above makes clear, winning the Southern Region with great margins would be the key to winning the presidency for any candidate. The only region with lower levels of volatility is the Central Region, mainly due to significantly more institutionalized nature of MCP (Kalua 2011). The party created a strong legacy as the defender of Central Region interest during the one-party era and has never been seriously challenged in its role as the Central Region hegemon. Nevertheless, this analysis has shown how stronghold mobilization persists despite volatility. Parties are generally able to mobilize strong regional cleavages, but these cleavages have to be mobilized on an election-to-election basis.

6.7 Conclusion

This chapter has discussed the regionalized character of Malawi elections across time. Whereas polarized voting patterns in Zambia grew stronger with the demise of the MMD and a more effective regionalized opposition, Malawian elections have remained mostly regionalized since the introduction of multipartyism. Such differences may be partly explained by the regionally exclusive character of the Malawi one-party state, the clear regional favoring of the Central Region, and the conspicuous exclusion of the populous Southern Region. The electoral regional patterns described here have several important repercussions for patterns of electoral violence that will be investigated in the following chapter, especially as it pertains to the 2014 election.

First, since the introduction to multipartyism, winning the Southern Region with great margins has been the key to winning national elections. The region is populous and tends to vote more homogeneously than the Central Region, its most prominent regional rival. However, the mobilization of the Southern Region was uncertain in the 2014 election. With UDF likely to command strong support in the Eastern Region, DPP needed to carry the other parts of the Southern Region with great margins. Also, with PP making strong claims to represent the Southern Region, it was important for the DPP to protect territoriality in the parts of the Southern Region that it won comfortably in 2009.

Second, PP had strength in the Northern Region, but this region has minimal political clout. It was clear that PP would not be able to win a national majority without the ability to mobilize Southern voters and make a claim inside areas that were traditional DPP heartland. Moreover, PP's hold of the Northern Region was all but secure. DPP won the region in great numbers in 2009 and could still make some claims to be the north's regional advocate. Frustrating the ruling party in some of its Northern strongholds could dismantle its chances to put together a majority.

Third, while local competition has been low in every Malawian election and was likely to continue in 2014, political realignment put regional mobilization in doubt. Apart from the Central Region that had been consistently and predictably (although without being able to ever win a national election) mobilized by the MCP, regional political mobilization was less predetermined in other parts of Malawi. Parties had strong incentives to protect their strongholds from inroads by other parties making strong regional appeals.

Lastly, the incumbent party was extremely weak organizationally and did not enjoy the sort of incumbent advantages that the ruling party in Zambia did. Conversely, the main opposition party had held the presidency as recently as two years prior to the election and had amassed great resources from systemic corruption. This unusual situation means that Malawi did not have the same sort of asymmetry in coercive capacity between the ruling party and the opposition as observed in Zambia.

7

Campaign Violence in Malawi

The previous chapter highlighted the importance of regionalism in Malawian elections and described the strategies used to win national elections. In particular, the chapter stressed how Malawian parties have relied on stronghold mobilization and actively tried to mobilize regional cleavages. How do modes of political mobilization affect the use of violence in election campaigns?

In this chapter, I argue that stronghold mobilization and the localist nature of politics in Malawi have been conducive to violence, particularly in non-competitive constituencies. The geographical patterns in violence observed in Malawi over time have many similarities with the findings from Zambia. While high-scale violence has not been common in Malawian elections, low-scale violence to control space is systemic and has featured almost constantly in Malawian electoral contests.

The historical analysis of violence in Malawi shows that the level of election violence has been relatively stable over time and has corresponded to a constant level of geographic polarization. In particular, parties have used low-scale violence to defend their electoral strongholds from the intrusion of "outside" forces. No-go zones in Malawian politics have been widespread and even explicitly articulated. The chapter will particularly describe the dynamics of such no-go zone politics through the lens of the notorious incident of violence against a Joyce Banda rally in Thyolo District in the 2014 election.

The chapter identifies three major regional clusters of election violence in the 2014 election. These clusters are rather different in many respects; they are located in different parts of the country and have varying political majorities. However, all of these clusters are highly uncompetitive. Focus groups from these clusters reveal that the bulk of the violence in these hotspots was perpetrated by the local hegemon in an attempt to monopolize space.

The emphasis on no-go zones and territoriality is remarkably similar to Zambia. Indeed, much of the violence is highly reminiscent of violent episodes describes in Chapter 4 from regions such as Zambia's Southern or Luapula Province. However, there are also important differences. In particular, while Malawi's low-scale violence has devastated local democracy, the level of violence remains lower in Malawi than in Zambia. An important explanation

Controlling Territory, Controlling Voters. Michael Wahman, Oxford University Press.
© Michael Wahman (2023). DOI: 10.1093/oso/9780198872825.003.0007

for lower levels of violence in Malawi is the absence of incumbent central-ized repressive capacity. While the Patriotic Front (PF) in Zambia was able to use its superior economic resources and access to government institutions to perpetrate violence in opposition strongholds, the People's Party (PP) in Malawi was unable to do so. Weak central repressive capacity also had conse-quences for geographic patterns of violence. Contrary to Zambia, opposition strongholds did not stand out as particular hotspots for violence.

The chapter will be concluded with statistical analysis of subnational varia-tions in election violence in the 2014 election. The analysis will use the Malawi Election Monitor Survey (MEMS). The analysis confirms that violence was particularly common in noncompetitive constituencies. However, the anal-ysis does not find that opposition strongholds were particularly affected by campaign violence.

7.1 Election Violence in Malawi's Multiparty History

Very little has been written on the topic of political violence in Malawi. The country has not experienced large-scale ethnic conflict or civil war. In terms of elections, violence has never escalated to the level that it has seriously threat-ened internal security. Nevertheless, one would be mistaken to conclude that violence plays no or only a marginal role in Malawian elections. Every election in Malawi has featured some degree of violence both before and after elec-tions and much of this violence has been territorial. However, while localized violence has been a constant in Malawian elections, there has been some vari-ation over time in the ruling party's willingness and ability to use centralized violence to contest territoriality in the areas where they have lacked in strength.

Although large-scale conflict never erupted during the one-party govern-ment under Kamuzu Banda, the regime was nevertheless highly repressive. The government invested significant resources in repressive capacity through-out the territory, not least by maintaining the para-military Malawi Young Pio-neers (MYP). These resources were certainly put on display during the 1993 referendum on multipartyism. The ruling Malawi Congress Party (MCP) fre-quently used MYP for targeted repression. While the repressive campaign was ultimately unsuccessful, violence was widely used to practically de-campaign the opposition during much of the campaign. MYP youth frustrated cam-paigns and limited crucial rallies organized by Banda's pro-democratic rivals. Such violence was designed to undermine the opposition momentum and con-fuse voters about the national mood that had steadily grown in favor of deep political transformation. For a dying dictatorship, violence was a strategy to install a sense of continuous political control at a time when authority was quickly eroding. While violence was used throughout the territory, it was particularly common in MCP heartlands in the Central Region (Dzimbiri 1994) and served to maintain the government party's territoriality.

With the military's disarmament of the MYP after the referendum (see Chapter 6), the MCP's centralized repressive capacity was significantly curtailed. Nevertheless, localized territorial violence was an important part of the electoral environment in 1994. During registration, machete-waiving MCP party activists attacked opposition leaders in the MCP-dominated Central Region (Cammack 1999). As the campaign progressed, violence and intimidation in relation to campaign events escalated and involved perpetrators from all parties. While cursory accounts of the 1994 election were understandably more focused on the historic democratic transition and electoral turnover, more detailed and reflective accounts of the campaign also noted that regionalism contributed to an often hostile and restricted campaign environment. In particular, the use of no-go zones was noted already in the inaugural election. It was commonplace for chiefs to restrict campaign access to perceived "outsider" parties. Opposition parties, as well as the government party, often used violence to prevent rivals from conducting rallies and meetings inside their regional strongholds (Kaspin 1995; Cammack 1999).

While the transition from the MCP government to the newly elected United Democratic Front (UDF) government happened without violent resistance from the outgoing regime, the end of MCP was not the end of organized violence. UDF invested in building more centralized repressive capacity after their electoral victory. The Muluzi regime emulated the repressive strategies of the MCP regime. Muluzi became notorious for paying young party activists in the so-called "Young Democrats"[1] to perpetrate violence against the opposition with impunity (Khembo 2004; Lwanda 2006). In the 1999 election, Malawi's most geographically polarized election to date, there were significant levels of territorial violence in the Southern Region. Hussein (2009: 357) describes how violence was used to uphold no-go zones in parts of the region. These strategies made it impossible for the opposition to campaign in certain localities. Violent territorial tendencies were particularly pronounced in Balaka and Mangochi, the home region of President Muluzi. Territorial violence was also perpetrated by the opposition. In particular, Muluzi's campaign in the Northern Region was frequently subjected to violence. The government

---

[1] An organization with apparent similarities with the MYP.

had to call upon the military to enable continued campaigning in the North. Reports emerged that UDF supporters in the Northern Region had been asked to move south because they did not support the Alliance for the Restoration of Democracy (AFORD) (Becher 2016: 278).

Summarizing violence in the 1994 and 1999 elections, Chirwa et al. (2000: 62) describe violence as a campaign strategy clearly related to the localist character of Malawian political campaigns:

> Both elections [1994 and 1999] have witnessed rigorous campaign activities by the three major parties, the MCP, UDF, and AFORD. Political parties draw their support mainly from rallies and campaign meetings. Campaign activities generally bring a colorful festive atmosphere. However, campaigns have not been free from violence and intimidation. Rallies of parties that are not predominant in the region tend to be disrupted by the supporters of the dominant party in that region.

Territorial violence was also noted in the 2004 and 2009 elections and the use of no-go zones persisted after the end of the Muluzi presidency. Geographic restriction of campaigns had become such an accepted form of electoral campaigning that parties even explicitly designated no-go areas. For instance, observers noted signs along the road touting messages like "Welcome to the north, the home of the DPP" or "Machinga the home of the UDF and no other party" (Hussein 2009). The common use of territorial violence over consecutive election cycles has also been acknowledged by Becher (2016: 2), who notes that: "almost all of my interviewees pointed to the importance of an emerging thinking in terms of strongholds which made it difficult for parties to campaign outside their home areas as rallies would be disrupted by the locally dominant party."

Malawi also had significant post-election violence both in 1999 and 2004. After Muluzi was declared the winner in the 1999 election, several mosques[2] were burned in the Northern Region and UDF supporters were violently harassed (Hussein 2009). In the 2004 election, the opposition engaged in widespread looting and vandalism in Southern Region. Police responded with teargas and fired sharp ammunition against protesters, resulting in several fatalities. In total, the police made more than 100 arrests in relation to the post-election violence of 2004 (Khembo 2004; Opitz et al 2013). Malawi has also had significant levels of intraparty violence during party nominations, not

[2] Muluzi was himself a Muslim and originated from the predominantly Muslim parts of eastern Malawi.

least within party strongholds. Party primaries within DPP in the 2009 election became particularly violent and resulted in several people, both voters, and candidates, being hospitalized (Patel and Mpesi 2010).

7.1.1 Comparing Election Violence in Malawi over Time 1994–2014

The brief introduction above indicates the constant territorial nature of violence in Malawi. Locally dominant parties have routinely used violence to protect their strongholds, but most of this violence has been low-scale and localized. The police and military have not been major perpetrators of electoral violence, mainly because the coercive apparatus in Malawi has been generally professionalized and independent of the executive since democratization. Indeed, if the military had not pursued the disarmament of the MYP before the introduction to multipartyism, Malawi could have embarked on a very different trajectory with a system of highly repressive centralized coercion. Nevertheless, centralized violence was more common in early than more recent elections and has been particularly connected to incumbent party strength and organization. MCP in the 1994 election and UDF in 1999 and 2004 stand out in this remark, both these parties had developed infrastructure at a central level to allow for violence outside traditional strongholds.

While comparative subnational analysis is not possible (without relying on media event data), data do exist to gauge differences in violence between elections at the aggregate level. This analysis may help us to understand the level of consistency and volatility in election violence across time. It can also shed light on possible correlations between levels of violence and the extent of geographic polarization. Figure 7.1 displays levels of election violence coded by V-Dem (Coppedge et al. 2020). Despite some smaller variations, the most striking pattern in Figure 7.1 is the high level of consistency over time.[3] The consistency can be understood by the relative stability in the structure of political competition and coercive resources. Most Malawian elections have featured similar regional coalitions pitted against each other (Boone et al. 2022). Regionalism has been strong, creating incentives for territorial violence, but at no stage has any party had strong authoritarian control over the state's

---

[3] Only 2004 stands out with somewhat higher levels of violence. This higher score in 2004 is likely related to post-election violence in the Southern Region.

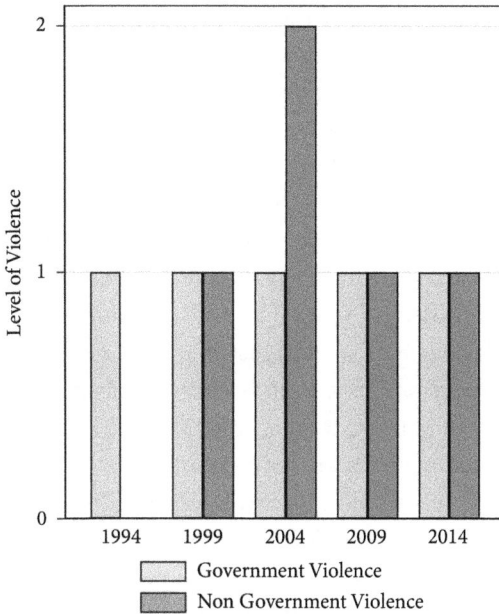

Figure 7.1 V-Dem Government and Nongovernment Violence in Malawi, 1994–2014.

Note: Source V-Dem v7.1, reported reversed versions of v2elintim_ord (government election violence) and v2epleace_ord (non-government election violence). Government violence: 0=None, 1=Restrained, 2=Some, 3=Frequent, 4=Strong. Non-government violence: 0=None, 1=Almost no violence, 2=Limited violence, 3=Significant violence, 4=Widespread violence.

coercive apparatus or central institutions. Violence has remained a tool associated with significant costs for central elites and has mostly been outsourced to local actors to maintain territorial control. This description portrays every election since 1994.

The somewhat crude coding by V-Dem may still obscure some meaningful differences noted in more qualitative and in-depth accounts. In particular, the 2009 election has been described as less affected by violence than previous multiparty contests (Cammack 2010). The relative peacefulness of the 2009 election can be explained by two major factors. First, the incumbent DPP was never seriously threatened in this election as the party rode high on a wave of economic success. DPP also benefitted greatly from party unity and an expanding elite-coalition as well as a particularly weak opposition. Thus, the party in power did not have strong incentives to use resources for large-scale repression. Secondly, compared to other elections in Malawi's history, the 2009 contest was significantly less regionally divided (Ferree and Horowitz 2010).

DPP had managed to nationalize the party and make inroads in areas where the party was traditionally weaker.

The generally low levels of violence noted in the V-Dem data may, however, be somewhat deceptive. As noted in the introduction, Malawian voters still have high levels of fear of election violence. This fear has been relatively constant over time, according to Afrobarometer data (Afrobarometer 2017). In 2011, 20% of Malawian respondents stated that they feared violence during elections "A lot." This share did not change in 2014. In 2017, 17% stated that they feared election violence "A lot." If we include those who say that they fear election violence "somewhat," we find that roughly 30% of Malawians fear violence in elections across all three rounds of the Afrobarometer that asked the question. Moreover, it is important to note that data from V-Dem and other cross-country sources have tended to underestimate the extent of violence in the case of Malawi. For instance, according to the V-Dem survey, the 2014 election was "Almost free from violence. There were only a few incidents of isolated violent acts, involving only a few people. No one died and very few were injured." This assessment is obviously wrong, with three documented incidents of fatal outcomes in the pre-election period.[4]

7.2 Election Violence in the Malawi 2014 Election

The discussion below will describe the local dynamics of election violence in the 2014 Malawian election. I particularly want to highlight how violence enforced territoriality in the localist context of the 2014 election. As with Zambia, I rely on a number of focus groups and interviews with domestic election observers, in combination with newspaper articles and NGO reports to develop a better understanding of the use of violence during the campaign. In particular, I conducted three focus groups with election observers from the National Initiative for Civic Education (NICE) in May–June 2015 in Mangochi (Southern Region), Mulanje (Southern Region), and Rumphi Districts (Northern Region). The three districts were all affected by violence but were dominated by different parties.[5] All participants in each focus group represented different constituencies in the district. Focus groups lasted for approximately two hours. I also conducted semi-structured interviews with NICE district officers in Ntcheu (Central Region), Phalombe (Southern Region), Zomba (Southern Region), Thyolo (Southern Region),

---

[4] Deadly violence was also noted in the 1994, 1999, and 2004 elections.
[5] Mangochi was dominated by UDF, Mulanje by DPP, and Rumphi by PP.

Neno (Southern Region), Mwanza (Southern Region), and Blantyre districts (Southern Region).[6]

Compared to the relatively peaceful nature of the 2009 election, violence in 2014 was a much more prominent and acknowledged part of the campaign. Much of this violence was low-scale, but a general atmosphere of intimidation and confrontations between supporters of various parties limited political campaigns and created significant tension. The violence described by most of the focus groups was predominantly perpetrated by youth party members paid by local politicians. These youth members were decisively less organized than the party cadres in Zambia. Compared to the Zambian example, most of the perpetrators of violence had less of a long-term commitment to the political party they campaigned for. Instead, they were more likely to hang around political campaigns for material benefits during the election (and possibly beyond). In every aspect, the organization for violence was significantly less institutionalized in Malawi than Zambia and parties had invested fewer resources in building such organization. This is somewhat of a deviation from early Malawi elections, where the MYP and the Young Democrats filled similar roles as organized groups of cadres in Zambia.

Figure 7.2 shows the occurrence of violence in the 2014 election. The left panel shows campaign violence, and the right panel post-election violence. In terms of campaign violence, three clusters are noteworthy. First, districts like Thyolo, Phalombe, and Mulanje in the Southern Region (the Southern hotspot). Second, Mangochi in the eastern part of the Southern Region (the Eastern hotspot) and, third, the central parts of the Northern Region (the Northern hotspot). My focus groups covered all these three hotspots, and participants in all focus groups recognized the spatial character of violence. Moreover, in each one of these hotspots, the most common perpetrator of violence and intimidation was identified as the locally dominant party: DPP in the Southern hotspot, PP in the Northern hotspot, and UDF in the Eastern hotspot.

The Southern hotspot was not only recognized in MEMS but also by several Malawi NGOs, including the Malawi Election Support Network (MESN) (The Nation 2014b). Districts like Thyolo, Phalombe, and Mulanje are all in the center of the DPP heartland, where the DPP was eager to defend its role as the locally dominant party. As the previous chapter illustrated, winning the Southern Region has historically been the key to winning national majorities. However, the region was also of key importance for PP. Joyce Banda

---

[6] I particularly prioritized the Southern Region due to its higher prevalence of violence.

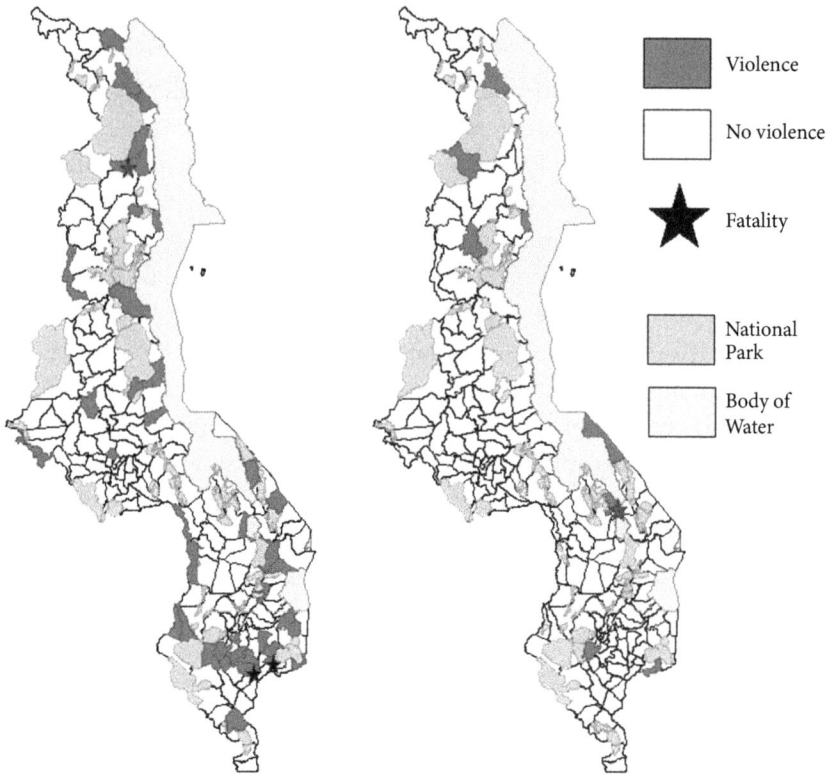

Figure 7.2 Map of Election Violence in Malawi, 2014.

Note: The figure is a reprint of Inken von Borzyskowski and Michael Wahman, "Systematic Measurement Error in Election Violence Data." British Journal of Political Science 51 (1): 230–252. Reproduced with permission. Left map shows violence in the pre-electoral period, right map shows violence in the post-election period. Data are from MEMS.

was herself a southerner, and the incumbent's chances of re-election were dependent on making inroads in the South and disturbing DPP's territorial control.

While the Southern hotspot was dominated by DPP, PP dominated the Northern hotspot. Members of the focus group in Rumphi identified territorial motives by the incumbent party in perpetrating violence. While DPP had carried the Northern Region with great margins in 2009, PP had built a strong organization in the region before 2014. However, without any party with a long-standing attachment to the region, PP needed to actively mobilize the region and create a strong sense of local advocacy.

The Eastern hotspot was dominated by the UDF. In fact, this was the only part of the country where the party had a strong presence. The UDF's national weakness also made the region a target for other parties, particularly PP. However, UDF was equally incentivized to use its local capacity to maintain the local electoral narratives and portray a sense of false national viability.

In other words, a cursory inspection of the map might indicate that, like in the case of Zambia, party strongholds were more affected by violence than more competitive areas. In general, members of focus groups in Mulanje, Mangochi, and Rumphi alike tended to agree with a spatial understanding of election violence. Violence was often discussed in terms of "controlling an area," "preventing campaigning," "parties fighting over territory," or "defending a stronghold" rather than as a form of repression targeted at individual voters with the aim to deter turnout or change their vote choice. Violence was seen as an integral part of the campaign used by parties in a strategic manner to regulate access to space.

Although not the main preoccupation of this book, it might also be worth quickly discussing episodes of post-election violence. Several episodes happened in Blantyre during election day, including DPP supporters setting up roadblocks, lighting fires, and attacking election officials. These episodes were generally directed toward the poor management of the election and severe delays in opening up polling stations in the Southern Region. The second, particularly serious, incident happened in Mangochi on May 23. In this incident, the police ended up shooting and killing a protester after members of UDF had taken to the streets to riot and burn tires. Riots erupted as a show of frustration with the conduct of the election and initial results (Focus group, Mangochi, 05/07/2015). The violence in Mangochi is indicative of the localist nature of Malawi election campaigns. UDF was the clearly dominant party in Mangochi.[7] However, outside eastern region of Malawi, the party had virtually no foothold (winning only 14% of the national vote). The perception that UDF had been rigged out of a national election victory seems to have been created by a significant extrapolation of the regional electoral environment. While voters residing in any other part of the country would most likely not have perceived a general momentum for the UDF, it is easy to understand why voters in Mangochi would be under such an impression.

---

[7] Winning 63% of the vote, compared to 18% to the runner-up DPP (Patel and Wahman 2015).

7.2.1 The Thyolo Incident

The notorious Thyolo violence mentioned in the very beginning of this book is worth particular attention, not only because it set the tone for much of the campaign, but also because it illustrates many of the mechanisms of territorial violence. The incident happened on March 16, 2014, at Goliati grounds within Thyolo Central constituency. Thyolo remains the epicenter of the DPP heartland and is absolutely crucial for the DPP's ability to win national majorities. According to the logic of stronghold mobilization, the party must mobilize voters in mass, create a sense of electoral momentum, and win the district with great margins to secure a national majority. In fact, for consecutive elections, Thyolo had been less competitive than any other district in Malawi. In 2014, Peter Mutharika won 91% of the presidential vote in the district.[8] Part of the DPP's dominance in Thyolo can be explained by the fact that both Peter Mutharika and his late brother, former President Bingu Mutharika, were born here. The DPP ended up picking up 213,000 votes in the district in 2014. The only district where DPP won more votes was Blantyre (225,000 votes), another DPP stronghold. According to the 2018 Census, the total population of Blantyre district is almost twice the size of Thyolo district.[9]

The incident at Goliati grounds was connected to a rally with President Banda. During the rally, supporters of the DPP attacked the crowd and pelted stones at President Banda's motorcade. When a large fight erupted, police intervened. In the commotion, one voter was killed by a lethal shot, and one police officer was hacked to death. Several other crowd members were also severely injured and rushed to the hospital for urgent care. The exact order of events has been disputed. Some influential members of DPP, including Peter Mutharika himself, have argued that the violence was a reaction to provocations by the PP. According to this version of the story, PP supporters had provoked aggression in local voters by uprooting party flags belonging to DPP. However, spokespeople from the PP, including Joyce Banda, have argued that the attack was premeditated and that DPP leadership were themselves involved in the planning of the attack (The Nation 2014a).

Regardless of the exact details of the event, the violence in Thyolo was certainly perceived as an expression of territorial politics and a way to shape

---

[8] The least competitive districts apart from Thyolo were the two neighboring districts of Mulanje and Phalombe. Both these districts were also overwhelmingly dominated by DPP and are also part of the Lomwe Belt (Patel and Wahman 2015; Lora-Kayambazinthu 2019).
[9] The census report does not provide data on population 18 and below the figures quoted above are the total population.

the local environment, particularly among members of PP. After the incident, PP regional governor for the Southern Region, Isaac Nyakamera commented: "Why should DPP make Thyolo a no-go area for other parties?" (The Nation 2014d). The suspicion among members of the PP was that DPP was looking to state an example and discourage any attempts of campaigning by the governing party within a region that was supposed to turn out in great numbers for Peter Mutharika, the local son. Local media quoted one local DPP supporter as saying:

> The discussion was about the political threat that the visit by the Head of State would pose to the DPP and its leadership because they consider the area a "no-go-area" for other political parties. The members' view was that Goliati is one of the DPP's major strongholds and it would be a "political embarrassment" should President Banda attract a large crowd there.
>
> (Nyasa Times 2014a)

In fact, the incident in Thyolo was not a great surprise. DPP has regularly employed territorial strategies to safeguard the district from political competition. In 2011, former President Bakili Muluzi was ambushed in the area (Nyasa Times 2014b). In 2012, DPP youths attacked PP youths at a presidential development rally, leading to eight people being injured. The aggressors had questioned the PP youth's right to travel on a road that had been constructed by the late President Bingu Mutharika (Nyasa Times 2012). The result has been an environment of fear, with little tolerance for freedom of expression and freedom of campaigning. In short, a form of subnational authoritarianism. The violence seen in instances such as the Banda rally is no more than the tip of the iceberg of an electoral environment entrenched in intimidation.

7.2.2 No-Go Zones

The Thyolo incident was generally understood as an expression of territorial politics, where one party (in this case, DPP) tried to enforce "no-go zone politics" towards a party understood as a regional outsider. While Thyolo was the most extreme example of such dynamics, most reported incidents in the MEMS data conform to this pattern. In Thyolo's neighboring districts Mulanje and Phalombe, most violent episodes escalated after parties, mostly DPP and PP, had uprooted each other's party flags. Such incidents may seem trivial in the context of African election violence, wherein the destruction of campaign material is not usually a cause for major concern. However, this kind of violence is indicative of the sort of low-scale territorial violence that is common in geographically polarized electoral systems. Party flags are displayed on shops, infrastructure, trees, and private dwellings. They fill an important function in Malawi election campaigns to show signs of local viability. They are, in a sense, the physical embodiment of territorial control. A party that can fly its flags in a geographic area is able to show its ability to protect its physical presence in a given location. For instance, focus group participants in Mulanje attested to the fact that PP were frequently prevented from campaigning and that this was a deliberate strategy to maintain territorial control. DPP youth cadets had often pre-empted PP campaigns by uprooting flags belonging to the government party in an attempt to create a sense of hostility and conflict in preparation for major campaign events. According to one member of the Mulanje focus group, "DPP never tolerated the presence of PP inside their stronghold" (Focus group, Mulanje, 05/04/2015). In another DPP stronghold, Mwanza, PP was regularly prevented from campaigning as DPP supporters blocked roads and stirred tension whenever campaign activities were planned (National Initiative for Civic Education 2013).

Mangochi, the main stronghold of UDF, is another region where no-go zone politics has been prevalent both in 2014 and earlier elections (Chingaipe 2018: 157). In the 2014 election, there were several recorded incidents of UDF supporters disturbing political rallies, particularly those held by PP. In another incident, a PP governor was seriously assaulted by UDF cadets (Nyasa Times 2014c). In the post-election report issued by the Malawi Election Support Network (MESN 2014: 31), the organization notes that the designation of no-go zones in Mangochi led to several episodes of violence. One civil society activist in Mangochi relates violence in the area to fear among UDF supporters that Joyce Banda's appeal among women voters could break UDF's territorial control in the district: "Some sections of the Muslim community in Mangochi are not happy with Muslim women supporting President Joyce Banda and her PP. The perception here is that Muslims must belong to the UDF and no other party." (Nyasa Times 04/12/2014). The practice of no-go zone politics in Mangochi was repeated in the 2019 election when cars belonging to the UTM party were burned during campaigning by Vice President Saulos Chilima. These incidents in Mangochi prompted the Malawian Catholic Archbishop, Thomas Luke Msusua, to announce that there must be no no-go zones in Malawian political campaigns and that parties must "allow everyone to hold their rallies anywhere they want" (Nyasa Times 2018).

In 2014, the government party also enforced its territoriality through violence inside its own strongholds. Several of the episodes of violence in northern Malawi were perpetrated by the PP. Commonly, such violence was used to prevent DPP from campaigning. For instance, in a widely publicized event in Mzuzu, a truck belonging to the main opposition party was torched (The Nation 2014c).

Territorial politics and violence as a means to prevent parties from entering into "other parties' territories" was such a concern in the 2014 election that MESN even attempted to collect data on the issue. In a report issued during the election campaign in which MESN had sent long-term observers to observe specific anticipated election hotspots, the organization found at least seven places designated as a no-go area for other parties. In more general terms, violence by locally strong parties against perceived outsiders was also acknowledged in the Malawi 2020 rerun. For instance, one domestic election observer report notes:

Supporters of the DPP-UDF alliance and the Tonse Alliance [i.e. both the government party and the opposition] often appropriate the political space and projected a sense of misguided entitlement that motivated them to act with impunity against candidates and members of the opposing party, uprooting flags and removing other campaign material of rivaling parties and acting violently against opponents especially in areas regarded as strongholds of support bases of the party.

(PAC et al. 2020: 5)

The explicit or implicit notion of parties as "owners" of space is a reminder of the importance of territorial cleavages and localism in Malawi politics. The use of no-go zones and physical defense of territory also highlights the importance of violence as a tool for maintaining territoriality. Furthermore, the fact that parties go to such lengths to regulate space confirms the argument that regional cleavages are not structurally determined but that parties use campaigns to translate regional cleavages into political mobilization. What several of the violent incidents in Malawi highlight is that parties do not take strongholds for granted. On the contrary, defending strongholds from political disruption is key to winning national majorities in polarized electoral systems.

7.2.3 Incumbent and Opposition Violence

In Zambia (Chapter 4), I observed a pattern where election violence was particularly prominent in opposition strongholds. In the 2014 Malawi election, this pattern was not quite as obvious. In many ways, PP was an unusual government party. The party was organizationally weak, clearly struggling to maintain its role as the perceived frontrunner, and did not enjoy the sort of incumbent advantages that is commonly expected for government parties (Dulani and Chunga 2015). PP was also faced by a formidable opposition in the shape of DPP. DPP was a party that had just recently been in office after winning a landslide election in 2009 and had created a level of nationalization previously unknown to Malawi politics (Ferree and Horowitz 2010). DPP had further enriched itself and its top-brass by systematic and extensive plundering of the state coffers during years in office (commonly referred to as the cashgate scandal) (Zimmerman 2015).

Whereas MCP and UDF were more typical opposition parties in the sense that they had little capacity to campaign aggressively outside their own territory, DPP adopted many of the strategies recognized from the PF campaign in Zambia. For instance, DPP was known to bus supporters to rallies in cities such as Lilongwe and Mzuzu, often from their more rural strongholds in southern Malawi (Nyasa Times 2014d).

The more nationalized nature of the campaign of the two most well-resourced parties, DPP and PP, had consequences for the patterns of violence observed in MEMS. In the cases where perpetrators could be identified by the observers in the survey, they tended to be either the locally strong party inside their own strongholds or PP or DPP outside their strongholds. MCP or UDF did not generally have capacity to perpetrate violence outside their strongholds. It is certainly also the case that DPP and PP were the two main protagonists of the 2014 election and that much of the violence was an expression of this main rivalry. However, whereas in the case of Zambia, the opposition rarely conducted violence outside its own stronghold, this was not the case in Malawi. Indeed, MEMS recorded incidents in districts such as Machinga and Karonga where DPP had been engaged in violence against the locally dominant parties (PP and UDF).

The statistical models will investigate whether there was more violence in DPP-dominated constituencies than in other constituencies controlled by PP or other less nationally competitive opposition parties. The case of Malawi makes it probable that the enhanced risk of violence in opposition strongholds is due to the incumbent party's ability to wage a nationalized repressive campaign. In cases such as Malawi where the resource strength between the main opposition and government party is unusually equal, we may not observe the same patterns of violence concentration in opposition strongholds.

7.3 Measuring and Analyzing Subnational Variations in Malawian Election Violence

In Zambia, I found that party strongholds were particularly prone to pre-electoral violence. Can we find systemic evidence of the same in Malawi, relying on the constituency-level MEMS survey of domestic election observers? The methodology of MEMS mirrors that of ZEMS (see Chapter 4).[10] With MEMS, I relied on Malawi's largest observer network, the National Initiative for Civic Education (NICE). NICE is a non-partisan organization with permanent offices in every one of Malawi's 28 districts. Through their regional representatives, they engage in long-term observation in every constituency of the country as well as sustained civic education activities. On election day, they deployed a total of 4500 observers. For each of the 193 constituencies, I asked the national secretariat of NICE to identify three particularly suitable observers. These are observers with intimate knowledge of the entire electoral cycle and without known partisan biases. The observers were interviewed by phone by a team of five trained enumerators representing the Institute for Policy Interaction (IPI), a think tank based in Blantyre, Malawi. Surveys started three weeks after the announcement of the 2014 election and lasted for a total of eight weeks. In total, enumerators finished 579 interviews with election observers.

Each respondent was asked the question: "Thinking *only* about the election in your constituency. To what extent have you personally experienced or received *credible* reports of pre-electoral violence during the general election campaign (i.e., physical violence targeted at voters, party officials, candidates, monitors, election officials, or property)" (this question is identical to the one asked in ZEMS). In the case that the respondent did indicate violence, they were later contacted by an enumerator in the team that asked for more details about the violence, including "How many violent events occurred in your constituency," we also asked for a qualitative narrative of event(s) in

---

[10] Also, see Chapter 1 (as well as von Borzyskowski and Wahman 2021) for a more general justification for the approach utilized here.

the constituency: "Please describe for each event: What happened? When did it happen? Who were involved (perpetrator/victim)? Was anyone injured or killed (how many)? Where in the constituency did this happen?" I code a constituency as having had violence if at least one observer indicates violence.[11]

As with ZEMS, I used the narratives provided in the survey to code both the number of events (none, one, or many) and the severity of violence (none, low-severity, high-severity), using the same coding criteria as in the analysis on Zambia (see Chapter 4). The empirical approach used in the statistical analysis of election violence in Malawi will also follow the same logic as in my analysis of Zambia. As with Zambia, I will use two different dependent variables, intensity and frequency, and estimate ordered probit models with standard errors clustered on region. I will also dichotomize the election violence variable and estimate logistic regressions (again with standard errors clustered on region). Post-estimations of the logistic regression results will be estimated, keeping covariates at their mean. I will also run Ordinary Least Squares (OLS) regressions as robustness checks and present these results in the Appendix. The list of control variables will also be repeated from the Zambian chapter: competition, history of election violence, population density, nightlight (logged), and ethnic fractionalization.[12] Data on population density and ethnic fractionalization are aggregated from the 2008 Malawi Population and Housing Census with assistance from the National Statistics Office of Malawi in Zomba.

A major benefit with the competition data for Zambia was that I could use the 2015 Zambian election results as a highly accurate pre-election estimation of party support. However, no similar data exist for Malawi. Instead, the best option is to use the results from the 2009 election. This is not without some limitations, as there were important realignments after 2009, with the creation of PP and the split of DPP. Using data from the 2014 election would be problematic as these can be considered post-treatment. Nevertheless, as I have argued together with coauthors in other related work (Boone et al. 2022), fundamental cleavages in Malawi have remained the same despite party realignment. As a consequence, while the party winning a certain constituency will not be the same in every election (as acknowledged in Chapter 6), constituencies that tend to bloc-vote tend to do so in every election.

---

[11] Intercoder reliability for pre-election violence is 0.74 for pre-electoral violence using Kuder-Richardson (1937) statistics.

[12] The groups recorded in the data include Chewa, Lambya, Lomwe, Ngonde, Ngoni, Nyakuysa, Nyanja, Sena, Senga, Tonga, Tumbuka, Yao, and Other.

7.3.1 Results

The results from the statistical analysis are displayed in Table 7.1. Model 1 displays the results in relation to severity and model 2 in relation to frequency. As with Zambia, whether we use frequency or severity as the main dependent variable seems to have a very small substantial effect on the results.

Looking particularly at model 1 (Table 7.1), I find a strong negative and statistically significant relationship between levels of competition and election violence severity. In other words, the higher the level of competition in 2009 at the constituency level, the lower the probability of higher severity violence in 2014. The predicted probabilities of different severity categories across varying levels of competition are plotted in Figure A7.1 of the Appendix. Model 2 (Table 7.1) also shows that more competitive constituencies were significantly less likely to have high categories of violence frequency. The results in regard to competition are robust both for severity and frequency if we re-estimate the model using standard OLS regression (Table A7.1 of the Appendix).

In relation to the control variables, only one of these controls are significant, population density. More densely populated constituencies were more likely to experience both more severe and more frequent violence. This is perhaps expected, given much of the literature. However, it is also an interesting contrast to Zambia. In Malawi much violence occurred in semi-urban areas of the Southern Region. Interesting to note is also that Malawi has not historically had the same sort of competitive urban politics that has been characteristic for much of Africa, including Zambia (Wahman and Boone 2018). The three main cities of Blantyre, Lilongwe, and Mzuzu have often followed broader regional patterns, much unlike cities like Lusaka. In other words, territorial politics has also been a part of urban electoral campaigns in Malawi.

I re-estimate the model using a logistic regression and a dichotomous dependent variable in Table 7.2. The results are robust for this change in model estimation. In Figure 7.3, I simulate the predicted probability of pre-electoral violence across varying levels of competition. In Figure A7.2 of the Appendix, I estimate the probability of different frequency of violence dependent on levels of competition. The first takeaway in comparison to Zambia is that the results reaffirm that levels of violence are lower in Malawi than in Zambia. Whereas low competition constituencies in Zambia were more likely to have violence than not have violence, no violence is the most likely value along all levels of competition in Malawi. Nevertheless, we see a meaningful decrease in the probability of violence as the level of competition increases. Going from the

Table 7.1 Analysis of relationship between competition and constituency-level campaign violence.

	Model 1 Severity	Model 2 Frequency
Competition	−1.246***	−1.238***
	(.235)	(.256)
History EV	−.151	−.658
	(.518)	(.515)
Population Density (log)	.285***	.314***
	(.096)	(.117)
Nightlight (log)	−.038	.254
	(.269)	(.237)
Literacy	.250	.176
	(.561)	(.323)
Ethnic Fractionalization	−.118	−.097
	(.155)	(.213)
N	192	192
Pseudo R²	.05	.07

Notes: ***≤p.01 **≤p.05 *≤p.1. Entries are ordered probit coefficients with standard errors in parentheses. Standard errors clustered by region.

Table 7.2 Analysis of relationship between competition and constituency-level campaign violence (Logistic Regression).

	Model 3
Competition	−2.194***
	(.515)
History EV	−.757
	(.796)
Population Density (log)	.513***
	(.135)
Nightlight (log)	−.153
	(.470)
Literacy	.017
	(.658)
Ethnic Fractionalization	−.133
	(.324)
N	192
Pseudo R²	.06

Notes: ***≤p.01 **≤p.05 *≤p.1. Entries are logistic regression coefficients with standard errors in parentheses. Standard errors clustered by region.

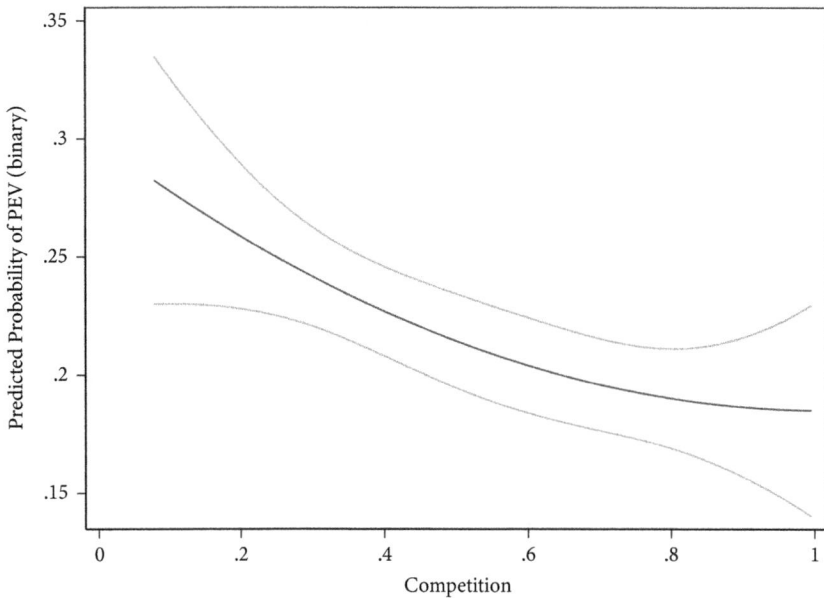

Figure 7.3 Post-estimation of Relationship between Competition and Election Violence.

Note: Post-estimations based on model 3 in Table 7.2. Outer boundaries show 95% confidence interval.

lowest observed value of competition (Mzimba South West, Northern Region: 0.004) to the highest observed value of competition (Lilongwe Kumachenga, Central Region: 0.995), the probability of violence occurring decreases from 28% to 18%.

Turning to the results on opposition votes, I look particularly at the main opposition party, the DPP. Malawi is different from Zambia in that the election was not as clear of a two-horse race. Nevertheless, it was clear going into the election that DPP was the more formidable challenge to PP. This conclusion was also supported in a credible pre-election opinion poll by Afro-barometer released closely before the election (Dionne and Dulani 2014). For this reason, if election violence is particularly common in opposition strongholds, we should particularly look at those constituencies that were important strongholds and vote accumulators for DPP.

Looking at the results in models 4 and 5 (Table 7.3), I do not find that constituencies with a high number of DPP votes in 2009 had significantly more severe or more frequent violence in 2014. This is also true when I estimate the model dichotomizing the dependent variable (Table 7.4) or estimate the model

Table 7.3 Analysis of relationship between opposition vote and constituency-level campaign violence.

	Model 4 Severity	Model 5 Frequency
DPP Votes 2009 (Thousand)	.018	.020
	(.014)	(.013)
History EV	−.295	−.839
	(.590)	(.588)
Population Density (log)	.149	.170
	(.201)	(.223)
Nightlight (log)	.051	.359
	(.362)	(.319)
Literacy	.319	.208
	(.993)	(.781)
Ethnic Fractionalization	−.082	−.074
	(.372)	(.428)
N	192	192
Pseudo R²	.04	.04

Notes: ***≤p.01 **≤p.05 *≤p.1. Entries are ordered probit coefficients with standard errors in parentheses. Standard errors clustered by region

Table 7.4 Analysis of relationship between opposition vote and constituency-level campaign violence (Logistic Regression).

	Model 6
DPP Votes 2009 (Thousand)	.035
	(.025)
History EV	−1.071
	(.910)
Population Density (log)	.282
	(.286)
Nightlight (log)	−.036
	(.589)
Literacy	.197
	(1.622)
Ethnic Fractionalization	−.138
	(.617)
N	192
Pseudo R²	.03

Notes: ***≤p.01 **≤p.05 *≤p.1. Entries are logistic regression coefficients with standard errors in parentheses. Standard errors clustered by region.

using OLS regression (Table A7.2). These findings suggest that the strength of the incumbent party vis-à-vis the opposition may have consequences for the partisan geography of election violence.

One important limitation here, that does call for some caution with these results, is that the 2009 election results do not perfectly match the political geography of 2014, particularly in the Northern Region where PP captured a lot of the electorate won by DPP in 2009. In the Appendix, I rerun the models excluding the Northern Region (Table A7.3). These models show more evidence of violence directed toward DPP areas, but the results are weak and mixed. I find that when excluding the Northern Region, constituencies with a high number of DPP votes in 2009 did not experience significantly more severe violence in 2014. In terms of frequency, I do find significantly more violence in constituencies with a high number of DPP votes in 2014, but this relationship is only significant at the 90% level. Also, as with the models on competition, I also re-estimate the models (Table A7.2 in the Appendix) using OLS regression. Again, I find no evidence that DPP strongholds were significantly more likely to experience violence.

7.4 Conclusion

This chapter has studied the geographic patterns of election violence in the 2014 Malawi election using both qualitative and quantitative data. I have argued that election violence in Malawi has, to a great extent, been territorial and parties have used election violence as a tool to enforce territoriality. These tendencies were highly visible in some remarkable incidents of election violence, such as the episode in Thyolo where two Malawians were tragically killed. The systematic use of no-go zone politics has seriously curbed political competition in Malawi. The Malawi case clearly illustrates the pernicious and often underappreciated consequences of low-scale violence on the quality of democracy.

In the statistical analysis, I show that constituencies with lower levels of historic competition are more prone to election violence. This finding corresponds with the findings in Chapter 4 on Zambia. However, contrary to my finding in Zambia, I do not find that election violence was particularly concentrated in opposition strongholds. These findings suggest that there may have been important differences between Malawi and Zambia in terms of incumbent–opposition power dynamics. The Malawian case is unusual in terms of incumbent weakness, but analyzing this case also shows some limits to the assumption that the incumbent party will always be the prime perpetrator of violence. Indeed, this does not seem to be the case in Malawi, where a strong opposition party showed considerable coercive capacity across the territory.

The next chapter will extend the findings from Malawi and Zambia to two additional cases, Kenya and Zimbabwe. These additional cases will serve to evaluate the plausibility of the electoral geography theory of violence for a larger set of geographically polarized electoral systems in Africa. In particular, it is important to see whether the territorial nature of violence is also evident in these additional cases and to what extent centralized repressive capacity has contributed to the more violent nature of election campaigns in Kenya and Zimbabwe.

8

Extending the Argument

This book has generalizing ambitions in its attempt to highlight how regionalism shapes electoral violence in geographically polarized electoral systems. Nevertheless, the empirical focus has been mainly restricted to two countries: Malawi and Zambia. The decision to prioritize depth over breath is deliberate. The book has introduced detailed data gathered from new constituency-level surveys and combined these data with qualitative accounts gathered from in-depth fieldwork. The in-depth approach of the book sets it apart from earlier work that has relied on aggregate-level data to study cross-national variations in election violence (e.g. Hafner-Burton et al. 2014; van Ham and Lindberg 2015; Fjelde Höglund 2016; Taylor et al. 2017; Birch 2020) or cross-national subnational research relying on event data (E.g. Reeder and Seeberg 2018; Choi and Raleigh 2021; Müller-Crepon 2021). In particular, I have argued that, although useful, event data suffers from certain geographic biases that may obscure violence occurring in more rural—less competitive—constituencies (von Borzyskowski and Wahman 2021).

The in-depth approach of the book is one of its comparative advantages, but it is also associated with some limitations. First, I have argued that the regionalized character of politics in geographically polarized electoral systems should be particularly conducive to election violence. In the cases of Malawi and Zambia, previous chapters have substantiated this claim by comparing elections over time. For instance, as Zambia grew more geographically polarized, campaign violence markedly increased. Nevertheless, previous chapters have not provided any evidence to suggest that the relationship between geographic polarization and election violence generalizes across the continent. Second, like every country, Malawi and Zambia have their idiosyncrasies. Most importantly, I have argued for the importance of studying violence as a tool of electoral manipulation in countries characterized by low-scale violence. As illustrated in Chapter 1, low-scale violence is the more common expression of election violence in Africa. Nevertheless, one might suspect that the form of territorial violence described in this book is less pervasive in countries where violence is more high-scale.

Controlling Territory, Controlling Voters. Michael Wahman, Oxford University Press.
© Michael Wahman (2023). DOI: 10.1093/oso/9780198872825.003.0008

This chapter will introduce further evidence to suggest the plausibility of the argument beyond the book's main cases. The chapter will do two things. First, it will offer descriptive statistics on the relationship between competition—at the national and local level—and aggregate levels of election violence across the continent. Second, I will use secondary accounts of electoral geography and patterns of election violence in two further geographically polarized cases, Kenya and Zimbabwe.

The evidence provided in this chapter is best understood as a plausibility probe of the further generalization of the book's main theoretical argument. The descriptive statistics are suggestive but not conclusive. Ultimately, the best test of the theory would be a more formal test building on cross-sectional time-series data and controlling for other possible confounders (such as electoral institutions, social heterogeneity, history of conflict, and levels of democracy). However, given a great dearth of disaggregated African election data,[1] missing data would be a serious concern when trying to model the relationship with a larger sample. As for the further case studies, ideally, I would present additional constituency-level data on election violence. However, without relying on event data, such data are not available.

These limitations withstanding, the chapter does provide suggestive evidence of the generalization of the book's argument. First, descriptive statistics show that polarized electoral systems have on average higher levels of election violence than other African countries where elections are more competitive at the local level. Secondly, the cases of Kenya and Zimbabwe further show the importance of localism in regionalized political systems. In both countries, parties have heavily relied on stronghold mobilization for winning national majorities. Moreover, secondary sources presented here have frequently alluded to the territorial nature of violence in both countries and suggested that electoral strongholds were main targets of campaign violence.

8.1 Cross-Country Evidence

Do African geographically polarized electoral systems have higher levels of election violence than locally more competitive ones? Table 8.1 divides sub-Saharan African countries into four different categories based on two variables: national-level and local-level competition. Levels of competition are not

---

[1] Especially from Presidential elections (Fridy 2009).

static but change between elections. However, I here re-use the same sample as in Figure 1.2 of Chapter 1.[2] Due to data restrictions, I am unable to include all African countries in the analysis. However, Table 8.1 contains data from 22 sub-Saharan African countries.[3] In the table, I distinguish between countries with high and low levels of national-level competition and countries with high and low levels of local competition. As a rough threshold, I categorize countries where the national election winner won at least 60% of the national vote as having low national competition. Similarly, countries where the constituency-level winner in presidential elections won, on average, at least 60% of the constituency-level vote are categorized as having low local competition.[4] *Geographically polarized electoral systems* occupy Box 2 (N = 10). Box 1 (N = 5) contains *Competitive electoral systems*, those where competition is high both at the national-level and in the average constituency. Box 3 (N = 0) includes what I label *Opposition fragmentation*; these are systems where one party is dominant nationally but where the typical constituency is competitive. I do not observe any such systems in the sample, but this category would be possible if a dominant nationalized ruling party face several locally strong regional opposition parties. Lastly Box 4 (N = 7) contains *Dominant-party electoral systems*, those where competition is low both nationally and in the average constituency.

For each of these four categories, I present three descriptive statistics. First, I show the average of two indices from V-Dem: The Government Electoral Intimidation Index and the Other Election Violence Index. Van Ham and Lindberg (2015) used these two statistics to capture levels of government-instigated election violence and nongovernment-instigated election violence.[5] For both of these indices, lower values equal *higher* levels of violence. Lastly, I show the average share of people who indicate that they fear election violence "a lot" in relation to elections according to the most proximate post-election Afrobarometer survey.[6]

---

[2] To recall, I used 2015 as my baseline year and used this year or the most recent previous election with available disaggregate data. I include only presidential and semi-presidential countries.

[3] If possible, I used constituency-level presidential election data. If such data were not available, I used district (admin 2-level) data. In the event that no such data was available, I excluded the country from the sample.

[4] The 60% threshold is undeniably somewhat arbitrary but corresponds with conservative thresholds often used to determine dominant-party regimes in the regimes and party-system literature (e.g., Howard and Roessler 2006).

[5] Note that these indices are not ideal for this purpose as they do not separate pre- and post-election violence. However, they do have the advantage of not relying on fatalities to register levels of election violence.

[6] Afrobarometer data were unavailable for the appropriate wave for Rwanda, Seychelles, and The Gambia.

Table 8.1 Electoral typology and violence across Africa.

National-Level Competition Local-Level Competition	High Local-level Competition	Low Local-level Competition
High National-Level Competition	**Box 1: Competitive Electoral Systems**	**Box 2: Geographically Polarized Electoral Systems**
	V-Dem GI: 3 V-Dem OEV: 3.4 AB Fear: 14.2% N=5	V-Dem GI: 2.7 V-Dem OEV: 2.7 AB Fear: 23.0% N=10
Low National-level Competition	**Box 3: Opposition Fragmentation**	**Box 4: Dominant-party Electoral Systems**
		V-Dem GI: 1.8 V-Dem OEV: 2.7 AB Fear: 13.9% N=7

Note: Scores show average scores across countries in category. V-Dem Government Intimidation Index (V-Dem GI): In this national election, were opposition candidates/parties/campaign workers subjected to repression, intimidation, violence, or harassment by the government, the ruling party or their agents. Scale 0–4, lower values indicate more violence. V-Dem Other Election Violence (V-Dem OEV): In this national election, was the campaign period election day, and post-election process free from other types (not by the government, the ruling party or their agents) of violence related to the conduct of the election and the campaigns? AB Fear: Percentage responding "A lot" to the question "During election campaigns in this country, how much do you personally fear becoming a victim of political intimidation or violence." Countries: High/High: Burkina Faso 2011, Cape Verde 2011, Liberia 2011, Senegal 2012, Seychelles 2015; High/Low: Benin 2011, Côte d'Ivoire 2011, Ghana 2012, Guinea 2015, Kenya 2013, Malawi 2014, Nigeria 2015, Sierra Leone 2012, Togo 2015, Zambia 2011; Low/Low: Cameroon 2011, Namibia 2014, Rwanda 2010, Tanzania 2010, The Gambia 2011, Uganda 2011, Zimbabwe 2013.

Looking first at levels of violence reported in the expert-based V-Dem survey, I find that the highest level of government intimidation is found in dominant-party electoral systems (Box 4). This is hardly surprising as many of these dominant-party systems are upheld by staggering levels of repression both during and beyond electoral periods. For instance, repression has been a dominant strategy for regime survival in countries like Cameroon (Morse 2018) and Rwanda (Samset 2011). In some cases, we can also observe that nationally dominant parties use electoral violence in a territorial way within dominant-party electoral systems to break territoriality inside opposition enclaves. In Tanzania, for instance, government-inflicted violence has been a mainstay of election campaigns in Zanzibar as the central government attempts to assert control inside the opposition stronghold (Cameron 2001; Cheeseman et al. 2021). McLellan (2020) argues that the rise of opposition enclaves in Tanzania such as Dodoma, Iringa, and Kilimanjaro, may account for the increase in election violence as the ruling Chama Cha Mapinduzi (CCM) tries to compensate for its loss of political authority. Table 8.1 also shows that levels of other forms of (non-government-instigated) election violence are similar in dominant-party electoral systems and geographically polarized electoral systems.

The most important comparison, however, is between geographically polarized electoral systems and competitive electoral systems. In this comparison, I find that geographically polarized electoral systems have substantially higher levels of both government and non-government-afflicted violence than competitive systems. Competitive systems such as Burkina Faso, Cape Verde, Liberia, Senegal, and the Seychelles have not been known for particularly high levels of election violence. Especially not compared to cases such as Kenya, Nigeria, and Côte d'Ivoire, countries that all fit into the geographically polarized category. While election violence may still be a useful strategy for political actors in such competitive electoral systems, it should be a less viable strategy for regulating access to space. Looking at perceptions of fear, I find that geographically polarized electoral systems have higher levels of fear than any other category. Geographically polarized electoral systems like Kenya, Côte d'Ivoire, and Togo belong to some of the countries with the highest level of election violence fear.

All in all, these descriptive statistics support the assertion that electoral violence has been an important element of electoral campaigns in geographically polarized electoral systems, if we compare them to more locally competitive systems. It is important to note that the results presented in the table depend on the elections included in the sample (with 2015 as a baseline year). However, if anything, this sample should provide a conservative estimate. For instance, Zimbabwe had unusually uncompetitive elections in 2013 and is here counted as a dominant-party regime. Typically, Zimbabwe has fit the mold of a geographically polarized electoral system with very high levels of election violence (as disused later in this chapter). Also, while Kenya and Nigeria are both classified as geographically polarized electoral systems, the included elections, Kenya 2013 and Nigeria 2015 were relatively peaceful by respective national standards.

8.2 Kenya and Zimbabwe

Can the argument presented earlier in this book be extended to Kenya and Zimbabwe, two other cases of geographically polarized electoral systems? To perform the analysis, I will rely on secondary accounts of electoral competition and election violence in Kenya and Zimbabwe. One distinct advantage of these two cases is that both countries (especially Kenya) have featured prominently in the election violence literature, enabling such an analysis.

In contrast to the cases of Malawi and Zambia—where violence has been mostly low scale—Kenya and Zimbabwe have both featured exceptionally high levels of lethal violence. The analysis will show that two important factors may explain the higher levels of violence in Kenya and Zimbabwe. First, both Kenya and Zimbabwe have significant economic land grievances, which have undoubtedly increased the motivation for citizens and elites to engage in the most serious violence (Boone and Kriger 2010; Boone 2011; Klaus 2020). Second, both cases, especially Kenya under Kenyan African National Union (KANU) and Zimbabwe under the Zimbabwe African National Union–Patriotic Front (ZANU–PF), had high levels of centralized repressive capacity. ZANU–PF, in particular, stands out here, with its authoritarian control and legacy of violent independence struggle. While some of these dynamics were in play in Zambia (but not Malawi), the scale of centralized repressive capacity in both Kenya and Zimbabwe is significantly higher. While Kenya and Zimbabwe differ from Malawi and Zambia in these regards, this chapter will particularly focus on the similarities in the distinctly spatial use of violence to enforce and contest territoriality in party strongholds.

8.2.1 Political Geography of Kenya

Is the type of regional electoral competition that spurred territorial election violence in Malawi and Zambia present in Kenya? I would argue that it is, to a high extent. However, in a literature with a strong emphasis on the micro-level importance of ethnicity, regionalism has been somewhat obscured as an analytical category (e.g. Bratton and Kimenyi 2008; Arriola 2013; Elischer 2013; Horowitz 2022). Nevertheless ethnicity and space are almost impossible to disentangle in much of Africa. Ethnic groups are spatially segregated, and the colonial categorization of ethnicity did in itself have a strongly spatial component. Ethnicity was institutionalized in a highly spatial manner through the recognition of neo-customary land tenure regimes that designated territory to ethnic groups through the use of "ethnic homelands" (Boone 2014). Sub-national boundaries, such as provinces, districts, and constituencies, were drawn to maximize ethnic homogeneity (Fox 1996).

It is held beyond any doubt that party nationalization in Kenya is extremely low by any standard (Ngau and Mbathi 2010; Wahman 2017). Like Malawi and Zambia, Kenya adopted and has maintained electoral institutions conducive to regional party-building, such as Single Member District (SMD) electoral systems and presidential elections in a single national constituency.[7] Election results in Kenya have quite consistently converged to the pattern of geographically polarized electoral systems. Figure 8.1 shows national-level and local-level (constituency) competition for presidential elections in the period 1991–2013. Across all of these contests, local-level competition has been remarkably low. In the average constituency, for every 100 votes picked up by the constituency presidential winner, the runner-up picked up only between 28 (2013) and 35 (2002) votes. While levels of competition at the local level have been almost constant across elections, there has been more variation in national-level competition. Nevertheless, national-level competition has still been considerable in all elections (except for the opposition landslide in 2002) (Barkan 2004). The national runner-up has typically won between 72% and 95% as many votes as the national winner.[8]

The cases of Malawi and Zambia showed that political parties actively try to mobilize regional cleavages. Research on Kenya reveals a similar spatial nature of political campaigns. Horowitz (2016) describes high reliance on ground campaigns to form strong bonds between parties and local communities and Horowitz and Long (2016) find that impressions of national viability are formed at the local level. In their formative work on the founding 1992 election, Throup and Hornsby (1997: 463) conclude that the "the 'big picture' was that the result was a combination of numerous smaller campaigns and conflicts ... There were at least 19 different electoral regions, quite different in style, issues, and competitors." This is a quintessential description of a non-nationalized electoral system where elections locally do not take on nationally unifying themes (Lipset and Rokkan 1967) and where localism prevails (Agnew 1987).

Similar to Malawi and Zambia, winning presidential candidates have relied heavily on votes from their respective strongholds. When KANU won the presidential elections in 1992 and 1997, 45–50% of their national vote came from their stronghold in the Rift Valley.[9] The Party for National Unity (PNU) won

---

[7] A couple of noteworthy constitutional provisions to mitigate the regionalization of politics, including a ban on ethnic parties (Moroff 2010) and a requirement for parties to win at least a minimal amount of support in a minimal number of subnational jurisdictions, have not fundamentally shifted political competition towards nationalization.

[8] Note that the accuracy of official election results particularly in 1992, 1997, and 2007 have been put into serious doubt (Brown 2001; Kanyinga 2009)

[9] Despite a very concerted effort by the Moi regime to register voters in the Rift Valley in the 1992 election, the Rift Valley only accounted for 15% of the registered voters in the 1992 election (Throup and Hornsby 1997).

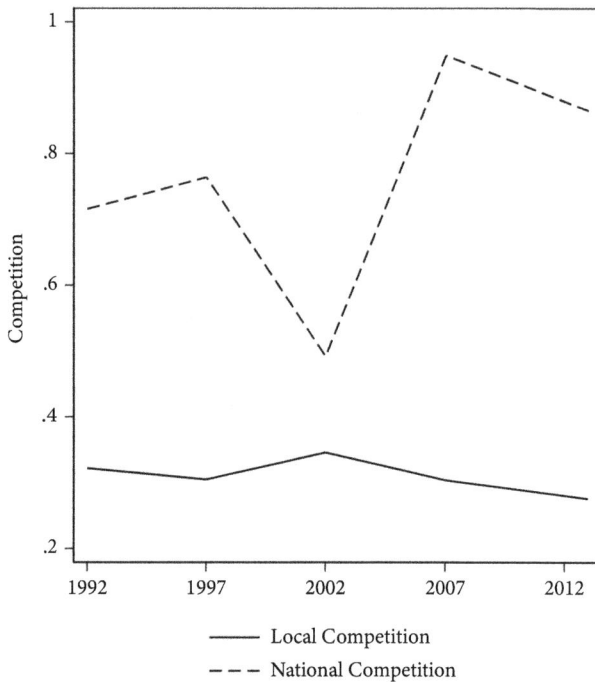

Figure 8.1 National and Local Competition in Kenya, 1992–2013.

Note: The figure shows the local average level of competition, measured as the average ratio between the constituency-level second vote-getter and the constituency-level first vote-getter, and the national-level competition measured as the ratio between the national first vote-getter and the second vote-getter.

roughly 40% of their national vote in Central Province in 2007, despite the province being home to only 12% of Kenya's population (Ngau and Mbathi 2010).[10] As in Zambia and Malawi, mobilizing core areas and controlling local narratives has been key to winning national majorities in Kenyan elections.

8.2.2 Campaign Violence in Kenya

Kenya has arguably informed our empirical and theoretical knowledge about election violence more than any other African country. Most existing work has studied election violence from the perspective of conflict rather than electoral manipulation, and a great deal of it has particularly focused on the devastating post-election violence of 2007 (e.g. Kanyinga 2009; Mueller 2011; Brown and Sriram 2012; Dercon and Guitérrez-Romero 2012; De Smedt 2009; Linke

---

[10] According to population projections from the 2005 census.

2022). The discussion below will concentrate on the 1992–2013 period. Earlier research has noted significant levels of variation in election violence across elections. Specifically, the 1992, 1997, and 2007 elections stand out as particularly violent, each resulting in thousands of deaths and violent displacements. The elections in 2002 and 2013 have been described as *relatively* peaceful. Lower levels of national competition in 2002 and 2013 have often been used as an explanation for these elections more peaceful nature (Burchard 2015; Klaus 2020).[11] Others have also pointed to the lack of an incumbent president standing for re-election (Taylor et al. 2017). In 2013, the lower levels of violence are often explained by the coalition between prominent Kikuyu and Kalenjin elites, the groups most frequently involved in ethnic clashes. However, neither 2002 nor 2013 were peaceful by African comparison. One study estimating the extent of violence in 2002 from media reports (with all its biases and estimation problems) found at least 129 reported deaths in election-related violence in the period January–December 2002 (Mugambi 2002). According to some estimations, more than 300 people were killed in the pre-electoral period of 2013 (Burchard 2015: 2). There has been a striking level of "normalization" of election violence in Kenya, where very high levels of violence have become accepted as a normal part of electoral competition (Cheeseman 2008).

Previous literature has had a focus on two primary factors and the interaction between them when analyzing Kenyan subnational variations in violence: ethnicity and land rights (e.g. Kanyinga 2009; Rutten and Owuor 2010; Boone 2011; Klaus and Mitchell 2015; Klaus 2020). Catherine Boone (2011; 2014) has demonstrated that much violence in Kenya has been concentrated in areas of politically allocated land rights, i.e., areas that do not follow the predominant pattern of neo-customary land rights in dedicated ethnic homelands. Later developments in this work show how insecure property rights may motivate the use of violence among ordinary citizens (Klaus 2020). The Rift Valley is a region particularly affected by such dynamics. In this region, colonial land appropriation and subsequent redistribution have led to insecurities and inter-group conflicts over land ownership (Kanyinga 2009).

While land insecurities and grievances enforce identities and create the motivation for violent mobilization, violence in a *campaign* environment fill strategic purposes within the structure of regionalized politics. Besides being a region where populations could easily be mobilized for violent purposes, the Rift Valley has also been a key part of national political strategies. As such,

---

[11] In fact, 2002 was the only Kenyan election that did not qualify as a geographically polarized electoral system due to the requirement of high levels of national competition.

the motivation for using land and ethnicity as a call for political mobilization within this environment has certainly been present. As noted above, any national electoral victory for KANU was contingent on an impressive performance inside their Rift Valley stronghold (Mugambi 2002). The Rift Valley is not the only political stronghold plagued by election violence. In her analysis of the 2007 election, Burchard (2015: 68) finds that constituencies with the *highest* levels of competition in presidential elections were *less* likely to experience violence in the pre-electoral period than constituencies with the *lowest* level of competition.[12] While Burchard summarizes this finding as proof that the relationship between competition and campaign violence is complex, the dynamics in this book may explain such empirical patterns. Indeed, these findings are highly compatible with those from Malawi and Zambia.

8.2.3 Zoning: Enforcing Territoriality

Ethnicity has been highly associated with space in the Kenyan context, not at least within designated "ethnic homelands." The practice of "electoral zoning" has been justified by the association between space and ethnicity and, by extension, the political parties claiming to represent a group/region (Becher 2016). With zoning, parties have claimed ownership over territory and denied local minorities the ability to practice their democratic rights during elections. The use of zoning in Kenya is comparable to the use of "no-go zones" in Zambia and Malawi, but even more extreme in its ethnic exclusion and calls for violence against what is perceived as regional outsiders.

Throughout Kenyan electoral history, the politicization of ethnicity has rested on strong spatial claims. The roots of much violence have been a contest over who "belongs" and may claim citizenship within a particular territory (Boone 2014). These disputes predate the introduction of multipartyism. The ideology of *Majimboism* is key to understanding many of these conflicts. At the dawn of independence, the Kenyan constitution followed the principle of Majimbo, where the bulk of power and resources were allocated to the regional level. In a rush to centralize power and bolster the economic and political dominance of the Kikuyu ethnic group, post-independence president, Jomo Kenyatta, abolished the principle of Majimbo in favor of a centralized state (Hassan 2020). At a later stage, as the presidency and leadership of KANU

---

[12] According to Burchard's analysis, 31% of the most competitive constituencies experienced violence, compared to 43% of the least competitive constituencies.

shifted from Kenyatta to Daniel Arap Moi, an ethnic Kalenjin, elites within KANU renewed calls for the reinstatement of majimboism. This vision of majimboism was built on strongly ethnic segregationist views, where ethnic groups could make exclusive territorial claims (Klopp 2001; Klaus 2020: 14). In particular, such views became strongly endorsed among sections of KANU elites in the Rift Valley—a majority Kalenjin province and a stronghold of Moi's KANU (Kanyinga 2009).

In the 1992 election, several Majimbo rallies were organized in the Rift Valley. The rallies led to horrendous ethnic clashes as rally leaders called for massive evictions of local Kikuyus. The consequence of the violence led to hundreds of deaths and thousands of displacements (Ndegwa 1998). The violence that transpired in the majimbo rallies and during early Kenyan elections in the Rift Valley unified the internally diverse Kalenjin group into one more homogeneous voting-bloc. While some parts of the Kalenjin community explored possible association with the opposition, politicians, and administrators issued public threats against anyone who attempted to "bring in" opposition politics (Lynch 2011).[13] Klopp argues that violence was a key to discouraging transethnic coalitions:

> There is the tendency to assume that trans-ethnic organizing is rare or a deviation from the norm. In fact, wheeling and dealing across fuzzy ethnic boundaries is common in a polyethnic society ... Kenya's majimbo bosses as much wished to avoid the strengthening of dissent in their strongholds by cleansing migrant swing voters and potential allies of dissenters as they wished to merely get rid of recalcitrant voters.
>
> (Klopp 2002: 275)

Leading KANU politicians attending the rallies declared key areas in the Rift Valley exclusive "KANU Zones" where opposition politicians were banned from campaigning (Ndegwa 1998; 610). Moi and the rest of the KANU establishment were keen to paint the violence in connection to the Majimbo rallies as "spontaneous" ethnic clashes. However, the evidence is clear that the government was involved in orchestrating and financing the violence, often using KANU youth and affiliated groups as agents. The security forces remained complicit in the face of violence, further suggesting government approval of grotesque expressions of violence for political gain (Throup and Hornsby 1997: 64; Brosché et al. 2020).

---

[13] Also see Barkan (1993).

In the 1992 and 1997 elections, KANU-dominated areas like the Rift Valley, Northeastern Province, and the Coast were particularly affected by campaign violence. Most of this violence was directed against ethnic minorities. Such minorities were construed as "guests" who should abide by certain rules of hospitality. Minorities, in this view, were not entitled to political citizenship or expected to engage directly in the political process (Jenkins 2020). Campaign environments in KANU zones were generally very hostile. Although official reporting tells stories of large-scale displacement, attacks, and killings directed towards outsiders and minorities, such reports most likely underestimate the scope of the repression (again emphasizing the problem of relying on media reporting to map violence). For instance, writing about KANU dominant constituencies like Baringo and Elegeyo-Marakwet (both in the Rift Valley), Throup and Hornsby (1997: 372) concluded: "There were few reports of violence or intimidation because it was so pervasive that it was unwise even for the press to inquire too far into what was happening. The evidence suggests that much of the harassment of non-Kalenjin communities in KANU areas was organized centrally, a continuation of the threats made against them during the 1991 majimbo rallies."

In preparation for the 1997 election, the government took further steps to make KANU strongholds inaccessible to the opposition, using their own violence to justify the securitization of the discourse around electoral competition. After the 1992 election, the government created so-called "security zones" in much of the Rift Valley and the Northeastern Province. The security zones were officially created to prevent ethnic clashes but were used to prevent journalists and opposition politicians from entering the KANU strongholds (Steeves 1999; Becher 2016: 231).

While KANU was known for using territorial violence to protect their home turf in early elections, the use of violence to enforce territoriality was not unique to KANU, nor did it stop after KANU's electoral defeat in 2002. In 1992–2002, the opposition also used violence to protect their strongholds, albeit to a lesser extent than the ruling party. Unsurprisingly, the main targets of such violence were scattered KANU supporters attacked my supporters affiliated with the locally dominant party. For instance, in 1992, Throup and Hornsby (1997: 383) describe how KANU had difficulty campaigning in Nyanza Province as supporters of FORD-K (the regionally dominant party) repeatedly attacked KANU rallies.

Describing the nature of campaign violence in 2007, Jenkins (2020: 377) states that: "Widespread intimidation, harassment, and the violent disciplining of political behavior by ordinary citizens became a defining feature of the pre-election period of 2007, and were legitimized by conceptions of territorialized belonging. Urban neighborhoods, villages, districts, and entire provinces were demarcated as ODM and PNU zones, and minority groups perceived as supporting the other party were subject to significant harassment." Notably, ODM frequently used territorial politics in Nairobi to control significant densely populated areas and create a sense of local dominance. In Nairobi's Kibera slum, Raila Odinga outperformed all competition, drawing impressive crowds to rallies and visually dominating the constituency. However, such spatial dominance was achieved through violence and a long-term campaign to cleanse the area of landlords, business owners, and local elites not aligned with the political interests of Odinga and his allies. Before the 2007 election, rallies of non-ODM candidates were simply not tolerated within the populous and electorally important area (De Smedt 2009).

8.2.4 State Repression and Vigilante Groups: Contesting Territoriality

Violence in Kenya has not only been used to enforce, but also to contest territoriality. Similar to the Zambian case, there is a strong relationship between central coercive capacity and such strategies. Violent repression against opposition strongholds was particularly common under the entrenched authoritarian rule of KANU. The Moi regime used provincial administrations across the country as a tool to perpetrate low-intensity violence against the opposition and violently shut down opposition meetings (Hassan 2017). To further enhance its repressive capacity in opposition zones, the Moi government strategically posted co-ethnic police officers inside opposition strongholds (ibid.). State harassment against the opposition grew particularly in the 1997 election (Barkan and Ng'ethe 1998).

Political parties in Kenya, particularly government parties, have also used external actors to perpetrate violence. Outsourcing violence to outside groups has enabled parties to extend their coercive reach to areas outside traditional party strongholds.[14] Most violence was concentrated in rural zones in Kenya's early multiparty elections. However, a noteworthy uptick in urban violence—particularly in Nairobi in the late 1990s and early 2000s—made for an important shift in the geographic distribution of campaign violence. The increase in urban violence has generally been associated with the proliferation of urban vigilante and militia groups. While there are many such groups, the

---

[14] Turnbull's (2020) work on another geographically polarized electoral system, Nigeria, offers further examples of how parties outsource violence to outside groups.

most notorious example is arguably the Mungiki. Mungiki traces its roots to Central Kenya, where it had served as a Kikuyu defense force, but it had established itself as a well-organized criminal group in the capital by the late 1990s (Lebas 2013). The Mungiki and other criminal gangs had come to control large sways of Nairobi's informal settlements, running bus services, controlling the rental markets, and extracting fees from local businesses. The groups became specialists in violence that could be enlisted by politicians at various levels in an effort to spatially dominate areas under the gang's violent control (Kagwanja 2003).

Both the opposition and the ruling party hired criminal gangs (Lebas 2013; Elfversson and Höglund 2019), but the legal protection offered by the ruling party made KANU an attractive ally during the dominant-party rule. The inaction of the police and local authorities in response to Mungiki violence speaks volumes about the symbiotic relationship between KANU and criminal gangs. Indeed, the relationship is highly reminiscent of how PF in Zambia cultivated support from cadres in Lusaka for electoral gain. Enlisting criminal gangs, KANU got a foothold in urban areas, providing an opportunity to contest territoriality in areas where the opposition was highly dominant. Mungiki and other groups were well known for disturbing opposition rallies and preventing campaigning in high-density areas where the gang had well-established territorial control:

> As KANU struggle to secure power in Nairobi's constituencies where the opposition currently hold sway, further violence in the run-up to the election scheduled for December 2002 seems unavoidable and indeed for KANU it may have utility. In Nairobi, the government does not have to manufacture an army to attack its opponents, as the followers of Mungiki are already undermining the opposition very effectively.
>
> (Anderson 2002: 554)

8.2.5 Zimbabwe

The analysis of electoral patterns and violence in Zimbabwe will focus on the period 2002–2013. This period represents the height of the electorally competitive period under the continuous rule of Robert Mugabe.[15] The overwhelming majority of violence in this period was perpetrated by ZANU–PF. Indeed, the

---

[15] I decided to not include the 2018 election, since there is still less secondary writing on violence in this election.

asymmetric violence between the ruling party and the opposition provides further evidence of how centralized coercive capacity affects the nature and magnitude of violence. Although the opposition Movement for Democratic Change (MDC) has also used violence in electoral contests this has been much rarer, and the nature of this violence is not particularly well documented in the secondary literature. For this reason, the analysis below will focus particularly on ZANU–PF perpetrated violence.

Before focusing on the narrower period of 2002–213, it is worthwhile giving a short background into the violent nature of the ZANU–PF regime and the emergence of political cleavages. Comparing Zimbabwe with Malawi, Zambia, and Kenya, there are obvious differences in the country's modern political history. While Malawi and Zambia, and also to a lesser extent Kenya,[16] gained independence in the 1960s through a mostly peaceful process, Zimbabwe's ultimate independence from white minority rule in 1980 came through organized and persistent violent resistance. With ZANU–PF winning the country's founding multiparty election, power was transferred to a political party that had reformed itself from a liberation army. ZANU–PF's legacy as a liberation army has often been evoked as one of the major explanations for the regime's continuous use of repression as a tool for regime survival (Bratton and Masunungure 2008; Frantzeskakis and Park 2022). Moreover, when taking power, ZANU–PF inherited a highly repressive state apparatus. The Rhodesian settler regime relied heavily on violence against the black majority population and developed a highly repressive legal environment enforced by a brutal police force and an extensive intelligence operation. While ZANU frequently condemned the legal order in the 1960s and 1970s as "fascist," legal scholar Welshman Nchube (1990: 3–10) concludes that the government decided to maintain most of the legal order and repressive state apparatus after independence.

The founding election in 1980 was contested primarily by two parties, Robert Mugabe's ZANU–PF and Joshua Nkomo's Zimbabwe African People's Union (ZAPU). Both ZANU and ZAPU originated from the militarized struggle against white minority rule and included a military wing (Zimbabwe African National Liberation Army (ZANLA) for ZANU and Zimbabwe People's Revolutionary Army (ZIPRA) for ZAPU. While ZANU–PF won an overwhelming victory in the founding election, securing 57/80 parliamentary seats, the country was regionally divided in 1980. ZAPU secured only

---

[16] Kenya did have significant violent resistance against colonialism, not least through the Mau Mau rebellion. However, compared to Zimbabwe, there is no direct translation from rebel groups to political parties.

20 seats, but 15 were in Matabeleland (Matabeleland North and Matabeleland South), where they secured 15/16 seats available. Some analysts understood the regional split as yet another expression of African ethnic voting. Gregory (1980), however, rejects this notion. He argues that ZANU–PF's regional support is better explained by its wartime organization. At the time of the election, ZANU–PF had already organized rural populations in large swaths of the country in the resistance movement. However, coercion was a vital tool to maintain party discipline within ZANLA-dominated areas (Kriger 2005:4) About ethnic voting, Gregory (1980: 68) concludes: "The crude nature of the electoral data makes it impossible to prove or disprove that 'tribal' identifications decisively influenced the outcome ... It is clear, however, that politicians in several minor parties who set out to exploit 'tribal' or 'sub-tribal' sentiments failed resoundingly."

After the 1980 election, repression against the remaining opposition intensified, and supporters of ZAPU were frequently targeted. Supporters and officials of ZANU–PF were known to question the right of ZAPU even to exist, particularly outside their stronghold in Matabeleland (Kriger 2005: 5). In 1983, the government deployed the military to Matabeleland and the Midlands provinces on a mission to suppress dissident movements. The deployment was motivated by an uptick in violence by ex-ZIPRA guerillas. However, rather than a targeted military operation, government forces proceeded to stage a full-blown massacre against civilians with or without ties to ZAPU. In the period 1983–1987, an estimated 20,000 people were killed in what is now known as the *Gukurahundi* (Ndlovu 2018). In the 1985 election, ZAPU held on to all their 15 seats in Matabeleland but lost all other seats outside the region.

The period 1987–2000 is characterized by total ZANU–PF dominance in Zimbabwean politics. After the 1987 peace accord, ZANU–PF and ZAPU merged into one party and the 1990 election turned Zimbabwe into a de facto one party-state. Under a new constitutional order, transforming Zimbabwe into a presidential democracy with significant executive powers, Robert Mugabe swept the presidential election with 83% of the vote. Only small pockets of opposition, predominantly in urban areas, remained (Sachikonye 1990).

Zimbabwe entered into a more competitive phase in the late 1990s. However, the regionalized character of Zimbabwean politics remained. Enhanced competitiveness is connected to a more effective opposition organized under the banner of the newly created MDC. The MDC emerged as a force combining discontent against the ZANU–PF regime from trade union activists, intellectuals, and student organizations (Lebas 2011). Morgan Tsvangirai, the Secretary General of the Zimbabwe Congress of Trade Unions (ZCTU) and a vocal critic of ZANU–PF's economic policies became the party leader.

8.2.6 Zimbabwe's Political Geography, 2002–2013

The concepts of regionalization, stronghold mobilization, and localism are also highly relevant in the case of Zimbabwe. Figure 8.2 shows local—and national-level competition for the 2002, 2008, and 2013 presidential elections. An important caveat about the data provided here is that they reflect official data presented by the Zimbabwe Electoral Commission (ZEC). It is held beyond doubt that most Zimbabwean elections have featured significant, often decisive, levels of fraud (Bratton et al. 2016). However, without the ability to estimate true vote returns, the data presented here will give a rough approximation of regional voting patterns and levels of competitiveness. The elections in 2002 and 2008 had electoral patterns typical for geographically polarized electoral systems. However, while local competition remained low in 2013 the election was not competitive nationally. Local-level competition has been consistently low. In 2002, for every 100 votes secured by the constituency presidential winner, the runner-up secured only 41, the corresponding figure for 2008 is 54 and 46 in 2013.

Although regional voting patterns have not been entirely static, there are some more long-standing patterns. Figure 8.3 shows the share of the total vote received by ZANU–PF for each province in the 2002, 2008, and 2013 elections.[17] Generally, ZANU–PF performed significantly better in rural Zimbabwe than in the two major urban regions of Harare and Bulawayo. Catastrophic performance by ZANU–PF in urban areas has been explained by several factors. The more pluralistic atmosphere of the cities allowed the opposition to organize and mobilize, using its strong association with civil society, church groups, and trade unions. Decades of economic mismanagement had also led to severe urban grievances. Urban voters had borne the brunt of the costs of structural adjustment with increases in food prices, a rapidly depreciating currency, and staggering youth unemployment (Dorman 2005; Bratton and Masunungure 2006). Urban resentment against the government undoubtedly grew stronger after 2005 with the government-initiated

---

[17] Vote shares for ZANU-PF were lower across the board in 2008 (when ZANU-PF lost the first round of voting) and higher in 2013 (when ZANU-PF won a large national majority).

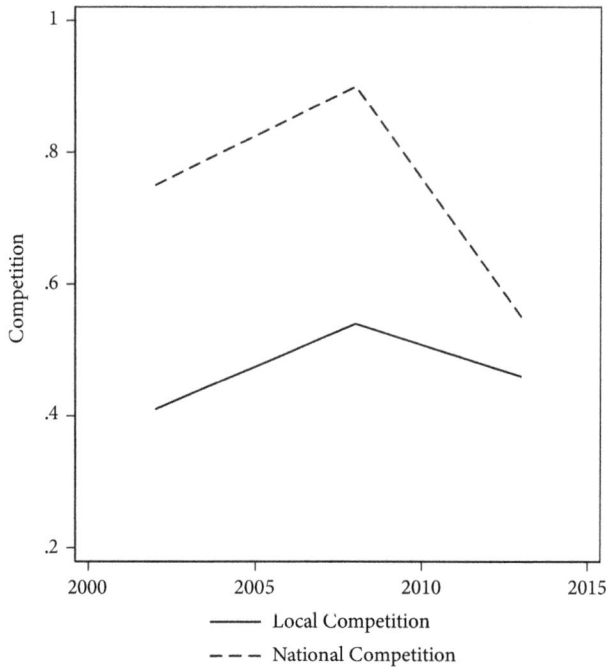

Figure 8.2 National and Local Competition in Zimbabwe, 2002–2013.

Note: The figure shows the local average level of competition, measured as the average ratio between the constituency-level second vote-getter and the constituency-level first vote-getter, and the national-level competition measured as the ratio between the national first vote-getter and the second vote-getter.

Operation Murambatsvina in the capital. The operation was formally motivated to curb urban informal economic activity but has generally been considered a form of retribution against urban dwellers who had come out in numbers to vote for the opposition in the 2002 election. The operation led to gross violations of human rights and large-scale displacement of the urban poor (Bratton and Masunungure 2006). With MDC's rural support mostly concentrated in Matabeleland, great vote margins and massive turnout in urban areas have been an essential part of the opposition's electoral strategy. In 2002, for instance, a quarter of all MDC votes came from Harare alone. It is, therefore, perhaps not surprising that the analysis below will show that Harare was a key site where ZANU–PF attempted to disturb opposition territoriality.

ZANU–PF's rural support was shored up in no small part through the promises of land to rural populations. Zimbabwe's farm invasions started soon after ZANU–PF's defeat in the 2000 constitutional referendum. The ruling party had made land and race central themes of electoral politics. Promising redistribution of white-owned commercial farm land, ZANU–PF attempted to

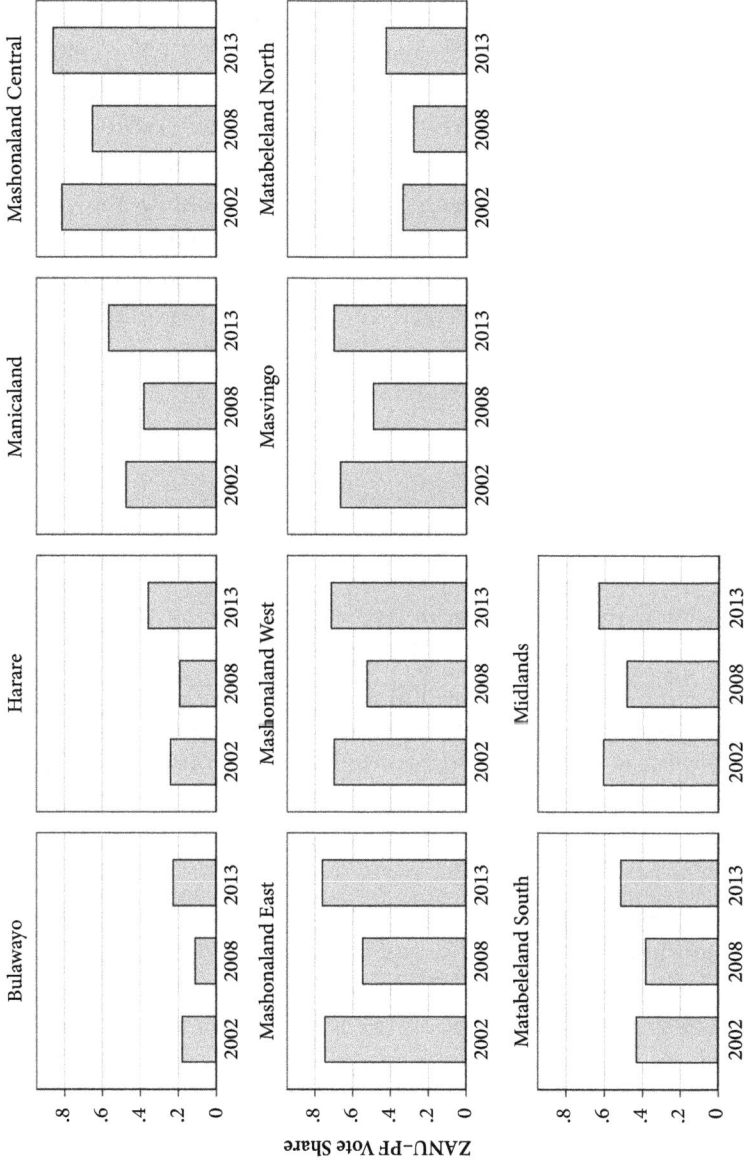

Figure 8.3 Share of Vote for ZANU-PF by Province, 2002–2013.

shore up clientelistic support in rural areas despite a failing economy (Boone and Kriger 2010). In 2002, approximately 85% of Mugabe's support came from the predominantly rural provinces of Manicaland, Mashonaland East, Mashonaland West, Masvingo, and Midlands (Raftopoulos 2002).

While not irrelevant, ethnicity is a fairly poor explanation for regional clustering in voting. ZANU–PF is not foremost an ethnic party. The salience of ethnicity varies subnationally and does not serve as the major cleavage for political mobilization. The ethnic categories in Zimbabwe are, as in most of Africa, complicated and amendable to political manipulation. The largest ethnic group, the Shona, has often been associated with the ZANU–PF, while the minority Ndebele has been associated with opposition interests. However, the Shona identity is an amalgamation of several different subgroups, linguistically and spatially dispersed. In several elections, some of these subgroups have voted for different parties (Lewanika 2019). Moreover, ethnic voting seems to poorly explain voting in multiethnic areas such as Harare, a city where a majority of the population belongs to Shona-affiliated groups known to support the ZANU–PF in other regions.

Apart from ethnicity, other factors may explain the creation of strong regional identities. Beardsworth (2018) describes regional grievances as an important factor that may create distinct regional identities. The unspeakable brutality of the ZANU–PF regime in the Gukuruhundi is one such historical event that has forged a strong anti-regime identity in Matabeleland. Still, perceptions of regional economic marginalization also play a part. Moreover, scholars have pointed to the organizational nature of the liberation struggle as a lasting correlate of regional voting trends (e.g., Gregory 1980; Tevera 1989). For instance, Friesen (2023) has shown a strong correlation between contemporary support for ZANU–PF and guerilla activity during the liberation war.

In terms of mobilization, parties have attempted both to turn out their electoral base to win national majorities and to weaken the opponent's base and undermine their regional strength. Campaigning in Zimbabwe has been dominated by local grassroot campaigns and rallies where parties have attempted to attach themselves to regional identities and make credible claims as defenders of regional interest (Beardsworth 2018; Lewanika 2019). The nature of campaigning in Zimbabwe reiterates the importance of localism in the African electoral context and the need for stronghold mobilization. This way, Zimbabwe does not differ from other geographically polarized electoral systems discussed in this book. Below, I will develop how violent territorial strategies have been a key ZANU–PF strategy for political survival.

8.2.7 Campaign Violence in Zimbabwe, 2002–2013

It is hard to overemphasize how integral violence has been to ZANU–PF's strategy for political survival. Indeed, for Zimbabwe, the concept of campaign violence is somewhat restricting as an analytical tool. While violence has peaked during times of elections (Reeder and Seeberg 2018), political repression has been a cornerstone in the creation of the Zimbabwean authoritarian state. It has in no way been restricted to electoral periods (Levitsky and Way 2010). In this sense, Zimbabwe, with its rather extreme levels of repression, stands out in comparison to Malawi and Zambia.

The formative work by Lebas (2006) stresses how violence has been used strategically by ZANU–PF. Zimbabwe shows how violence can polarize constituencies, increase partisan mobilization, and prevent fractionalization. Violent mobilization in Zimbabwe has also enhanced regional cleavages and political regionalization.

Similar to Zambia under PF and Kenya under KANU, but unlike Malawi under PP, ZANU–PF had significant centralized resources for violence. In fact, ZANU–PF stands out as the case where the asymmetry in violent capacity between the ruling party and the opposition is the largest. It is, therefore, not surprising that ZANU–PF and its affiliates have been responsible for most of the violence during election campaigns. The ruling party had access to several crucial groups to perpetrate violence on its behalf. The state, through the police and the military, has often been directly involved in perpetrating violence. Former freedom fighters, also known as "war veterans" have also been pivotal in bolstering the party's coercive capacity. The war veterans, who were instrumental in the farm invasions after 2000, have been kept under the clientelistic protection of the ruling party and have been instrumentally motivated to provide violent support to the government and protect the political status quo. War veterans have become an essential factor in Zimbabwean politics, exerting significant influence on government policy (not at least as it pertains to agriculture) (Bratton 1987). Along with the war veterans, ZANU–PF has also recruited and trained unemployed youth and criminal gangs for violent purposes (Makumbe 2002; Boone and Kriger 2010; McGregor 2013).

While violence has been an essential part of electoral competition in Zimbabwe, there has also been a significant variation in levels of violence across electoral contests. The election in 2002 featured exceptionally high levels of violence perpetrated both by the state and state-affiliated actors. The number of deaths in the run-up to the election is hard to confirm, but different sources indicate a fatality count in the region of 20–100 (Smiles 2003). Nevertheless, the razor-close 2008 election particularly stands out because of its extraordinarily high levels of violence. Violence particularly peaked after ZANU–PF's loss to MDC in the first round of voting. Unprecedented levels of violence in preparation for the presidential run-off led to MDC withdrawing from an election they would have won under free and fair competition. The electoral period resulted in hundreds of deaths and thousands of displacements. After mediation by a regional negotiation team led by South African President Thabo Mbeki, a coalition government was formed in which Mugabe assumed the role of President and Tsvangirai became the Prime Minister (Bratton 2014). The election in 2013 stands out as the least violent contest in the analyzed period. Lower levels of violence in 2013 are often explained by lower levels of national competition. According to Tendi (2013: 965), ZANU–PF consciously tried to minimize violence in 2013, believing that they could secure an electoral victory without large-scale violence and with the help of other less stigmatizing forms of electoral manipulation. Nevertheless, Masunungure (2014) describes how ZANU–PF often evoked the "ghost of 2008" as an electoral strategy. With large-scale violence in fresh memory, the ruling party used intimidation to foster compliance.[18]

8.2.8 The No-Go-Zone Politics of ZANU–PF

Zimbabwe provides a critical test of the theory laid out in this book. Indeed, the country has inspired much of the scholarship arguing that violence is a tool mainly to target close elections in swing districts (Robinson ad Torvik 2009). Similarly, finding no support for the general hypothesis that violence is particularly targeted at opposition strongholds in Zimbabwe, Rauschenbach and Paula (2019: 693) conclude that violence in Zimbabwe might not have been very spatial: "This suggests a possibility of cross-country variation in the targeting of intimidation; while in Zimbabwe targeting might have been used more discriminately at the individual level, in other countries targeting seems to take place more on the regional level." However, qualitative case study evidence, as well as more quantitative analysis is consistent with the interpretation that violence in Zimbabwe was highly spatial in nature and used mainly to maintain territorial control inside incumbent party strongholds.

---

[18] Beardsworth et al. (2019) make similar observations about the use of intimidation in the 2018 Zimbabwean election.

Re-emphasizing one of the main methodological arguments in this book about the difficulty of measuring subnational variations in election violence using media-based event data, Lebas (2006: 428) concludes:

> Unfortunately there are several problems with the aggregate data on political violence in Zimbabwe for the period 2000-2003 that makes cross-temporal and spatial analysis difficult .... If the data are assumed to have consistent bias due to collection problems, the number of violent incidents in ZANU–PF strongholds would be grossly underestimated, and the scale and intensity of violence in urban, predominantly MDC areas perhaps overstated. Instead, all available data suggest that violence was more serious and more systematically organized in ZANU–PF strongholds.

In fact, the sentiment that election violence was particularly concentrated in ZANU–PF strongholds, particularly in the 2002 and 2008 elections, is widely shared among Zimbabwe scholars (Raftopoluos 2002; Lebas 2006; Makumbe 2006; Lewanika 2019). Despite the reporting issues inherent in media-based event data, Fielding (2018) (using ACLED (Armed Conflict Location and Event Data Project) data) found the highest levels of violence in ZANU-PF strongholds leading up to the second round of the 2008 presidential election.

Case study work provides an informative account of the violence observed in ZANU–PF strongholds, its purpose, and organization. Such descriptions lend substantial support to the territorial understanding of violence promoted in this book. Indeed, violence in such areas has widely been perceived as a deliberate attempt to create no-go zones inside the ruling party's strongholds (Raftopoluos 2002; Lebas 2006; Makumbe 2006; Kibble 2013; Lewanika 2019). In fact, the extent to which ZANU–PF enforced territoriality in rural territories such as Mashonaland and Masvingo by far exceeds what I earlier observed in Malawi and Zambia. As concluded by Lewanika (2019: 24) "ZANU–PF's strategy was in the main, coercive clientelist mobilization, and was buttressed by ZANU–PF attempts to turn its core constituencies into what it termed 'one-party state constituencies.' To achieve this, ZANU–PF blocked, disrupted, and limited opposition campaigns." Both in 2002 and 2008, the opposition could not operate within much of rural Zimbabwe. War veterans erected illegal roadblocks along the roads of many ZANU–PF strongholds, demanding that ordinary citizens showed their ZANU–PF party cards to continue their journeys (Sachikonye 2002; Makumbe 2006). Lewanika (2019: 203) describes how ZANU–PF set up extremely sophisticated and encompassing surveillance systems in strongholds such as

Mt. Darwin to stifle any opposition activity that could disrupt the government party's hold of their most important strongholds. Villages were divided into 10×10 blocks, where every household was monitored by informants.

Although violence was less overt in the 2013 election, several accounts describe how intimidation of suspected MDC supporters in ZANU–PF strongholds made true competition impossible. Gallagher (2015) notes how voters in such areas refrained from talking about politics publicly and how MDC supporters abstained from putting on their party regalia in fear of victimization. These qualitative accounts coincide with my micro-level findings from Zambia, presented in Chapter 5. In Mashonaland, Tsvangirai found great difficulty in campaigning, as voters were actively disengaging with his campaign in fear of violent retribution from local ZANU–PF cadres (Zamchiya 2013: 960).

8.2.9   Contesting Territoriality in Urban MDC Strongholds

Lebas (2006: 426) notes that rural Zimbabwe was the target of most violence in earlier elections, but urban violence grew steadily in the 2000s. She attributes this growth of violence in MDC-controlled urban areas to the government's initiation of a youth training program in 2001. The training of new party cadets allowed for deployment of para-military forces across the territory and significantly bolstered the ruling party's centralized coercive capacity. Zimbabwe's farm invasions further entrenched the government's coercive capacity, creating a strong incentive among war veterans to perpetrate violence on behalf of the government (Boone and Kriger 2010). Accounts of campaign violence in 2002 and 2008 describe how war veterans were provided military uniforms, weapons, and small payments, and bussed into opposition strongholds to bolster ZANU–PF's campaign and provide security in such "alien" territory (Makumbe 2006) (the parallels with bussing of PF cadres in Zambia, described in Chapter 4, are clear).

ZANU–PF also leveraged its strong association with *Chipangano*, a criminal network operating in Harare and its suburbs, to reinforce its coercive capacity in the capital. Chipangano was engaged in the sort of extortionate business and rent-seeking that we already discussed in relation to Mungiki in Kenya or PF cadres in Zambia. Offering the group impunity, ZANU–PF could utilize Chipangano's preference for the political status quo and enlist their violence experts as agents of the ruling party's campaign (Kibble 2013; Lebas 2013; Mutongwizo 2018). ZANU–PF also used the state itself in its attempt to curb urban opposition mobilization. For instance, in 2001, army units were deployed to Harare's Budiriro suburb, a key opposition stronghold. Officers assaulted citizens indiscriminately in their homes and beer halls to remind the locals about the government's continued control (Amnesty International 2002: 27).

ZANU–PF's ability to inject themselves into the campaign in urban MDC strongholds likely had significant consequences for the electoral environment in areas that typically would have been completely dominated by the opposition. Several accounts of violence in Harare confirm that this violence was only enabled through ZANU–PF's centralized coercive resources. Without such resources, the government would have been unable to make an impact in Harare. For instance, McGregor (2013: 796) writes about the 2013 campaign: "Patterns of urban violence in Harare's high-density suburbs during the Inclusive Government were shaped by MDC's predominance, which made ZANU–PF supporters vulnerable to intimidation and violence unless they could draw on state forces and outside reinforcements or militia had presence." The strong coercive presence of ZANU–PF in the capital "benefitted ZANU–PF greatly as it resulted in other MDC activities losing momentum and operating more discretely" (Mutongwizo 2018: 2013). In other words, violence filled the purpose of breaking opposition territorial control.

Notably, several observers noted how violence was not only used to undermine the opposition within urban strongholds but also create a false sense of ZANU–PF viability. ZANU–PF struggled to attract large crowds to rallies in several parts of Harare (Makumbe 2006). However, Chipangano was frequently used to coerce voters to attend ZANU–PF rallies in the capital, artificially inflating the sense of government popularity. While this is not a use of violence that I came across in my other cases, it is completely consistent with the idea of using violence to create a sense of local viability.

8.3 Comparing Malawi and Zambia with Zimbabwe and Kenya

The previous chapters have analyzed the cases of Malawi and Zambia in some detail. How do these cases compare internally and with the reference cases of Zimbabwe and Kenya? First of all, the most important similarity across all four cases is that violence has served as a territorial tool. From the Rift Valley in Kenya to Thyolo in Malawi, to Southern Province in Zambia, and Mashonaland in Zimbabwe, these dynamics have been illustrated throughout this book. In all these cases, parties have used violence to enforce territoriality in electoral systems characterized by localism.

A significant difference between the countries is the magnitude of violence. First, comparing Zambia with Malawi, it is noteworthy that violence has increased in Zambia and that violence in contemporary Zambian politics is at a higher scale and more frequent than in Malawi. This difference cannot be explained by some form of ethnic essentialism or arguments about deep-rooted ethnic competition. If anything, Malawi has a history of more ethnic competition than Zambia, which had a more ethnically inclusive single-party regime. The difference can also not be explained by varying levels of historic conflict, since neither one of the two countries has a history of civil war and both countries received independence through a mostly peaceful process (although with some elements of violent protest in both). Neither can it be explained by variations in national-level competition, since both Zambia and Malawi are highly competitive at the national level.

Instead, the previous chapters have highlighted the importance of centralized capacity for violence as a major explanation for the higher levels of violence in Zambia than in Malawi. The centralized capacity for violence in Zambia also explains why the PF was more inclined to use violence to contest territoriality than PP in Malawi. Extending the argument to Kenya and Zimbabwe, we again see the importance of centralized capacity. KANU and ZANU–PF both used the military and the police to perpetrate violence on the government's behalf. Such violence was also perpetrated inside opposition strongholds, where the ruling party would have had low local capacity. We also see the establishment of organized party capacity for violence in Zambia, Zimbabwe, and Kenya. In Zambia, the book discussed the emerging cadre culture at length. In many ways, the real tipping point for Zambia was when the ruling party offered impunity for organized criminal gangs in exchange for increased repressive capacity. The similarity between the cadres in Zambia, gangs such as Mungiki in Kenya, and war veterans in Zimbabwe, is striking. Similar organized groups of cadres do not exist in Malawi, especially not in the 2014 election. It is hard to imagine that an embattled PP government would have been able to provide the same protection for such gangs.

This is not to say that centralized capacity is the only thing that separates Malawi, Zambia, Zimbabwe, and Kenya. As convincingly argued by several scholars, the extraordinary levels of violence in the case of Kenya is highly related to the country's political economy and fragility stemming from land disputes (Kanyinga 2009; Boone 2011; Klaus 2020). These underlying conflicts have enabled a level of violent mobilization that is unlikely in the cases of Malawi and Zambia. Similarly, historic conflicts in Zimbabwe, combined with decades of systematic human rights abuses and grand corruption by the government party, have made ruling elites more willing to engage in the most extreme forms of violence (Sachikonye 2011; Bratton 2014; Birch 2020). It is quite possible that the eventual defeat of PF in 2021 reduced the chances of Zambia finding itself in a similar downward spiral where violence and corruption in the past beget even more violence and corruption in the future.

8.4 Conclusion

This chapter has illustrated two main things. First, violence as an electoral tool has been common across Africa in geographically polarized electoral systems. Second, the territorial nature of violence is not unique to Malawi and Zambia. In both Kenya and Zimbabwe, analysis of secondary literature showed how parties used violence to both enforce and contest territoriality in election campaigns, serving the logic of localist electoral mobilization common for regionalized African elections.

In Kenya, KANU systematically used violence in areas such as Rift Valley and Northeastern Province to protect their strongholds from opposition activity. Using the language of ethnic exclusionism, opposition campaigning and transethnic mobilization were disabled inside areas that more or less single-handedly handed national electoral victories to the ruling party. The practice of electoral zoning continued after the end of the KANU-era and has become an integral part of electoral campaigning in Kenya. In Zimbabwe, sophisticated surveillance systems were set up by ZANU–PF inside their rural strongholds. Such coercive control turned much of the Zimbabwean countryside into essentially a one-party system. In both Kenya and Zimbabwe, particularly ruling parties have also been able to leverage their centralized coercive capacity to perpetrate violence in opposite strongholds. Governing parties have used the state, paramilitary groups, and criminal gangs. The use of such violence was clear in early Kenyan elections in Nairobi or in 2002 and 2008 in Harare.

While the analysis provided in this chapter should be understood as preliminary, it is highly suggestive. The trends observed in Malawi and Zambia appear generalizable across other geographically polarized electoral system. The findings also further suggest that the main arguments presented in this book are not restricted to cases characterized predominantly by low-scale violence but also extend to cases where violence is of a higher magnitude.

9

Conclusion

This book has introduced a political geography theory of election violence
in geographically polarized electoral systems. Drawing mainly on the cases of
Zambia and Malawi, I have argued that in electoral systems where regionalism is the major political cleavage, campaign violence becomes a territorial
tool used to influence local electoral environments. This concluding chapter
highlights the wider implications of the book's arguments and main findings.
In particular, it focuses on the implications for research on election violence,
African political geography, and sub-national authoritarianism. In all of these
sections, I will also suggest possible avenues for further research that flows
naturally from the findings presented here. Lastly, the chapter will discuss the
potential policy implications of the book. I will specifically concentrate on how
central stakeholders may reduce, manage, and document election violence in
African geographically polarized electoral systems.

9.1 Implications for Research on Election Violence

This book's theoretical and empirical contributions have several implications for future work on election violence. These implications extend beyond
research on sub-national variations in election violence. Indeed, the arguments in this book should also be of interest to those studying individual-level
behavioral effects of election violence as well as those interested in cross-
national variations in election violence.

The book's emphasis on the territorial nature of campaign violence suggests that the effects of violence operate above the individual level. While
earlier research has recognized spatial variations in electoral violence, space
has mostly been used as a stand-in for other spatially clustered variables such
as ethnicity or partisanship. I argue that violence is not simply a tool to directly
affect individual-level behavior, it has a much broader effect on entire local
electoral environments. In locations where violence or the threat of violence is
considerable, campaigns will be restricted. Violence will create an unlevel electoral playing field, giving some actors better opportunities to stage effective

Controlling Territory, Controlling Voters. Michael Wahman, Oxford University Press.
© Michael Wahman (2023). DOI: 10.1093/oso/9780198872825.003.0009

campaigns, mobilize citizens, and create strong local electoral appeals. This argument has important implications for the way that we understand the strategic use of violence. We cannot assume that violence will only be used in locations where parties try to dissuade voters from turning out to the polls; it can also be a way to manage and maintain strengths in vital strongholds.

The book focused particularly on the interaction between local political campaigns and national-level politics. However, the concept of territoriality can also be applied to much more local electoral campaigns. For instance, territorial politics has been an important part of parliamentary elections within electoral constituencies. In a recent survey with 208 parliamentary candidates standing in the 2021 Zambian election, I found that 55% of candidates experienced that they could not move around and campaign freely in their constituency. Most of the candidates were more concerned with violence when visiting areas of the constituency that were dominated by rival candidates (Wahman 2022). The territorial nature of campaign violence might also affect campaigns in primary elections, a part of the electoral cycle that is often neglected in the election violence research but has often been associated with significant levels of violence (Seeberg et al. 2018). Future research on the territorial nature of lower-level elections would add considerably to our understanding of the contemporary use of election violence in political campaigns.

For more behavioral and individual-level work on election violence, the argument presented in this book is important. Observational studies of political behavior in violent electoral contexts need to take into account the geographic context in which a voter resides. We cannot expect a voter aligned with the locally dominant party to be equally exposed to violence as someone aligned with the local minority party. For experimental studies, the findings of this book suggest that we need to consider the external validity of individual-level treatments. Violence does not only affect elections through the direct effect on individuals but also through its indirect effect on electoral environments. For instance, while we might find that voters react negatively to information about a candidate's involvement in election violence, it is hard to infer that violence is counterproductive if the same violence profoundly affects the entire local environment in which campaigns are conducted.

The book has also provided a strong argument for taking low-scale violence seriously. The literature has been mostly preoccupied with studying the most extreme cases of violence in a handful of countries. These cases are important, especially if we are interested in understanding how elections can polarize societies and exacerbate conflict. However, if we are interested in election violence as a tool of electoral manipulation, there is no reason to believe that only lethal violence affects the conduct of elections and election campaign environments. Crucially, if parties want to affect elections through the use of violence but avoid the high costs that violence may incur in terms of both internal and external legitimacy, they would be better off engaging in low-scale, less eye-catching violence (Cheeseman and Klaas 2019). The cross-country analysis of the relationship between perceptions of fear and registered deadly violence (presented in Chapter 1) shows virtually no correlation between the two. The book did not hypothesize or theorize how fear of violence is reproduced within an electoral environment, but this would be an important task for future research.

The discussion above also has important methodological consequences for how we measure election violence sub-nationally and cross-nationally. A particular weakness of media-based event data is that such data are notoriously ill-equipped to capture low-scale violence and violence occurring in less competitive, more remote, areas (von Borzyskowski and Wahman 2021). This book introduced a new way to measure sub-national variations in election violence, using surveys with domestic election observers. This strategy could be replicated in other contexts. It is fair to assume that the results from the statistical analysis would have been rather different if the analysis had used more conventional strategies for measuring sub-national election violence. Researchers conducting both sub-national and country-level research must be aware of the limitations of election violence data. For sub-national-level research, we should consider the potential sources of geographic bias. For national-level research, we should be careful to assume that elections will only be affected by violence in countries with multiple fatal election violence events.

Lastly, the book has important implications for the cross-national study of variations in election violence. One of the most robust findings in this literature is the strong correlation between national-level competition and higher levels of election violence (Hafner Burton et al. 2014; Taylor et al. 2017). Chapter 8 of this book provides some preliminary evidence to suggest that cross-national variations are not only dependent on national-level competition but also sub-national competition. Future research studying the impact of party nationalization and local competition on election violence can add significantly to our understanding of why some countries have higher levels of violence during elections than others. A possible hypothesis deriving from this work is that the combination of low-level local competition and high-level national competition is especially conducive to election violence.

9.2 Implications for Research on Electoral Geography

The book also has important implications for our understanding of African electoral geography. It introduces the concept of geographically polarized electoral systems and argues that we should understand electoral competition in such systems from the perspective of competition over the mobilization of regional cleavages. Although much research on African elections has recognized the spatial clustering of vote choice, much of this research has understood such clustering as a symptom of uneven distribution of segmental cleavages, particularly ethnicity. In this book, I argue that space matters in a much more fundamental way. Regionalism may be a structuring cleavage in many African electoral systems. Still, the mobilization of regional cleavages is a political process where political parties must create strong links to a particular region. Parties attempt to create a sense among voters of local viability and local development advocacy. They also need to show that they care about locally salient issues. Interpretations of elections in non-nationalized electoral systems are created locally in localist political mobilization. Research on African elections has just started to scratch the surface of what localism actually means for political competition.

The dearth of mainstream electoral geography work in Africa is surprising, given the very obvious regional divisions in African elections. The weak emphasis on electoral geography is perhaps a reflection of data available. In African studies, we have long had access to superb and comparable (longitudinal and cross-country) public opinion data through the Afrobarometer. In contrast, sub-national election data have been much harder to come by. For this reason, researchers may have been prone to study African voting from the micro- rather than the meso-level. More research is needed to establish the basic regional basis of electoral mobilization in Africa and to understand variations in voting across space. More work is also needed to unlock the relationship between regional electoral blocs and spatial economic variations.[1]

In the chapters on the political geography of Malawi and Zambia, the book also dispels the myth that parties can rely on dependable regional blocs to turn out voters in great numbers. First, there is a considerable degree of party volatility at the local level. Contrary to what some might expect, all of this volatility is not caused by party system instability. Second, there is a significant variation over time in the extent to which parties can mobilize varying regions. This book has focused on violence as a tool to prevent rival parties

---

[1] For one good illustration of such work, see Momba (1985).

from contesting local electoral narratives. Still, more work is needed on other strategies that parties use to enable strong regional mobilization. Some excellent recent work has focused on the role of rallies in this process (e.g. Paget 2019; Brierley and Kramon 2020) or local elite endorsements (Arriola et al. 2022), but much of this process is still unknown.

The discussions in this book also open many interesting avenues of research for work on political nationalization. The concept of nationalization has often been misconstrued to imply the absence of uniform party support across space. However, nationalization is, in fact, a much larger concept. If national-level cleavages are unevenly distributed across space, a country could be nationalized despite high regional variation in party support. Instead, the characterizing feature of non-nationalized electoral systems is the lack of unifying national political themes that play out in a regular way across the territory (Lipset and Rokkan 1967). The feature that makes African electoral systems non-nationalized is not so much the uneven support of different parties across space as the fact that voters in different localities may vote for the same party for rather different reasons. Africa is an interesting laboratory for studying the process of electoral nationalization. The continent exhibits interesting variations in electoral systems and political decentralization, and new technologies may shift some political conversations against more nationally unifying themes.

9.3 Implications for Research on Sub-national Authoritarianism

The book adds significantly to conversations about sub-national authoritarianism in Africa (van de Walle 2007 and Boone 2014) and beyond (McMann 2006; Gibson 2013; Giroudy 2015). While some types of electoral manipulation (e.g., aggregation fraud or the biasing of national-level institutions) occur at the national level, much of the manipulation that matters in contemporary African elections is conducted locally using local party capacity. Some of this manipulation may relate to the counting of the vote (Asunka et al. 2019) or vote buying (Kramon 2018). This book emphasizes electoral violence, including forms of low-scale violence, as a tool for upholding sub-national authoritarianism.

Election violence does not only distort local political campaigns and competition, but also severely reduces the quality of democracy. No-go zones have been a major problem in Malawi, Zambia, Zimbabwe, and Kenya. Voters living in no-go zones do not enjoy access to real democracy; they cannot access alternative messages in an open marketplace of ideas. In many cases, they are deprived of the ability to effectively keep governments accountable or critically discuss the track record of the incumbent.

Democratic citizenship cannot be reduced to the simple act of voting; an engaged citizenry is one of the hallmarks of a healthy democracy (Almond and Verba 1963; Putnam 2000). Violence tends to exacerbate political inequalities. The findings in Chapter 5 show that women and local partisan minorities are more afraid of violence than men and those in the local partisan majority. Violence is a tool of political exclusion and one that tends to amplify the position of those with power at the expense of those without. It is certainly troubling that many of the landmark improvements in participation accomplished by Africa's transition to multipartyism may be challenged by the use of violence at the local level. More research would help us better understand the participatory effects of violence and how such effects affect citizens to different degrees. However, one important takeaway from this book is that we should not assume that vulnerability is equal across space. Moreover, power relations can also vary. For instance, while opposition voters in Zambia's 2016 election were the main targets of violence throughout the campaign, it was voters with affiliation to the government party in the opposition-dominated Southern Province that became the main targets of violence in the aftermath of the election.

The argument in this book also has important implications for our understanding of sub-national variations in political competition and how this may pertain to urban/rural divides. While urban areas have often been considered the hotspots for electoral violence, particularly high-scale violence, the arguments here show how violence has been a highly effective tool in rural Africa for effectively closing the democratic space. From Thyolo in Malawi to Mashonaland in Zimbabwe, parties have been able to control rural electorates by restricting political pluralism through violence.

9.4 Implications for Policy

This book has not been primarily concerned with evaluating potential solutions for reducing levels of violence in geographically polarized electoral systems. Nevertheless, there are several possible lessons for those working actively on programming to strengthen African democracy and curb electoral violence. First, and most importantly, this book is a plea to take low-scale violence seriously. The two main cases studied in this book, Malawi and Zambia, do not stand out as particularly violent by African standards. Perhaps, as a consequence, policymakers and the international donor community have often failed to adequately prioritize these issues when designing election programming. Professionals in the international community often come to countries like Malawi and Zambia with experiences from significantly more politically violent contexts and have a fairly high acceptance of violence as a part of political competition. However, as this book has argued, violence does not have to be lethal to devastate the democratic process and affect political participation. In order to truly strengthen the democratic processes, we need to fully evaluate the extent to which violence stands in the way of a more inclusive and competitive electoral environment.

Domestic NGOs and observers played an important part in the production of this book. In particular, my partnership with the National Initiative for Civic Education (NICE) in Malawi and the Foundation for Democratic Process (FODEP) and the Southern African Centre for Constructive Resolution of Disputes (SACCORD) enabled the collection of all the quantitative data presented on sub-national variations in election violence. Domestic election observation networks could play a much more important role in documenting violence throughout the electoral process. Provided the right resources and methodological tools, they could collect the necessary data to accurately map the real hotspots of violence. The key to this strategy is to ensure a method for data collection that does not make any predetermined judgments on where violence may occur. As this book has argued, media reports are heavily biased toward recognizing violence in urban areas and known hotspots. Such reports are also likely to underestimate the extent of violence. Several international monitoring reports that I read throughout the process of writing this book recognize that their missions have been unable to fully capture the extent of violence that occurred during the election, particularly in more remote areas (e.g., EU 2008: 19). The inability of stakeholders to accurately document low-scale violence makes violence a fairly low-cost tool of manipulation for perpetrating actors. With a better system for documenting violence over time, international monitors would be in a much better position to accurately assess the extent to which electoral violence shaped electoral environments.

The cases in this book also highlight the need to put more pressure on the judiciary and the electoral commission to actually hold the perpetrators of election violence accountable. Worryingly often, actors at different levels can perpetrate violence with impunity. To take one example, the Electoral Commission of Zambia (ECZ) has the prerogative to disqualify candidates (at national or local levels) that instigate violence (Electoral Process Act No. 35 of 2016). Similarly, the judiciary may retrospectively nullify elections based on breaches of the electoral code of conduct, including the instigation of violence. However, these tools have not been adequately used in the Zambian context.[2] Although such provisions have to be used parsimoniously not to become a source of incumbent bias, a debate is needed on how these provisions should be used in order to seriously restrain political actors from engaging in electoral violence. Along the same lines, the narratives from both Malawi and Zambia illustrate that the actual perpetrators of violence rarely get prosecuted for their violent offences. Civil society and the media need the resources to demand that those engaged in violence are held accountable.

Lastly, it is also worth pointing out the policy initiatives that have worked well in the contexts studied here. In particular, I would highlight initiatives that recognize the role of local actors in preventing the escalation of violence. Malawi, in particular, established local Multiparty Liaison Committees (MPLCs) in preparation for the 2014 election. These MPLCs were set up by the Malawi Electoral Commission (MEC) at the district level. MPLCs contained representatives from the political parties and their youth wings, faith-based organizations, traditional chiefs, the police, and civil society (Travaglianti 2017). MPLCs could resolve local disputes at an early stage before violence ensued. During many of my conversations with monitors on the ground, key informants attested to the success of MPLCs and their ability to engage local actors in mitigating conflict. Given the main findings of this book, it is imperative to consider policy solutions that derive from the local environments that political actors compete to control.

---

[2] The High Court of Zambia did nullify the elections in Lusaka Central and Munali constituencies in 2016, citing violence, among other things. However, these decisions were later reversed by the Constitutional Court (Kerr and Wahman 2021).

Appendix

Supplementary Tables and Figures: Chapter 3

Table A3.1 Analysis of relationship between competition and stated voting.

	Model 1 Voted
Competition	.041
	(.382)
Local partisan majority	1.031
	(.228)
Competition* Local partisan majority	1.438***
	(.468)
Constituency Population density (log)	−.114
	(.468)
Lived Poverty Index	.079
	(.075)
Constituency nightlight	−.003
	(.008)
N	1,159
Pseudo R^2	.044

Notes: ***≤p.01 **≤p.05 *≤p.1. Entries are logistic coefficients with standard errors in parentheses. Standard errors clustered by province.

Supplementary Tables and Figures: Chapter 4

Table A4.1 Analysis of relationship between competition and constituency-level campaign violence (OLS Regression).

	Model 1 Severity	Model 2 Frequency
Competition	−.642**	−.465*
	(.249)	(.226)
History EV	−.002	.017
	(.214)	(.226)
Population Density (log)	.015	.023
	(.097)	(.078)
Nightlight (log)	.568	.097
	(.616)	(.626)
Literacy	−.160	.212
	(.775)	(.657)
Ethnic Fractionalization	.449	.306
	(.388)	(.336)
N	156	156
R^2	.05	.04

Notes: ***≤p.01 **≤p.05 *≤p.1. Entries are OLS regression coefficients with standard errors in parentheses. Standard errors clustered by province.

Table A4.2 Analysis of relationship between opposition vote and constituency-level campaign violence (OLS Regression).

	Model 3 Severity	Model 4 Frequency
Competition	.041***	.030***
	(.009)	(.006)
History EV	−.042	−.011
	(.212)	(.222)
Population Density (log)	−.022	−.004
	(.082)	(.071)
Nightlight (log)	.535	.071
	(.485)	(.551)
Literacy	.182	.456
	(.689)	(.602)
Ethnic Fractionalization	.049	.016
	(.370)	(.349)
N	156	156
R^2	.09	.07

Notes: ***≤p.01 **≤p.05 *≤p.1. Entries are OLS regression coefficients with standard errors in parentheses. Standard errors clustered by province.

Table A4.3 Logistic Regression with quadradic PF vote share.

	Model 5 Election Violence
PF Vote Share 2015	−.037
	(.023)
PF Vote Share 2015∧2	.000
	(.000)
History EV	−.300
	(.701)
Population Density (log)	.064
	(.235)
Nightlight (log)	.865
	(1.323)
Literacy	.480
	(1.878)
Ethnic Fractionalization	.673
	(1.138)
N	156
Pseudo R^2	.02

Notes: *** ≤p.01 ** ≤p.05 * ≤p.1. Entries are logistic coefficients with standard errors in parentheses. Standard errors clustered by province.

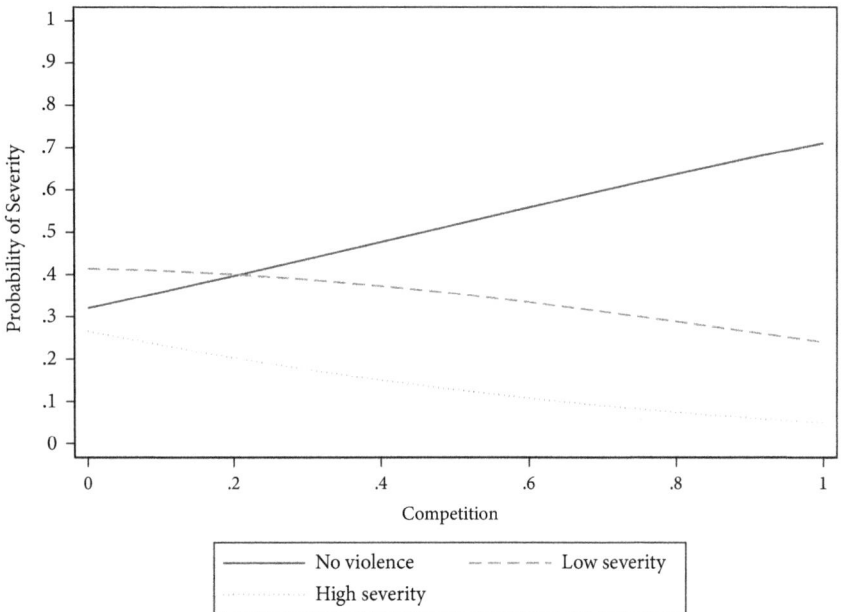

Figure A4.1 Post-estimation of Relationship between Competition and Severity of Violence.

Note: Post-estimation based on Model 1 in Table 4.1

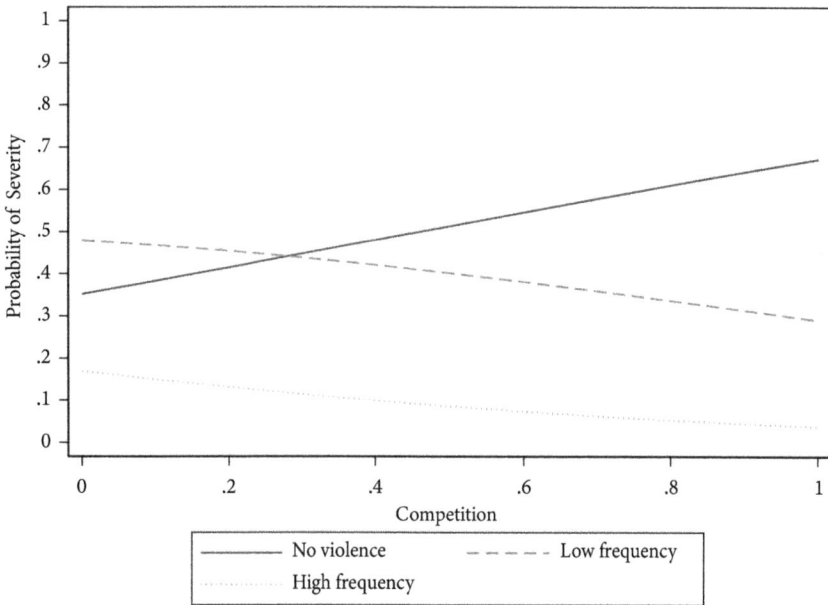

Figure A4.2 Post-estimation of Relationship between Competition and Frequency of Violence.

Note: Post-estimation based on Model 2 in Table 4.1

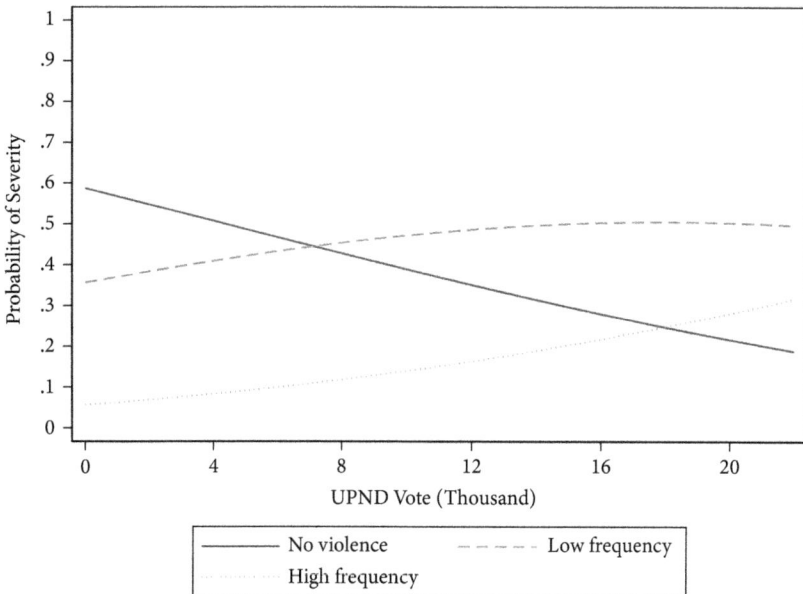

Figure A4.3 Post-estimation of Relationship between Opposition Vote and Severity of Violence.

Note: Post-estimation based on Model 4 in Table 4.3

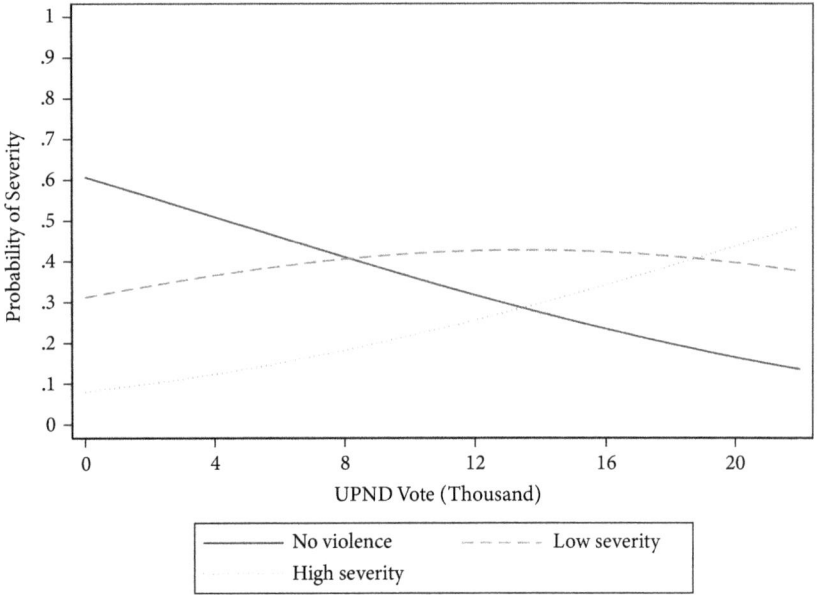

Figure A4.4 Post-estimation of Relationship between Opposition Vote and Frequency of Violence.

Note: Post-estimation based on Model 5 in Table 4.3

Supplementary Tables and Figures: Chapter 5

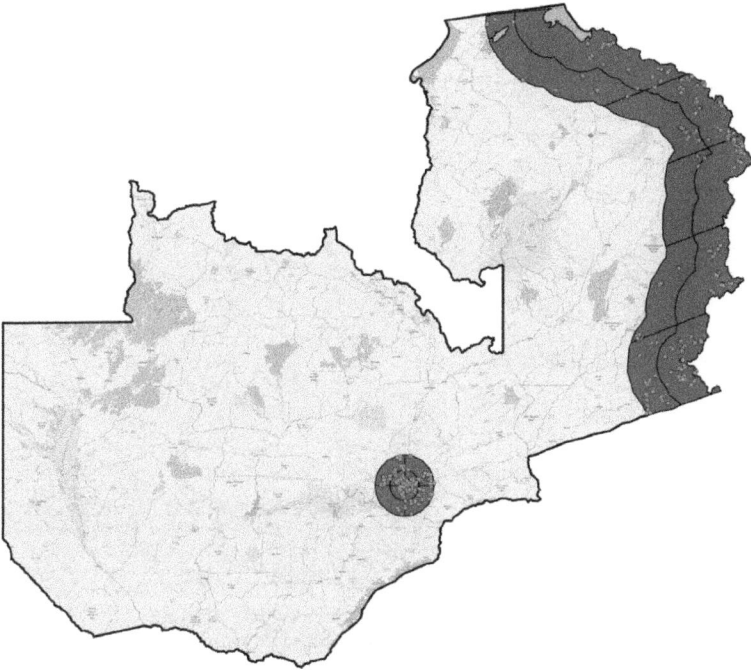

Figure A5.1   Original Sampling GLD LGPI Survey 2019.

Note: Shaded areas show the radius of the original sample areas in LGPI. Circles indicate respondent clusters.

Supplementary Tables and Figures: Chapter 7

Table A7.1 Analysis of relationship between competition and constituency-level campaign violence (OLS Regression).

	Model 1 Severity	Model 2 Frequency
Competition	−.411***	−.415***
	(.014)	(.009)
History EV	−.010	−.274
	(.257)	(.236)
Population Density (log)	.103	.115
	(.050)	(.065)
Nightlight (log)	.023	.240
	(.122)	(.086)
Literacy	.074	.031
	(.197)	(.042)
Ethnic Fractionalization	−.031	−.024
	(.067)	(.084)
N	192	192
R^2	.07	.10

Notes: ***≤p.01 **≤p.05 *≤p.1. Entries are OLS coefficients with standard errors in parentheses. Standard errors clustered by region.

Table A7.2 Analysis of relationship between opposition vote and constituency-level campaign violence (OLS Regression).

	Model 3 Severity	Model 4 Frequency
DPP Votes 2009 (Thousand)	.007	.008
	(.004)	(.004)
History EV	−.076	−.353
	(.277)	(.266)
Population Density (log)	.057	.068
	(.073)	(.089)
Nightlight (log)	.047	.269
	(.130)	(.082)
Literacy	.138	.081
	(.393)	(.266)
Ethnic Fractionalization	−.032	−.031
	(.138)	(.164)
N	192	192
R^2	.04	.07

Notes: ***≤p.01 **≤p.05 *≤p.1. Entries are OLS coefficients with standard errors in parentheses. Standard errors clustered by region.

Table A7.3 Analysis of relationship between opposition vote and constituency-level campaign violence (Excluding Northern Region).

	Model 5 Severity	Model 6 Frequency
DPP Votes 2009 (Thousand)	.024	.026
	(.019)	(.016)
History EV	−5.003***	−5.120
	(.283)	(.350)
Population Density (log)	.238	.244
	(.337)	(.346)
Nightlight (log)	.258	.500
	(.525)	(.529)
Literacy	−.756	−.612
	(.451)	(.403)
Ethnic Fractionalization	−.168	−.216
	(.280)	(.311)
N	159	159
Pseudo R²	.05	.06

Notes: ***≤p.01 **≤p.05 *≤p.1. Entries are ordered probit coefficients with standard errors in parentheses. Standard errors clustered by region.

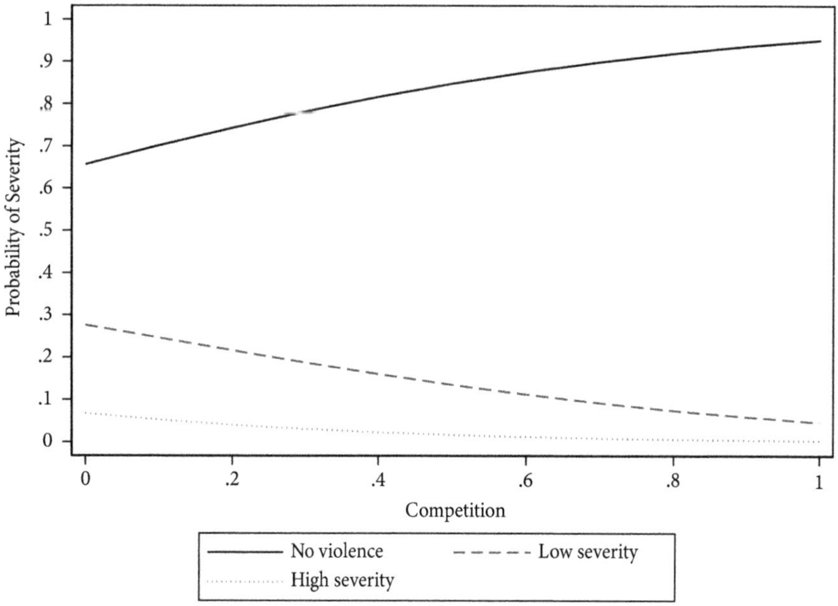

Figure A7.1 Post-estimation of Relationship between Competition and Severity of Violence.

Note: Post-estimations based on model 1 in Table 7.1

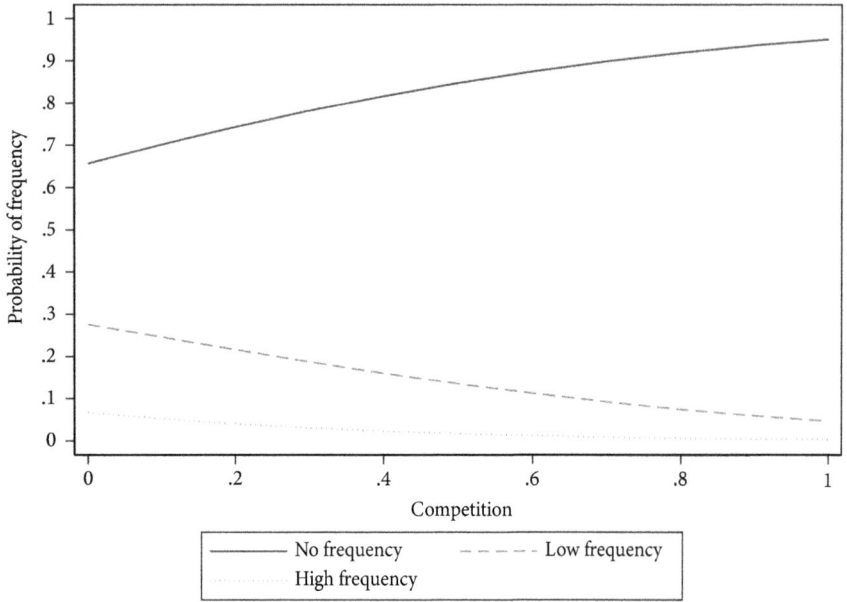

Figure A7.2 Post-estimation of Relationship between Competition and Frequency of Violence.

Note: Post-estimations based on model 2 in Table 7.1

References

Abrahamsen, Rita and Gerald Bareebe. 2016. "Uganda's 2016 Elections: Not Even Faking It Anymore." *African Affairs* 115 (461): 751–765.

Afrobarometer. 2017. Zambia: Round 7. *Afrobarometer.*

Agnew, John. 1987. *Place and Politics: The Geographical Mediation of State and Society.* New York: Routledge.

Agnew, John. 1995. "The Rhetoric of Regionalism: The Northern League in Italian Politics, 1983–94." *Transactions of the Institute of British Geographers* 20 (2): 156–172.

Agnew, John. 1996. "Mapping Politics: How Context Counts in Electoral Geography." *Political Geography* 15 (2): 129–146.

Albrecht, Holger. 2015. "The Myth of Coup-proofing: Risk and Instances of Military Coup d'état in the Middle East and North Africa, 1950–2013." *Armed Forces and Society* 41 (4): 659–687.

Aldrich, John. 1996. *Why Parties?* Chicago: University of Chicago Press.

Alesina, Alberto and Ekaterina Zhuravskaya. 2011. "Segregation and the Quality of Government in a Cross Section of Countries." *American Economic Review* 101 (5): 1872–1911.

Almond, Gabriel A. and Sidney Verba. 1963. *The Civic Culture: Political Attitudes and Democracy in Five Nations.* Princeton: Princeton University Press.

Al Jazeera. 2014. "Banda Throws Malawi into New Political Crisis." May 24, 2014. https://www.aljazeera.com/news/2014/5/24/banda-throws-malawi-into-new-political-crisis. [last accessed October 5, 2022]

Amnesty International. 2002. "Zimbabwe: Toll of Impunity." Report AFR 46/034/2002.

Anderson, David M. 2002. "Vigliantes, Violence and the Politics of Public Order in Kenya." *African Affairs* 101 (405): 531–555.

Andreassen, Bård-Anders, Gisela Geisler, and Arne Tostensen. 1992. "Setting a Standard for Africa? Lessons from the 1991 Zambian Election." *Chr. Michelsen Institute Report,* 1992: 5.

Andrews, Sarah. 2015. "Agricultural Clientelism in the 2014 Campaign," in Patel, Nandini and Michael Wahman (Eds.) *The Malawi 2014 Election: Is Democracy Maturing?* Lilongwe: National initiative for Civic Education, pp. 176–194.

Angerbrandt, Henrik. 2018. "Deadly Elections: Post-Election Violence in Nigeria." *Journal of Modern African Studies* 56 (1): 143–167.

Arriola, Leonardo. 2009. "Patronage and Political Stability in Africa." *Comparative Political Studies* 42 (10): 1339–1362.

Arriola, Leonardo. 2013. *Multiethnic Coalitions in Africa.* New York: Cambridge University Press.

Arriola, Leonardo R., Donghyun Danny Choi, and Matthew K. Gichohi. 2022. "Increasing Intergroup Trust: Endorsements and Voting in Divided Societies." *Journal of Politics* 84 (4): 2107–2122.

Asante, Richard and Emmanuel Gyimah-Boadi. 2004. *Ethnic Structure, Inequality and Public Sector in Ghana.* New York: United Nations Research Institute for Social Development.

Asunka, Joseph, Sarah Brierley, Miriam Golden, Eric Kramon, and George Ofosu. 2019. "Electoral Fraud and or Violence: The Effect of Observers on Party Manipulation Strategies." *British Journal of Political Science* 49 (1): 129–151.

Balcells, Laia and Jessica A. Stanton. 2021. "Violence against Civilians during Armed Conflict: Moving beyond the Macro- and Micro Level." *Annual Review of Political Science* 24 (1): 45–69.

Baldwin, Kate. 2013. "Why Vote with the Chief? Political Connections and Public Goods Provision in Zambia." *American Journal of Political Science* 57 (4): 794–809.

Baldwin, Kate. 2014. "When Politicians Cede Control of Resources: Land, Chiefs and Coalition-building in Africa." *Comparative Politics* 46 (3): 253–271.

Bangura, Ibrahim and Mimmi Söderberg Kovacs. 2018. "Competition, Uncertainty, and Violence in Sierra Leone's Swing District," in Söderberg Kovacs, Mimmi and Jesper Bjarnesen (Eds.) *Violence in African Elections: Between Democracy and Big Man Politics.* London: ZED, pp. 114–134.

Barkan, Joel D. 1993. "Lessons from a Flawed Election." *Journal of Democracy* 4 (3): 85–99.

Barkan, Joel D. 2004 "Kenya after Moi." *Foreign Affairs* 83 (1): 100–114.

Barkan, Joel D. and Njunguna Ng'ethe. 1998. "African Ambiguities: Kenya Tries Again." *Journal of Democracy* 9 (2): 32–48.

Basedau, Matthias, Gero Erdmann, Jan Lay, and Alexander Stroh. 2011. "Ethnicity and Party Preference in Sub-Sharan Africa." *Democratization* 18 (2): 462–489.

Bates, Robert. 1981. *Markets and States in Tropical Africa.* Berkeley: University of California Press.

Bates, Robert H. and Steven A. Block. 2013. "Revisiting African Agriculture: Institutional Change and Productivity Growth." *Journal of Politics* 75 (2): 372–384.

Baylies, Carolyn and Morris Szeftel. 1992. "Introduction: The Making of the One-party State," in Gretzel, Cherry, Carolin Beylies, and Morris Szeftel (Eds.) *The Dynamics of the One-Party State in Zambia.* Manchester: Manchester University Press, pp. 1–29.

Beardsworth, Nicole. 2018. *Electoral Coalition-building among Opposition Parties in Zimbabwe, Zambia, and Uganda from 2000 to 2017.* Unpublished Doctoral Dissertation: Warwick University.

Beardsworth, Nicole. 2019. "Opposition Coalitions," in Lynch, Gabrielle and Peter Von-Doepp (Eds.) *Routledge Handbook of Democratization in Africa.* London: Routledge, pp. 289–320.

Beardsworth, Nicole. 2020. "From a 'Regional Party' to the Gates of State House: The Resurgence of the UPND," in Tineneji, Banda, O'Brien Kaaba, Marja Hinfelaar, and Muna Ndulo (Eds.) *Democracy and Electoral Politics in Zambia,* Leiden: Brill, pp. 34–68.

Beardsworth, Nicole, Nic Cheeseman, and Simukai Tinhu. 2019. "Zimbabwe: The Coup that was, and the Election that Could have Been." *African Affairs* 118 (472): 580–596.

Beardsworth, Nicole, Alastair Fraser, Danielle Resnick, and Gilbert Siame. 2021. "Briefing Paper 6: Party Cadres, the Politicisation of Local Government, and Zambia's 2021 Election." *The Zambia Electoral Analysis Project (ZEAP) Briefing Papers Series*, Westminster Foundation for Democracy and Southern African Institute for Policy and Research.

Becher, Anika. 2016. *Explaining Ethnic and Election Violence: Kenya and Malawi in Comparative Perspective.* Baden-Baden: Nomos.

Beck, Linda. 2008. *Brokering Democracy in Africa: The Rise of Clientelist Democracy in Senegal.* New York: Palgrave MacMillan.

Bekoe, Dorina A. and Stephanie M. Burchard. 2017. "The Contradictions of Pre-Electoral Violence: The Effects of Violence on Voter Turnout in Sub-Saharan Africa." *African studies Review* 60 (2): 73–92.

Birch, Sarah. 2007. "Electoral Systems and Electoral Misconduct." *Comparative Political Studies* 40 (12): 1533–1556.

Birch, Sarah. 2011. *Electoral Malpractice*. Oxford: Oxford University Press.

Birch, Sarah. 2020. *Electoral Violence, Corruption, and Political Order*. Princeton: Princeton University Press.

Birch, Sarah, Ursula Daxecker, and Kristine Höglund. 2020. "Electoral Violence: An Introduction." *Journal of Peace Research* 57 (1): 3–14.

Bjarnegård, Elin. 2018. "Making Gender Visible in Election Violence: Strategies for Data Collection." *Politics and Gender* 14 (4): 690–695.

Bleck, Jamie and Nicolas van de Walle. 2018. *Electoral Politics in Africa since 1990: Continuity and Change*. New York: Cambridge University Press.

Bob-Milliar, George M. 2014. "Party Youth Activists in Low-Intensity Violence in Ghana: A Qualitative Study of Party Foot Soldiers' Activism." *African Studies Quarterly* 15 (1): 125–152.

Bogaards, Matthijs and Sebastian Elischer. 2016. "Competitive Authoritarianism in Africa Revisited." *Zeitschrift für Vergleichende Politikwissenscheft* 10: 5–18.

Boone, Catherine. 2003. *Political Topographies of the African State: Territorial Authority and Institutional Choice*. Cambridge: Cambridge University Press.

Boone, Catherine. 2009. "Electoral Populism where Property Rights are Weak: Land Politics in Contemporary Sub-Saharan Africa." *Comparative Politics* 41 (2): 183–196.

Boone, Catherine. 2011. "Politically Allocated Land Rights and the Geography of Election Violence: The Case of Kenya in the 1990s." *Comparative Political Studies* 48 (2): 173–202.

Boone, Catherine. 2014. *Property and Political Order in Africa*. Cambridge: Cambridge University Press.

Boone, Catherine. 2016. Spatial Inequality in African Political Economy Dataset. LSE RIIF 2016 (#1-BRD-B079)

Boone, Catherine. 2018. "Property and Land Institutions," in Cheeseman, Nic (Ed.) *Institutions and Democracy in Africa: How the Rules of the Game Shape Political Development*. Cambridge: Cambridge University Press.

Boone, Catherine and Norma Kriger. 2010. "Multiparty Elections and Land Patronage: Zimbabwe and Côte d'Ivoire." *Commonwealth & Comparative Politics* 48 (2): 173–202.

Boone, Catherine and Rebecca Simson. 2019. "Regional Inequalities in African Political Economy: Theory, Conceptualization and Measurement, and Political Effects." *LSE Department of International Development Working Paper*, March 2019.

Boone, Catherine and Michael Wahman. 2015. "Rural Bias in African Electoral Systems: Legacies of Unequal Representation in African Democracies." *Electoral Studies* 40: 335–346.

Boone, Catherine, Wahman, Michael, Kyburz, Stephan, and Andrew Linke. 2022. "Regional Cleavages in African Politics: Persistent Electoral Blocs and Territorial Oppositions." *Political Geography*, 99: 102741.

Borzyskowski, von Inken. 2019. *The Credibility Challenge: How Democracy and Aid Influences Election Violence*. Ithaca: Cornell University Press.

Borzyskowski, von Inken and Patrick M. Kuhn. 2020. "Dangerously Informed: Voter Information and Pre-Electoral Violence in Africa." *Journal of Peace Research* 57 (1): 15–29.

Borzyskowski, von Inken and Michael Wahman. 2021. "Systematic Measurement Error in Election Violence Data: Causes and Consequences" *British Journal of Political Science* 51 (1): 230–252.

Brancati, Dawn and Jack L. Snyder. 2013. "Time to Kill: The Impact of Election Timing on Post conflict Stability." *Journal of Conflict Resolution* 57 (5): 822–853.

Bratton, Michael. 1987. "The Comrades and the Countryside: The Politics of Agricultural Policy in Zimbabwe." *World Politics* 39 (2): 174–202.

Bratton, Michael. 1992. "Zambia Starts Over." *Journal of Democracy* 3 (2): 81–94.

Bratton, Michael. 2008. "Vote Buying and Violence in Nigerian Elections." *Electoral Studies* 27: 621–631.

Bratton, Michael. 2014. *Power Politics in Zimbabwe*. London: Lynne Rienner Press.

Bratton, Michael, Ravi Bhavnani, and Tse-Hsin Chen. 2012. "Voting Intentions in Africa: Economic or Partisan." *Commonwealth & Comparative Politics* 50 (1): 27–52.

Bratton, Michael, Boniface Dulani, Eldred Masunungure. 2016. "Detecting Manipulation in Authoritarian Elections: Survey Based Methods in Zimbabwe." *Electoral Studies* 42: 10–21.

Bratton, Michael and Mwangi S. Kimenyi. 2008. "Voting in Kenya: Putting Ethnicity in Perspective." *Journal of Eastern African Studies* 2 (2): 272–289.

Bratton, Michael and Eldred Masunungure. 2006. "Popular Reactions to State Repression: Operation Murambatsvina in Zimbabwe." *African Affairs* 106 (422): 21–45.

Bratton, Michael and Eldred Masunungure. 2008. "Zimbabwe's Long Agony." *Journal of Democracy* 19 (4): 41–55.

Bratton, Michael and Nicolas van de Walle. 1992. "Popular Protest and Political Reform in Africa." *Comparative Politics* 24 (4): 419–442.

Bratton, Michael and Nicolas van de Walle. 1997. *Democratic Experiments in Africa: Regime Transitions in Comparative Perspective*. Cambridge: Cambridge University Press.

Brierley, Sarah and Eric Kramon. 2020. "Party Campaign Strategies in Ghana: Rallies, Canvassing and Handouts." *African Affairs* 119 (477): 578–603.

Briggs, Ryan C. 2012. "Electrifying the Base? Aid and Incumbent Advantage in Ghana." *Journal of Modern African Studies* 50 (4): 603–624.

Brown, Stephen and Chandra Lekha Siriam. 2012. "The Big Fish Won't Fry Themselves: Criminal Accountability for Post-election Violence in Kenya." *African Affairs* 111 (443): 244–260.

Brosché Johan, Hanne Fjelde, and Kristine Höglund. 2020. "Electoral Violence and the Legacy of Authoritarian Rule in Kenya and Zambia." *Journal of Peace Research* 57 (1): 112–125.

Burchard, Stephanie M. 2015. *Electoral Violence in Sub-Saharan Africa: Causes and Consequences*. London: Routledge.

Burchard, Stephanie M. 2020. "Get Out the Vote-Or Else: The Impact of Fear of Election Violence on Voters." *Democratization* 27 (4): 588–604.

Burnell, Peter. 2001. "The Party System and Party Politics in Zambia: Continuities Past, Present, and Future." *African Affairs* 100 (399): 239–269.

Butler, David and Donald Stokes. 1969. *Political Change in Britain: Forces Shaping Electoral Choice*. London: MacMillan.

Bwalya, Edgar. 2002. *The Electorate's View on the 2001 Zambian Presidential, Parliamentary and Local Government Elections: Before, During and After the Elections*. Lusaka: The University of Zambia.

Bwalya, John and Brij Maharaj. 2018. "Not to the Highest Bidder: The Failure of Incumbency in the Zambia 2011 Elections." *Journal of Contemporary African Studies* 36 (1): 71–86.

Cameron, Greg. 2001. "The Tanzanian General Elections on Zanzibar." *Review of African Political Economy* 28 (88): 282–286.

Cammack, Diana. 1999. "The Democratic Transition in Malawi: From Single Party Rule to a Multiparty State," in Daniel, John, Roger Southall, and Morris Szeftel (Eds.) *Voting for Democracy: Watershed Elections in Contemporary Anglophone Africa*. London: Routledge, pp. 187–210.

Cammack, Diana. 2010. "The Politics of Chameleons Revisited: The Burden of Malawi's Political Culture," in Ott, Martin and Fidelis Edge Kanyongolo (Eds.) *Democracy in Progress: Malawi's 2009 Parliamentary and Presidential Elections*. Zomba: Kachere Books, pp. 153–184.

Cammack, Diana. 2012. "Malawi in Crisis, 2011–12." *Review of African Political Economy* 39 (132): 375–388.

Caramani, Daniel. 2004. *The Nationalization of Politics: The Formation of National Electorates and Party Systems in Western Europe*. Cambridge: Cambridge University Press.

Carrier, Neil and Hassan H. Kochore. 2014. "Navigating Ethnicity and Electoral Politics in Northern Kenya: The Case of the 2013 Election." *Journal of Eastern African Studies* 8 (1): 135–152.

Carter Center. 2002. *Observing the 2001 Zambian Elections: Final Report*. Atlanta: Carter Center.

Chan, Stephen. 1992. "Democracy in Southern Africa: The 1990 Elections in Zimbabwe and 1991 Elections in Zambia." *The Roundtable* 322: 183–201.

Cheeseman, Nic. 2008. "The Kenyan Election of 2007: An Introduction." *Journal of Eastern African Studies* 2 (2): 166–184.

Cheeseman, Nic. 2015. *Democracy in Africa: Success, Failures, and the Struggle for Political Reform*. Cambridge: Cambridge University Press.

Cheeseman, Nic and Marja Hinfelaar. 2010. "Parties, Platforms, and Political Mobilization. The Zambian Presidential Election of 2008." *African Affairs* 109 (434): 51–76.

Cheeseman, Nic and Brian Klaas. 2019. *How to Rig an Election*. New Haven: Yale University Press.

Cheeseman, Nic, Hilary Matfess, and Aitalali Amani. 2021. "Tanzania: The Roots of Repression." *Journal of Democracy* 32 (2): 77–89.

Chhibber, Pradeep and Ken Kollman. 1998. "Party Aggregation and the Number of Parties in India and the United States." *American Political Science Review* 92 (2): 329–342.

Chikadza, Kondwani Farai. 2021. "Political Competition, Electoral Strategies and Political Development in Malawi: Evidence from the 2019 Tripartite Elections," in Kanyongolo, Edge and Nandini Patel (Eds.) *Malawi's 2019 Tripartite Elections*. Pretoria: Pretoria University Press, pp. 161–188.

Chingaipe, Henry. 2018. "Malawi" in Chirambo, Kondwani and Thibaud Kurtz (Eds.) *Preventing and Mitigating Electoral Conflict and Violence*. Brussels: European Centre for Electoral Support, pp. 148–188.

Chinsinga, Blessings. 2010. "Malawi's Political Landscape 2004–2009," in Ott, Martin and Fidelis Edge Kanyongolo (Eds.) *Democracy in Progress: Malawi's 2009 Parliamentary and Presidential Elections*. Zomba: Kachere Books, pp. 115–152.

Chinsinga, Blessings. 2015. "The Political Economy Context," in Patel, Nandini and Michael Wahman (Eds.) *The Malawi 2014 Election: Is Democracy Maturing?* Lilongwe: National initiative for Civic Education, pp. 17–38.

Chirambo, Reuben. 2001. "Protesting Politics of 'Death and Darkness' in Malawi." *Journal of Folklore Research* 38 (3): 205–227.

Chirambo, Reuben. 2004. "'Operation Bwezani': The Army, Political Change, And Dr. Banda's Hegemony in Malawi." *Nordic Journal of African Studies* 13 (2): 146–162.

Chirwa, Wiseman, Nandini Patel, Fidelis Kanyongolo. 2000. *Democracy Report for Malawi.* Stockholm, International IDEA.

Chirwa, Wiseman Chijere. 2001. "Dancing Towards Dictatorship: Political Songs and Popular Culture in Malawi." *Nordic Journal of African Studies* 10 (1): 1–27.

Chiyamwaka, Baldwin. 2015. "The Media: Did they Inform or Misinform?" in Patel, Nandini and Michael Wahman (Eds.) *The Malawi 2014 Election: Is Democracy Maturing?* Lilongwe: National initiative for Civic Education, pp. 135–156.

Choi, Hyun Jin and Clionadh Raleigh. 2021. "The Geography of Regime Support and Political Violence." *Democratization* 28 (56): 1095–1114.

Christian Churches Monitoring Group (CCMG). 2021. CCMG 2021 LTO Report 5 (June 5-June 20). *CCMG*, Lusaka: Zambia.

Collier, Paul and Pedro C. Vicente. 2012. "Violence, Bribery, and Fraud: The Political Economy of Elections in Sub-Saharan Africa." *Public Choice* 153 (1): 117–147.

Commission of Inquiry into Voting Patterns and Electoral Violence (CIVPEV). 2019. *Final Report of the Commission of Inquiry into Voting Patterns and Electoral Violence.* Lusaka: Republic of Zambia.

Commonwealth. 2006. "Zambia: Presidential, National Assembly, and Local Government Elections." London: Commonwealth Secretariat.

Conroy-Krutz, Jeffrey. 2018. "Individual Autonomy and Local-Level Solidarity in Africa." *Political Behavior* 40: 593–627.

Coppedge, Michael, John Gerring, Carl Hendrik Knutsen, Staffan I. Lindberg, Staffan Jan Teorell, David Altman et al. 2020. "V-Dem Codebook V.10" V-Dem Working Papers.

Daddieh, Cyril K. 2001. "Elections and Ethnic Violence in Côte d'Ivoire: The Unfinished Business of Succession and Democratic Transition." *African Issues* 29 (1–2): 14–19.

Davenport, Christian. 1997. "From Ballots to Bullets: Aan Empirical Assessment of How National Elections Influence State Use of Political Repression." *Electoral Studies* 16 (4): 517–540.

Daxecker, Ursula. 2014. "All Quiet on Election Day? International Election Observation and Incentives for Pre-Election Violence in African Elections." *Electoral Studies* 34: 232–243.

Daxecker, Ursula. 2020. "Unequal Votes, Unequal Violence: Malapportionment and Election Violence in India." *Journal of Peace Research* 57 (1): 156–170.

Daxecker, Ursula and Rauschenbach. Forthcoming. "Election Type and the Logic of Pre-election Violence: Evidence from Zimbabwe." Unpublished manuscript.

De Smedt, Johan. 2009. "'No Raila, No Peace!' Big Man Politics and Election Violence in Kibera." *African Affairs* 108 (433): 581–593.

De Miguel, Carolina. 2017. "The Role of Electoral Geography in the Territorialization of Party Systems." *Electoral Studies* 47: 67–83.

Dercon, Stefan and Roxana Gutiérrez-Romero. 2012. "Triggers and Characteristics of the 2007 Kenyan Electoral Violence." *World Development* 40 (4): 731–744.

Dionne, Kim Yi and Boniface Dulani. 2013. "Constitutional Provisions and Executive Concession: Malawi's 2012 Transition in Comparative Perspective." *African Affairs* 112 (446): 111–137.

Dionne, Kim Yi and Boniface Dulani. 2014. "On the Eve of Malawi's Election." Washington Post/Monkey Cage. https://www.washingtonpost.com/news/monkey-cage/wp/2014/05/19/on-the-eve-of-malawis-election/ [last accessed January 3, 2021].

Dorman, Sara Rich. 2005. "'Make Sure They Count Nicely this Time': The Politics of Election and Election Observation in Zimbabwe." *Commonwealth and Comparative Politics* 43 (2): 155–177.

Dulani, Boniface. 2006. "Consolidating Malawi's Democracy? An Analysis of the 2004 Malawi Elections." *African Insight* 36 (1): 3–12.

Dulani, Boniface and Joseph Chunga. 2015. "When is Incumbency No Longer an Advantage? Explaining President Joyce Banda's Defeat," in Patel, Nandini and Michael Wahman (Eds.) *The Malawi 2014 Election: Is Democracy Maturing?* Lilongwe: National initiative for Civic Education, pp. 236–257.

Dulani, Boniface, Adam S. Harris, Jeremy Horowitz, and Happy Kayuni. 2021. "Electoral Performance among Multi-Ethic Voters in Africa." *Comparative Political Studies* 54 (2): 280–311.

Dunning, Thad. 2011. "Fighting and Voting: Violent Conflict and Electoral Politics" *Journal of Conflict Resolution* 55 (3): 323–339.

Dzimbiri, Lewis B. 1994. "The Malawi Referendum of June 1993." *Electoral Studies* 13 (3): 229–234.

Electoral Institute for Sustainable Democracy in Africa (EISA). 2016. *EISA Election Observer Mission Report No. 50.* Johannesburg: EISA.

Elfversson, Emma and Kristine Höglund. 2019. "Violence in the City that Belongs to No One: Urban Distinctiveness and Interconnected Insecurities in Nairobi (Kenya)." *Conflict, Security & Development* 19 (4): 556–574.

Elischer, Sebastian. 2013. *Political Parties in Africa: Ethnicity and Party Formation.* Cambridge: Cambridge University Press.

Erdmann, Gero and Neo Simutanyi. 2003. *Transitions in Zambia: The Hybridisation of the Third Republic.* Lilongwe: Konrad-Adenauer-Stiftung

European Union (EU). 2008. *Final Report: EU EEM Zambia Presidential By-Election, 30 October 2008.* EU: Lusaka.

Ferree, Karen and Jeremy Horowitz. 2010. "Ties the Bind? The Rise and Decline of Ethno-Regional Partisanship in Malawi, 1994–2009." *Democratization* 17 (3): 534–563.

Fielding, David. 2018. "The Geography of Violence During a Presidential Election: Evidence from Zimbabwe." *European Journal of Political Economy* 55: 538–558.

Fjelde, Hanne. 2020. "Political Party Strength and Electoral Violence." *Journal of Peace Research* 57 (1): 140–155.

Fjelde, Hanne and Kristine Höglund. 2016. "Electoral Institutions and Electoral Violence in Sub- Saharan Africa." *British Journal of Political Science* 46 (2): 297–320.

Fjelde, Hanne and Kristine Höglund. 2022. "Introducing the Deadly Electoral Conflict dataset." *Journal of Conflict Resolution* 66 (1): 162–185.

Foundation for Democratic Process (FODEP). 2002. *Zambia's 2001 Tripartite Elections.* Lusaka: FODEP.

Foundation for Democratic Process (FODEP). 2006. *Zambia's 2006 Tripartite Elections.* Lusaka: FODEP.

Fox, Roddy. 1996. "Bleak Future for Multi-Party Elections in Kenya." *Journal of Modern African Studies* 34 (4): 597–607.

Franck, Raphaël and Ilia Rainer. 2012. "Does the Leader's Ethnicity Matter? Ethnic Favoritism, and Health in Sub-Sharan Africa." *American Political Science Review* 106 (2): 294–325.

Frantzeskakis, Nikolaos and Brandon Beomseob Park. 2022. "Armed and Dangerous: Legacies of Incumbent-military Ties and Electoral Violence in Africa." *Electoral Studies* 80: 1–7.

Fraser, Alastair. 2017. "Post-populism in Zambia: Michael Sata's Rise, Demise and Legacy." *International Political Science Review* 38 (4): 456–472.

Fridy, Kevin. 2009. "Africa's Disappearing Election Results: Why Announcing the Winner is Simply not Enough." *Journal of African Elections* 8 (2): 88–101.

Friesen, Paul. 2023. "The Partisan Consequences of Liberation Mentality: Ruling Party Support in Zimbabwe Across Space and Time." *Party Politics* 29 (2): 306–321.

Gadjanova, Elena. 2021. "Status-quo and Grievance Coalitions: The Logic of Cross-ethnic Campaign Appeals in African Highly Diverse States." *Comparative Political Studies* 54 (3/4): 652–685.

Gallagher, Julia. 2015. "The Battle for Zimbabwe in 2013: From Polarisation to Ambivalence." *Journal of Modern African Studies* 53 (1): 27–49.

Galli, Giorgio and Alfonso Prandi. 1970. *Patterns of Political Participation in Italy.* New Haven, Yale University Press.

Gibson, Edward. 2013. *Boundary Control: Subnational Authoritarianisms in Federal Democracies.* New York: Cambridge University Press.

Giraudy, Agustina. 2015. *Democrats and Autocrats. Pathways of Subnational Undemocratic Regime Continuity within Democratic Countries.* Oxford: Oxford University Press.

Gloppen, Siri, Edge Kanyongolo, Nixon Khembo, Nandini Patel, Lise Rakner, Lars Svåsand, Arne Tostensen and Mette Bekken. 2006. "The Institutional Context of the 2004 General Elections in Malawi." *CMI Report* 2006: 21.

Goldring, Edward and Michael Wahman. 2016. "Democracy in Reverse: The 2016 General Election in Zambia." *Africa Spectrum* 3 (1): 107–121.

Goldring, Edward and Michael Wahman. 2018. "Fighting for a Name on the Ballot: Constituency-Level Analysis of Nomination Violence in Zambia." *Democratization* 25 (6): 996–1015.

Goldsmith, Arthur A. 2015. "Elections and Civil Violence in New Multiparty Regimes: Evidence from Africa." *Journal of Peace Research* 52 (5): 607–621.

Golosov, Grigorii V. 2016. "Factors of Party System in Nationalization." *International Political Science Review* 37 (2): 246–260.

Gonzalez-Ocantos, Ezequiel, Chad Kiewiet de Jonge, Carlos Meléndez, David Nickerson, and Javier Osorio. 2020. "Carrots and Sticks: Experimental Evidence of Vote Buying and Voter Intimidation in Guatemala." *Journal of Peace Research* 57 (1): 46–61.

Gonzalez-Ocantos, Ezequiel, Chad Kiewiet de Jonge, Carlos Meléndez, Javier Osorio, David W. Nickerson. 2012. "Vote Buying and Social Desirability Bias: Experimental Evidence from Nicaragua." *American Journal of Political Science* 56 (1): 202–217.

Grebe, Jan. 2010. "And They are Still Targeting: Assessing the Effectiveness of Targeted Sanctions against Zimbabwe." *Africa Spectrum* 45 (1): 3–29.

Gregory, Martyn. 1980. "The Zimbabwe Election: The Political and Military Implications." *Journal of Southern African Studies* 7 (1): 17–37.

Gutiérrez-Romero, Roxana. 2014. "An Inquiry into the Use of Illegal Electoral Practices and Effects on Political Violence and Vote Buying." *Journal of Conflict Resolution* 58 (8): 1500–1527.

Gutiérrez-Romero, Roxana and Adrienne Lebas. 2020. "Does Election Violence Affect Vote Choice and Willingness to Vote? Conjoint Analysis of a Vignette Experiment." *Journal of Peace Research* 57 (1): 77–92.

Hafner-Burton, Emilie, Susan D. Hyde and Ryan Jablonski. 2014. "When do Governments Resort to Violence." *British Journal of Political Science* 44 (1): 149–179.

Hale, Henry. 2010. *Why Not Parties in Russia?* Cambridge: University of Cambridge Press.

van Ham, Caroline and Staffan I. Lindberg. 2015. "From Sticks to Carrots: Electoral Manipulation in Africa, 1986–2012." *Government and Opposition* 50 (3): 521–548.

Hansen, Karen Tranberg and Wilma Nchito. 2013. "Where Have All the Vendors Gone? Of Redrawing Boundaries in Lusaka's Street Economy." In Hansen Karen Tranberg, Walter E. Little, and Lynne Milgram (Eds.) *Street Economies in the Urban Global South*. Santa Fe: School for Advanced Research, pp. 72–97.

Harbers, Imke, Cécile Richetta, Enrike van Wingerden. 2023. "Shaping Electoral Outcomes: Intra-and Andi-systemic Violence in Indian Assembly elections." *British Journal of Political Science*, 53 (2): 424–440.

Harding, Robin. 2020. *Rural Democracy: Elections and Development in Africa*. Oxford: Oxford University Press.

Hassan, Mai. 2015. "Continuity Despite Change: Kenya's New Constitution and Executive Power." *Democratization* 22 (4): 587–609.

Hassan, Mai. 2017. "The Strategic Shuffle: Ethnic Geography, The Internal Security Apparatus, and Elections in Kenya." *American Journal of Political Science* 61 (2): 382–395.

Hassan, Mai. 2020. "The Local Politics of Resource Distribution," in Cheeseman, Nic, Karuti Kanyinga, and Gabrielle Lynch (Eds.) *The Oxford Handbook of Kenyan Politics*. Oxford: Oxford University Press, pp. 482–496.

Hechter, Michael. 1975. *Internal Colonialism: The Celtic Fringe in British National Development*. Berkeley: University of California Press.

Helle, Svein-Erik. 2016. "Defining the Playing Field: A Framework for Analysing Fairness in Access to Resources, Media and the Law." *Zeitschrift für Vergleichende Politikwissenschaft* 10: 47–78.

Herbst, Jeffrey. 2000. *States and Power in Africa: Comparative Lessons in Authority and Control*. Princeton: Princeton University Press.

Hern, Erin. 2019. *Developing States, Shaping Citizenship: Service Delivery and Political Participation in Zambia*. Ann Arbor: University of Michigan Press.

Hichilema, Hakainde. 2016/06/13. https://www.facebook.com/hakainde.hichilema/posts/ we-are-deeply-saddened-by-reports-of-violent-incidents-against-our-members-acros/ 1113579005390920/ [last accessed January 31, 2023].

Hicken, Allen and Noah L. Nathan. 2020. "Clientelism's Red Herrings: Dead Ends and New Directions in the Study of Non-programmatic Politics." *Annual Review of Political Science* 23 (1): 277–294.

Hicken, Allen and Heather Stoll. 2011. "Presidents and Parties: How Presidential Elections Shape Coordination in Legislative Elections." *Comparative Political Studies* 44 (7): 854–883.

Hinfelaar, Marja, O'Brien Kaaba, and Michael Wahman. 2021. "Electoral Turnovers and the Disappointment of Enduring Presidential Power: Constitution Making in Zambia." *Journal of Eastern African Studies*, 15 (1): 63–84.

Hinfelaar, Marja, Danielle Resnick, and Sishuwa Sishuwa. 2020. "Cities and Dominance: Urban Strategies for Settlement Maintenance and Change- Zambia Case Study." *ESID Working Paper*, 136.

Hodder-Williams, Richard. 1974. "Dr. Banda's Malawi." *Journal of Commonwealth & Comparative Politics* 12 (1): 91–114.

Hoffman, Barak D. and James D. Long. 2013. "Parties, Ethnicity, and Voting in African Elections." *Comparative Politics* 45 (2): 127–146.

Horowitz, Donald L. 2001. *The Deadly Ethnic Riot*. Berkeley: University of California Press.

Horowitz, Jeremy. 2016. "The Ethnic Logic of Campaign Strategy in Diverse Societies: Theory and Evidence from Kenya." *Comparative Political Studies* 49 (3): 324–356.

Horowitz, Jeremy 2022. *Multiethnic Democracy: The Logic of Elections and Policymaking in Kenya*. Oxford: Oxford University Press.

Horowitz, Jeremy and James Long. 2016. "Strategic Voting, Information, and Ethnicity in Emerging Democracies: Evidence from Kenya." *Electoral Studies* 44: 351–361.

Houle, Christian, Chuncho Park and Paul D. Kenny 2019. "The Structure of Ethnic Inequality and Ethnic Voting." *Journal of Politics* 81 (1): 187–200.

Howard, Marc. Morjé and Philip. G. Roessler. 2006. "Liberalizing Electoral Outcomes in Competitive Authoritarian Regimes." *American Journal of Political Science* 50 (2): 365–381.

Human Rights Watch. 1996. "Zambia: Elections and Human Rights in the Third Republic." *Human Rights Watch Reports* 8 (4).

Hussein, Mustafa Kennedy. 2009. "Opposition Politics in Malawi: Hopeful Signs Amid the Warnings." *South African Journal of International Affairs* 16 (3): 347–269.

Höglund, Kristine. 2009. "Electoral Violence in Conflict-Ridden Societies: Concepts, Causes, and Consequences." *Terrorism and Political Violence* 21 (3): 417–427.

Höglund, Kristine. 2017. "Explaining Ethnic and Election Violence: Malawi and Kenya Compared." *Africa Spectrum* 52 (2): 132–134.

Ichino, Nahomi and Noah L. Nathan. 2013. "Crossing the Line: Local Ethnic Geography and Voting in Ghana." *American Political Science Review* 107 (2): 344–361.

Ishiyama, John. 2012. "Explaining Ethnic Bloc Voting in Africa." *Democratization* 19 (4): 761–788.

Ismail, Jamil Abdi and James Deane. 2008. "The 2007 General Election in Kenya and Its Aftermath: The Role of Local Language Media." *Press/Politics* 13 (3): 319–327.

Jablonski, Ryan. 2014. "How Aid Targets Voters: The Impact of Electoral Incentives on Foreign Aid Distribution." *World Politics* 66 (2): 293–330.

Jenkins, Sarah J. 2020. "Violence as an Electoral Strategy," in Cheeseman, Nic, Karuți Kanyinga, and Gabrielle Lynch (Eds.) *The Oxford Handbook of Kenyan Politics*. Oxford: Oxford University Press, pp. 369–382.

Johnston, Ron, David Manley, Kelyn Jones and Rybe Rohla, R. 2020. "The geographical polarization of the American electorate: a country of increasing electoral landslides?" *GeoJournal* 85 (1): 187–204.

Kaaba, O'Brien and Privilege Haang'andu. 2020. "Democracy and Electoral Politics in Zambia," in Banda, Tineneji, O'Brien Kaaba, Marja Hinfelaar, and Muna Ndulo (Eds.) *Democracy and Electoral Politics in Zambia*, Leiden: Brill, pp. 172–194.

Kagwanja, Peter Mwangi. 2003. "Facing Mount Kenya or Facing Mecca? The Mungiki, Ethnic Violence, and the Politics of the Moi Succession in Kenya, 1987–2002." *African Affairs* 102 (106): 25–49.

Kalipeni, Ezekiel. 1997a. "Regional Polarisation in Voting Patterns: Malawi's 1994 Elections." *African Journal of Political Science* 2 (1): 152–167.

Kalipeni, Ezekiel. 1997b. "Contained Urban Growth in Post-Independence Malawi." *East African Geographic Review* 19 (2): 49–66.

Kalua, Phaniso. 2011. "The Extent of Political Party Institutionalization in Malawi: The Case of United Democratic Front (UDF) and Malawi Congress Party (MCP)." *Forum for Development Studies* 38 (1): 43–63.

Kalyvas, Stathis N. 2006. *The Logic of Violence in Civil War*. Cambridge: Cambridge University Press.

Kanyinga, Karuti. 2009. "The Legacies of the White Highlands: Land Rights, Ethnicity and the post–2007 Election Violence in Kenya." *Journal of Contemporary African Studies* 27 (3): 325–344.

Kapesa, Robby, Owen Sishone, and Bwalya, John. 2020. "Ethnic Mobilization, Horizontal Inequalities, and Electoral Conflict," in Banda, Tineneji, O'Brien Kaaba, Marja Hinfelaar, and Muna Ndulo (Eds.) *Democracy and Electoral Politics in Zambia*, Leiden: Brill, pp. 212–241.

Kasara, Kimuli. 2007. "Tax me if you Can: Ethnic Geography, Democracy, and the Taxation of Agriculture in Africa." *American Political Science Review* 101 (1): 159–172.

Kaspin, Deborah. 1995. "The Politics of Ethnicity in Malawi's Democratic Transition." *Journal of Modern African Studies* 33 (4): 595–620.

Kayuni, David. 2015. "Vote Brokers? An Assessment of the Influence of Traditional Leaders on a Candidate's Vote," in Patel, Nandini and Michael Wahman (Eds.) *The Malawi 2014 Election: Is Democracy Maturing?* Lilongwe: National initiative for Civic Education, pp. 195–215.

Kuder, G. Frederic and Marion Webster Richardson. 1937. "The Theory of the Estimation of Test Reliability." *Psychometrika* 2 (3): 151–160.

Kerr, Nicholas and Michael Wahman. 2021. "Electoral Rulings and Public Trust in African Courts and Elections." *Comparative Politics* 53 (2): 257–290.

Khembo, Nixon. 2004. "The Autonomy of Electoral Democracy in Malawi: Neo- Authoritarianism in a Multiparty State," in Minnie, Jeannete (Ed.), *Outside the Ballot Box: Preconditions for Elections in Southern Africa*. Windhoek: Media Institute of Southern Africa.

Kibble, Steve. 2013. "Zimbabwe Between the Referendum and the Elections." *Strategic Review for Southern Africa* 35 (1): 93–117.

Kim, Eun Kyung. 2017. "Party Strategy in Multidimensional Competition in Africa: The Case of Zambia." *Comparative Politics* 50 (1): 21–43.

Kim, Eun Kyung. 2018. "'Sector Based Choice': A New Approach to Explaining Core and Swing Voters in Africa." *International Political Science Review* 21 (1): 28–50.

King, Gary. 1998. *Unifying Political Methodology: The Likelihood Theory of Statistical Inference*. Ann Arbor: Michigan University Press.

Klaus, Kathleen. 2020. *Political Violence in Kenya: Land, Elections, and Claim Making*. Cambridge: Cambridge University Press.

Klaus, Kathleen and Matthew Mitchell. 2015. "Land Grievances and the Mobilization of Electoral Violence: Evidence from Côte d'Ivoire and Kenya." *Journal of Peace Research* 52 (5): 622–635.

Klopp, Jacqueline M. 2001. "'Ethnic Clashes' and Winning Elections: The Case of Kenya's Electoral Despotism." *Canadian Journal of African Studies* 35 (3): 473–513.

Klopp, Jacqueline M. 2002. "Can Moral Ethnicity Trump Political Tribalism? The Struggle for Land and Nation in Kenya." *African Studies* 61 (2): 269–284.

Koter, Dominika. 2013. "King Makers: Local Leaders and Ethnic Politics in Africa." *World Politics* 65 (2): 187–232.

Koter, Dominika. 2017. *Beyond Ethnic Politics in Africa*. Cambridge: Cambridge University Press.

Kramon, Eric. 2018. *Money for votes: The causes and consequences of electoral clientelism in Africa*. Cambridge: Cambridge University Press.

Kriger, Norma. 2005. "ZANU(PF) Strategies in General Elections, 1980–2000: Discourse and Coercion." *African Affairs* 104 (414): 1–34.

Kuenzi, Michelle, John P. Tuman, Moritz P Rissmann and Gina Lambright. 2019. "The economic determinants of electoral volatility in Africa." *Party Politics* 25 (4): 621–631.

Kydd, Andrew H. and Barbara F. Walter. 2006. "The Strategies of Terrorism." *International Security* 31 (1): 49–80.

Langston, Joy and Guillermo Rosas. 2018. "Risky Business: Where do Presidential Campaigns Visit?" *Electoral Studies* 55: 120–130.

Larmer, Miles. 2008. "Enemies Within? Opposition to the Zambian One-Party State, 1972–1980," in Gewald, Jan-Bart and Marja Hinfelaar (Eds.) *One Zambia, Many Histories*. Leiden: Brill, pp. 98–125.

Larmer, Miles and Alastair Fraser. 2007. "Of Cabbages and King Cobra: Populist Politics and Zambia's 2006 Election." *African Affairs* 106 (425): 611–637.

LeBas, Adrienne. 2006. "Polarization as craft: Party formation and state violence in Zimbabwe." *Comparative Politics* 38 (4): 419–438.

Lebas, Adrianne. 2011. *From Protest to Party*. Oxford: Oxford University Press.

LeBas, Adrienne. 2013. "Violence and Urban Order in Nairobi, Kenya and Lagos, Nigeria." *Studies in Comparative International Development* 48: 240–262.

Lehoucq, Fabrice E. and Iván Molina. 2002. *Stuffing the Ballot Box: Fraud, Electoral Reform and Democratization in Costa Rica*. Cambridge: Cambridge University Press.

Lemon, Anthony. 2007. "Perspectives on Democratic Consolidation in Southern Africa: The Five General Elections of Southern Africa." *Political Geography* 26 (7): 824–850.

Letsa, Natalie Wenzell. 2019. "The Political Geography of Electoral Autocracies: The Influence of Party Strongholds on Political Beliefs in Africa." *Electoral Studies* 60 (August): 1–12.

Levitsky, Steven and Lucan Way. 2010. *Competitive Authoritarianism: Hybrid Regimes after the Cold War*. Cambridge: Cambridge University Press.

Lewanika, McDonald. 2019. *Campaigns, Coercion, and Clientelism: ZANU-PF Strategies in Zimbabwe's Presidential Elections 2008–2013*. Unpublished Doctoral Dissertation: London School of Economics.

Lindemann, Stefan. 2011. "Inclusive Elite Bargaining and the Dilemma of Unproductive Peace: a Zambia Case Study." *Third World Quarterly* 32 (10): 1843–1869.

Linke, Andrew. 2022. "Post-Election Violence in Kenya: Leadership, Legacies, Demography, and Motivations." *Territory, Politics, Governance* 10 (2): 180–199.

Lipset, Seymour Martin. 1960. *Political Man*. London: Hainemann.

Lipset, Seymour Martin, and Stein Rokkan. 1967. "Cleavages, structures and Voters Alignments: An introduction', in Seymour Martin Lipset and Stein Rokkan, (Eds.) *Party Systems and Voter Alignments*. New York: Free Press, pp. 1–50.

Lora-Kayambazinthu, Edrinnie Elizabeth. 2019 "Elhomwe Revitalization Efforts: Myth or Reality." *Anthological Linguistic* 61 (1): 12–43.

Lusaka Times. 2011. "MMD, PF Cadres Clash." August 26, 2011. https://www.lusakatimes.com/2011/08/26/mmdpf-cadres-clash/ [last accessed October 5, 2022]

Lusaka Times. 2015. "Kampyongo Defends Shiwangandu Attacks." January 4, 2015. https://www.lusakatimes.com/2015/01/04/kampyongo-defends-shiwangandu-attacks/ [last accessed October 5, 2022]

Lusaka Times. 2016a. "PF Cadres Again Attack UPND Campaign Team in Muchinga Province." June 14, 2016. https://www.lusakatimes.com/2016/06/14/pf-cadres-attack-upnd-campaign-team-muchinga-province/ [last accessed January 3, 2021]

Lusaka Times. 2016b. "Allow Others to Campaign in Southern Province- Kambwili." March 20, 2016. https://www.lusakatimes.com/2016/03/20/allow-others-campaign-southern-province-kambwili/ [last accessed January 3, 2021].

Lusaka Times 2016c. "Fight Back When You Are Attacked, GBM Instructs UPND Youth" June 16, 2016. https://www.lusakatimes.com/2016/06/16/fight-back-attacked-gbm-instructs-upnd-youths/ [last accessed January 3, 2021].

Lusaka Times 2016d. "A Minister Hired the Thugs Who Tried to Bring Down UPND Helicopter- Katuka" June 16, 2016. https://www.lusakatimes.com/2016/06/14/minister-hired-thugs-bring-upnd-helicopter-katuka/ [last accessed January 3, 2021].

Lusaka Times. 2021. "Explain where the Money Being Displayed by PF Cadres on Social Media in Coming from, HH Challenges BOZ." March 3, 2021. https://www.lusakatimes.com/2021/03/03/explain-where-the-money-being-displayed-by-pf-cadres-on-social-media-is-coming-from-hh-challenges-boz/ [last accessed January 3, 2021]

Lust, Ellen, Nicole Beardsworth, Matthais Krönke, Jeremy Seekings, and Michael Wahman. 2021. Zambia Election Panel Survey, Round 1. *The Program on Governance and Local Development and University of Cape Town.*

Lust, Ellen, Kao, Kristen., Landry, Pierre. F., Harris, Andrew, Dulani, Boniface, Lueders, Hans. 2020. The local governance and performance index (LGPI) 2019: Kenya, Malawi, Zambia. *The Program on Governance and Local Development.*

Lwanda, John. 2006. "Kwacha: The Violence of Money in Malawi Politics, 1954–2004." *Journal of Southern African Studies* 32 (3): 525–544.

Lynch, Gabrielle. 2011. *I Say to You: Ethnic Politics and the Kalenjin in Kenya.* London: University of Chicago Press.

Macola, Giacomo. 2008. "Harry Mwaanga Nkumbula, UNIP and the Roots of Authoritarianism in Nationalist Zambia," in Gewald, Jan-Bart and Marja Hinfelaar (Eds.) *One Zambia, Many Histories.* Leiden: Brill, pp. 17–44.

Mail & Guardian. 2015. "Malawi 'Theft' Balloons to R540m." February 12, 2015. https://mg.co.za/article/2015-02-12-malawi-theft-balloons-to-r540m/ [last accessed October 28, 2022].

Mainwaring, Scott, Carlos Gervasoni, and Annabella Estaña-Najera. 2017. "Extra- and Within- System Electoral Volatility." *Party Politics* 23 (6): 623–635.

Mair, Peter. 1997. *Party System Change: Approaches and Interpretations.* Oxford: Oxford University Press.

Makumbe, John. 2006. "Electoral Politics in Zimbabwe: Authoritarianism vs. the People." *African Development* 31 (3): 45–61.

Makumbe, John Mw. 2002. "Zimbabwe's Hijacked Election." *Journal of Democracy* 13 (4): 87–101.

Malawi Electoral Support Network (MESN). 2014. *Elections Report, 20th May, 2014, Tripartite Elections in Malawi.* Lilongwe: MESN.

Malik, Aditi. 2018. "Constitutional Reform and New Patterns of Electoral Violence: Evidence from Kenya's 2013 Election." *Commonwealth and Comparative Politics* 56 (3): 340–359.

Mamdani, Mahmood. 1996. *Citizen and Subject: Contemporary Africa and the Legacy of Late Colonialism.* Princeton: Princeton University Press.

Mansfield, Edward. D. and Jack Snyder. 2005. *Electing to Fight: Why Emerging Democracies Go to War.* Cambridge: MIT Press.

Martínez I Coma, Ferran and Lee Morgenbesser. 2020. "Election Turnout in Authoritarian Regimes." *Electoral Studies* 68: 102–122.

Masunungure, Eldred N. 2014. "The 'Menu of Manipulation' and the 2013 Zimbabwe Elections." *Journal of African Elections* 13 (2): 94–121.

Mattes, Robert. 2020. "Lived Poverty on the Rise: Decade of Living-standard Gains Ends in Africa." *Afrobarometer Policy Paper* No. 62.

May, Glenn Anthony. 1991. *Battle for Batangas: A Philippine Province at War.* New Haven: Yale University Press.

Mbowela, Noel and Ollen Mwalubunju. 2015. "A Scrutiny of Voter Participation and Civic and Voter Education." in Patel, Nandini and Michael Wahman (Eds.) *The Malawi 2014 Election: Is Democracy Maturing?* Lilongwe: National initiative for Civic Education, pp. 117–134.

McGregor, JoAnn. 2013. "Surveillance and the City: Patronage, Power Sharing and the Politics of Urban Control in Zimbabwe." *Journal of Southern African Studies* 39 (4): 783–805.

McLellan, Rachel. 2020. *The Politics of Local Control in Electoral Autocracies.* Unpublished Doctoral Dissertation: Princeton University.

McMann, Kelly M. 2006. *Economic Autonomy and Democracy: Hybrid Regimes in Russia and Kyrgyzstan.* New York: Cambridge University Press.

McMaster, Carolyn. 1974. *Malawi, Foreign Policy and Development.* London: Julian Friedmann Publishers.

Momba, Jotham C. 1985. "Peasant Differentiation and Rural Party Politics in Colonial Zambia." *Journal of Southern African Studies* 11 (2): 281–294.

Morgenstern, Scott, Stephen M. Swindle, Andrea Castagnola. 2009. "Party Nationalization and Institutions." *Journal of Politics* 71 (4): 1322–1341.

Moroff, Anika. 2010. "Party Bans in Africa: An Empirical Overview." *Democratization* 17 (4): 618–641.

Morse, Yonatan. 2018. *How Autocrats Compete: Parties, Patrons and Unfair Elections in Africa.* Cambridge: Cambridge University Press.

Moyo, Themba. 2002. "Language Politics and National Identity in Malawi." *South African Journal of African Languages* 22 (4): 262–272.

Mpesi, Andrew Mabvuto and Ragnhild L. Muriaas. 2012. "Food Security as a Political Issue: the 2009 Election in Malawi." *Journal of Contemporary African Studies* 30 (3): 377–393.

Mueller, Susanne. 2011. "Dying to Win: Elections, Political Violence, and Institutional Decay in Kenya." *Journal of Contemporary African Studies* 29 (1): 99–117.

Mugambi, Kiai. 2002. *Ghasia Watch: CDU Report on Electoral Violence in Kenya, January-December 2002.* Nairobi: CDU.

Mukuntu, Kabale Ignatius. 2019. "Electroal Violence and Youth Cadres in Zambia." *Journal of African Elections* 18 (1): 129–147.

Müller-Crepon, Carl. 2022. "Local Ethno-Political Polarization and Election Violence in Majoritarian vs. Proportional Systems." *Journal of Peace Research* 59 (2): 242–258.

Muñoz, Paula. 2019. *Buying Audiences: Clientelism and Electoral Campaigns When Parties are Weak.* Cambridge: Cambridge University Press.

Murunga, Godwin R. 2011. "Spontaneous or Premeditated? Post-election Violence in Kenya." *Nordiska Afrikainstitutet*, Discussion Paper 57.

Mutongwizo, Tariro. 2018. "Eclectic Ties and Election Touts: Chipangano's Cyclic Governance Agenda in Mbare- Zimbabwe," in Söderberg Kovacs, Mimmi and Jesper Bjarnesen (Eds.) *Violence in African Elections: Between Democracy and Big Man Politics.* London: ZED Books, pp. 197–214.

Mygakov, Mikhail, Peter Ordeshook, and Dimitri Shakin. 2009. *The Forensics of Election Fraud: Russia and Ukraine.* Cambridge: Cambridge University Press.

Nathan, Noah. 2019. *Electoral Politics and Africa's Urban Transition.* Cambridge: Cambridge University Press.

The Nation. 2014a. "JB in Blamegame Again." March 24, 2014. https://www.mwnation.com/jb-in-blame-game-again/ [last accessed April 11, 2021].

The Nation. 2014b. "MESN Uncovers Politically Motivated Violence." March 24, 2014. https://www.mwnation.com/mesn-uncovers-politically-motivated-violence/ [last accessed April 11, 2021].

The Nation. 2014c. "Thugs Attack DPP Vehicle in Mzuzu." March 20, 2014. https://www.mwnation.com/thugs-attack-dpp-vehicle-in-mzuzu/ [last accessed April 11, 2021].

The Nation. 2014d. "Thyolo Violence: Stones Thrown at JB Shock PP Bigwigs." March 22, 2014. https://www.mwnation.com/thyolo-violence-stones-thrown-at-jb-shock-pp-bigwigs/ [last accessed April 11, 2021].

National Assembly of Zambia. 2016. "Debates, Wednesday, 17th February, 2016." https://www.parliament.gov.zm/node/4972 [last accessed January 3, 2021].

National Democratic Institute (NDI)/Carter Center. 1992. *The October 31, 1991, National Elections in Zambia*. Washington DC: National Democratic Institute.

Nchube, Wichman. 1990. "State Security, the Rule of Law and Politics of Repression in Zimbabwe." *U-Landsseminariets Skriftserie*, Nr. 51, University of Oslo.

Ndegwa, Stephen N. 1998. "The Incomplete Transition: The Constitutional and Electoral Context in Kenya." *Africa Today* 45 (2): 193–211.

Ndlovu, Mphathisi. 2018. "Speaking for the Dead: Testimonies, Witnesses, and Representation of Gukurahundi Atrocities in New Media." *Journal of African Cultural Studies* 30 (3): 293–306.

Ndulo, Muna. 2016a. "Hichilema and Another vs. Lungu and Another." *SAIPAR Case Review* 1 (1): 13–18.

Ndulo, Muna. 2016b. "Professor Muna Ndulo Launches a Scratching Attack on the Three Constitutional Court Judges." *Lusaka Times*, November 11, 2016. https://www.lusakatimes.com/2016/09/11/professor-muna-ndulolaunches-scathing-attack-three-constitutional-court-judges/ [Last viewed 03/29/2018].

Ndulo, Muna B. and Robert B. Kent. 1996. "Constitutionalism in Zambia: Past, Present and Future." *Journal of African Law* 40 (2): 256–278.

Ngau, Peter and Musyimbi Mbathi. 2010. "The Geography of Voting in Kenya: The Analysis of the 2007 Presidential, Parliamentary, and Civic Voting Patterns," in Kanyinga, Karuti and Duncan Okello (Eds.) *Tensions and Reversals in Democratic Consolidation: The 2007 Kenyan Elections*. Nairobi: Society for International Development, pp. 139–174.

Nichter, Simeon. 2008. "Vote Buying or Turnout Buying? Machine Politics and the Secret Ballot." *American Political Science Review* 102 (1): 19–31.

Norris, Pippa. 2013. "The New Research Agenda on Studying Electoral Integrity." *Electoral Studies* 32 (4): 563–575.

Nyasa Times. 2012. "Malawi: DPP in Savage Attack to PP Supporters in Thyolo." November 13, 2012. https://www.nyasatimes.com/malawi-dpp-in-savage-attack-to-pp-supporters-in-thyolo/ [last accessed April 11, 2021].

Nyasa Times. 2014a. "DPP Planned Thyolo: JB Blames Mutharika." March 20, 2014. https://www.nyasatimes.com/dpp-planned-thyolo-violence-jb-blames-mutharika/ [last accessed April 11, 2021].

Nyasa Times. 03/21/2014b. "UDF Accused of Fomenting Violence in Mangochi." https://www.nyasatimes.com/udf-accused-of-fomenting-violence-in-mangochi/ [last accessed April 11, 2021].

Nyasa Times. 2014c. "PP Governor Assaulted." April 9, 2014. https://www.mwnation.com/pp-governor-assaulted/ [last accessed April 11, 2021].

Nyasa Times. 2014d. "Mutharika Appeals for Votes as DPP Imports Audience at Rally." 21 April, 2014. https://www.nyasatimes.com/mutharika-appeals-for-votes-as-dpp-import-audience-at-rally/ [last accessed April 11, 2021].

Nyasa Times. 2018. "Archbishop Msusa Tells Malawi Politicans there are 'No-go zones' for Other Parties." August 26, 2018. https://www.nyasatimes.com/archbishop-msusa-tells-malawi-politicians-there-are-no-go-zones-for-other-parties/ [last accessed April 11, 2021].

Omotola, Shola. 2010. "Explaining Electoral Violence in Africa's 'New' Democracies." *African Journal of Conflict Resolution* 10 (3): 51–73.

Omotola, J. Shola. 2009. "'Garrison' Democracy in Nigeria: The 2007 General Elections and the Prospects of Democratic Consolidation." *Commonwealth and Comparative Politics* 47 (2): 194–220.

Onapajo, Hakeem. 2014. "Violence and Votes in Nigeria: The Dominance of Incumbents in the Use of Violence to Rig Elections." *Africa Spectrum* 49 (2): 27–51.

Opitz, Christian, Hanne Fjelde, and Kristine Höglund. 2013. "Including Peace: The Influence of Electoral Management Bodies on Electoral Violence." *Journal of Eastern African Studies* 7 (4): 713–731.

Oyewole, Samuel and J. Shola Omotola. 2021. "Violence in Nigeria's 2019 General Elections: Trends and Geospatial Dimensions." *GeoJournal* 87: 2393–2403.

Paget, Dan. 2019. "The Rally-Intense Campaign: A Distinct Form of Electioneering in Sub-Saharan Africa and Beyond." *The International Journal of Press/Politics* 24 (4): 444–464.

Patel, Nandini. 2015. "Management of the Elections: Challenges and Outcomes," in Patel, Nandini and Michael Wahman (Eds.) *The Malawi 2014 Election: Is Democracy Maturing?* Lilongwe: National initiative for Civic Education, pp. 104–116.

Patel, Nandini and Andrew Mpesi. 2010. "Between choice and imposition: the politics of nomination," in Ott Martin and Edge Kanyongolo (Eds.) *Democracy in Progress: Malawi's 2009 Parliamentary and Presidential Elections*. Zomba: Kachere Books, pp. 295–316.

Patel, Nandini and Michael Wahman. 2015. "The Presidential, Parliamentary, and Local Elections in Malawi, May 2014." *Africa Spectrum* 50 (1): 79–92.

Pedersen, Mogens N. 1979. "The Dynamics of European Party Systems: Changing Patterns of Electoral Volatility." *European Journal of Political Research* 7 (1): 1–26.

Pettman, Jan. 1974. "Zambia's Second Republic: The Establishment of a One-party State." *Journal of Modern African Studies* 12 (2): 231–244.

Posner, Daniel N. 2005. *Institutions and Ethnic Politics in Africa*. Cambridge: Cambridge University Press.

Potts, Deborah. 1985. "Capital Relocation in Africa: The Case of Lilongwe in Malawi." *The Geographical Journal* 151 (2): 182–196.

Powell, G. Bingham Jr. 1986. "American Voter Turnout in Comparative Perspective." *American Political Science Review* 80 (1): 17–43.

Powell, Ellenor Neff and Joshua A. Tucker. 2014. "Revisiting Electoral Volatility in Post-Communist Countries: New Data, New Results and New Approaches." *British Journal of Political Science* 44 (1): 123–147.

Public Affairs Committee (PAC), Catholic Commission for Justice and Peace, and National Initiative for Civic Education (NICE). 2020. *Preliminary Observations and Recommendations on the Electoral Process for the Fresh Presidential Election (FPE)*. Lilongwe.

Putnam, Robert. 2000. *Bowling Alone: The Collapse and Revival of American Community*. New York: Simon & Schuster.

Raftopoulos, Brian. 2002. "Briefing: Zimbabwe's 2002 Presidential Election." *African Affairs* 101 (404): 313–426.

Rakner, Lise. 2010. "The Management of the 2009 Electoral Process: The Role of the Malawi Electoral Commission," in Ott, Martin and Fidelis Edge Kanyongolo (Eds.) *Democracy in Progress: Malawi's 2009 Parliamentary and Presidential Elections*. Zomba: Kachere Books, pp. 25–47.

Rakner, Lise and Lars Svåsand. 2004. "From Dominant to Competitive Party System: The Zambian Experience 1991–2001." *Party Politics* 10 (1): 49–68.

Rakner, Lise and Lars Svåsand. 2005. "Stuck in Transition: Electoral Processes in Zambia 1991–2001." *Democratization* 12 (1): 85–105.

Rakner, Lise and Nicolas van de Walle. 2009. "Democratization by Elections? Opposition Weakness in Africa." *Journal of Democracy* 20 (3): 108–121.

Rakner, Lise, Lars Svåsand and Nixon Khembo. 2007. "Fissions and Fusions, Foes and Friends: Party System Restructuring in Malawi in the 2004 General Election." *Comparative Political Studies* 40 (9): 1112–1237.

Raleigh, Clionadh, Andrew Linke, Håvard Hegre, and Joakim Karlsen. 2010. "Introducing ACLED: An Armed Conflict Location and Event Dataset." *Journal of Conflict Resolution* 47 (5): 651–660.

Rasmussen, Thomas. 1969. "Political Competition and One-Party Dominance in Zambia." *Journal of Modern African Studies* 7 (3): 407–424.

Rauschenbach, Mascha. 2015. *The Importance of Preaching to the Converted: The Strategic Use of Campaign Rallies, Campaign Promises, Clientelism, and Violence in African Elections.* Unpublished Doctoral Dissertation: University of Mannheim.

Rauschenbach, Mascha and Katrin Paula. 2019. "Intimidating Voters with Violence and Mobilizing them with Clientelism." *Journal of Peace Research* 56 (5): 682–696.

Reeder, Bryce and Merete Bech Seeberg. 2018. "Fighting your Friends? A Study of Intra-Party Violence in sub-Saharan Africa." *Democratization* 25 (6): 1033–1051.

Reno, William. 1998. *Warlord Politics and African States.* Bounder: Lynner Rienner Publishers.

Resnick, Danielle. 2013. *Urban Poverty and Party Populism in African Democracies.* New York: Cambridge University Press.

Resnick, Danielle. 2022. "How Zambia's Opposition Won." *Journal of Democracy* 33 (1): 70–84.

Riley, Liam and Emmanuel Chilanga. 2018. "'Things are Not Working Now': Poverty, Food Insecurity and Perceptions of Corruption in Urban Malawi." *Journal of Contemporary African Studies* 36 (4): 484–498.

Robinson, Amanda. 2020. "Ethnic Diversity, Segregation, and Ethnocentric Trust in Africa." *British Journal of Political Science* 50 (1): 217–239.

Robinson, James A. and Ragnar Torvik. 2009. "The Real Swing Voter's Curse." *American Economic Review* 99 (2): 310–315.

Roessler, Philip. 2011. "The Enemy Within: Personal Rule, Coups, and Civil War in Africa." *World Politics* 63 (2): 300–346.

Rokkan, Stein and Henry Valen. 1962. "The Mobilization of the Periphery: Data on Turnout, Party Membership and Candidate Recruitment in Norway." *Acta Sociologica* (January 1962): 111–158.

Rosenzweig, Steven C. 2021. "Dangerous Disconnect: Voter Backlash, Elite Misperception, and the Costs of Violence as an Electoral Tactic." *Political Behavior* 43: 1731–1754.

Rotberg, Robert I. 1971. *The Rise of Nationalism in Central Africa: The Making of Malawi and Zambia.* Cambridge: Harvard University Press.

Rueda, Miguel. R. 2017. "Popular Support, Violence, and Territorial Control in Civil Wars." *Journal of Conflict Resolution* 61 (8): 1626–1652.

Rundlett, Ashlea and Milan Svolik. 2016. "Deliver the Vote! Micromotives and Macrobehavior in Electoral Fraud." *American Political Science Review* 110 (1): 180–197.

Ruiz-Rufino, Rubén and Sarah Birch. 2020. "The Effect of Alternation in Power on Electoral Intimidation in Democratizing Regimes." *Journal of Peace Research* 57 (1): 126–139.

Rutten, Marcel and Sam Owuor. 2010. "Land, Ethnicity, and the 2007 Elections in Kenya," in Kagwanja, Peter and Roger Southall (Eds.) *Kenya's Uncertain Democracy*. London: Routledge, pp. 46–65.

Sachikonye, Lloyd M. 1990. "The 1990 Zimbabwe Elections: A Post-Mortem." *Review of African Political Economy* 17 (48): 92–99.

Sachikonye, Lloyd M. 2002. "Wither Zimbabwe? Crisis & Democratisation." *Review of African Political Economy* 29 (91): 13–20.

Sachikonye, Lloyd M. 2011. *When a State Turns on its Citizens: 60 Years of Institutionalised Violence in Zimbabwe*. Sunnyside: Jankana.

Sack, Robert. 1986. *Human Territoriality: Its Theory and History*. Cambridge: Cambridge University Press.

Salehyan, Idean, Cullen S. Hendrix, Jesse Hamner, Christina Case, Christopher Linebarger, Emily Stull and Jennifer Williams. 2012. "Social Conflict in Africa: A New Dataset." *International Interactions* 38 (4): 503–511.

Salehyan, Idean, and Christopher Linebarger. 2015. "Elections and Social Conflict in Africa, 1990–2009." *Studies in Comparative International Development* 50 (1): 23–49.

Samset, Ingrid. 2011. "Building a Repressive Peace: The Case of Post-genocide Rwanda." *Journal of Intervention and Statebuilding* 50 (3): 265–283.

Sata v. Lubinda and others, 2016/HP/EP0050. *High Court of Zambia*.

Scarritt, James R. 2006. "The Strategic Choice of Multiethnic Parties in Zambia's Dominant and Personalist Party System." *Commonwealth & Comparative Politics* 44 (2): 234–256.

Schedler, Andreas. 2002. "Elections without Democracy: The Menu pf Manipulation." *Journal of Democracy* 13 (2): 36–50.

Scott v. Mwanakatwe and others. 2016/CC/A018. *Constitutional Court of Zambia*.

Seeberg, Merete Bech. 2018. *State Capacity, Economic Control and Authoritarian Elections*. New York: Routledge.

Seeberg, Merete Bech. 2021. "How State Capacity Helps Autocrats Win Elections." *British Journal of Political Science* 51: 541–558.

Seeberg, Merete Bech, Michael Wahman, Svend-Erik Skaaning. 2018. "Candidate Nomination, Intra-Party Democracy, and Violence in Africa." *Democratization* 25 (6): 959–977.

Seekings, Jeremy. 2020. "Voters, Parties, and Elections in Zambia," in Banda, Tinenenji, O'Brien Kaaba, Marja Hinfelaar, and Muna Ndulo (Eds.) *Democracy and Electoral Politics in Zambia*. Leiden: Brill, pp. 116–146.

Shaw, Daron R. 1999. "The Method Behind the Madness: Presidential Electoral College Strategies, 1988–1996." *Journal of Politics* 61 (4): 893–913.

Siachiwena, Hangala. 2022. "A Silent Revolution." Journal of African Elections 20 (2): 32–56.

Simati, Meshack. 2020. *Post-Election Violence in Africa. The Impact of Judicial Independence*. London: Routledge.

Siqueira, Kevin and Petros G. Sekeris. 2012. "Politics and Insurgencies." *Economics and Politics* 24 (2): 157–181.

Sishuwa, Sishuwa. 2016. *"I am Zambia's Redeemer." Populism and the Rise of Michael Sata, 1955–2011*. Unpublished Doctoral Dissertation: University of Oxford.

Skage, Ingvild. 2016. *The Urban Poor as Citizens and Clients. Enacting Political Agency through Political Parties and Social Movements in Kenya and Zambia*. Unpublished Doctoral Dissertation: University of Bergen.

Smiddy, Kimberley and Daniel J. Young. 2009. "Presidential and Parliamentary Elections in Malawi, May 2009." *Electoral Studies* 28 (4): 662–666.

Smidt, Hannah. 2020. "Mitigating Election Violence Locally: UN Peacekeepers' Election Education Campaigns in Côte d'Ivoire." *Journal of Peace Research* 57 (1): 199–216.

Smiles, Joseph. 2003. "Zimbabwe: Review of the 2002 Election." *Journal of Contemporary History* 28 (3): 152–164.

Snyder, Jack. 2000. *From Voting to Violence: Democratization and Nationalist Conflict.* New York: W.W. Norton.

Snyder, Richard. 2001. "Scaling Down: The Subnational Comparative Method." *Studies in Comparative International Development* 36 (1): 93–110.

Von Soest, Christian and Michael Wahman. 2015. "Not all Dictators are Equal: Coups, Fraudulent Elections, and the Selective Targeting of Democratic Sanctions." *Journal of Peace Research* 52 (1): 17–31.

Somer, Murat, Jennifer L. McCoy, and Russell E. Luke. 2021 "Pernicious Polarization, Autocratization and Opposition Strategies." *Democratization* 28 (5): 929–948.

Staniland, Paul. 2014. "Review Essay: Violence and Democracy." *Comparative Politics* 47(1): 99–118.

Steeves, Jeffrey S. 1999. "The Political Evolution of Kenya: The 1997 Election and Succession Politics." *Commonwealth and Comparative Politics* 37 (1): 71–94.

Stokes, Susan C., Thad Dunning, Marcelo Nazareno. 2013. *Brokers, Voters, and Clientelism.* Cambridge: Cambridge University Press

Stoll, Heather. 2015. "Presidential Coattails: A Closer Look." *Party Politics* 21 (3): 417–427.

Straus, Scott. 2011. "'It's Sheer Horror Here' Patterns of Violence in the First Four Months of Cote d'Ivoire's Election Crisis." *African Affairs* 110 (440): 481–489.

Straus, Scott and Charlie Taylor. 2012. "Democratization and Electoral Violence in Sub-Saharan Africa, 1990–2008," in Bekoe, Dorina (Ed.) *Voting in Fear: Election Violence in Sub- Saharan Africa.* Washington DC: US Institute for Peace.

Sumbwa, Nyambe. 2000. "Traditionalism, Democracy and Political Participation: The Case of Western Province, Zambia." *African Study Monographs* 21 (3): 105–146.

Svåsand, Lars. 2015. "Political Parties: Fragmentation and Consolidation, Change and Stability," in Patel, Nandini and Michael Wahman (Eds.) *The Malawi 2014 Election: Is Democracy Maturing?* Lilongwe. National initiative for Civic Education, pp. 86 104.

Tao, Ran, Daniel Strandow, Michael Findley, Jean-Claude Thill, James Walsh. 2016. "A Hybrid Approach to Modelling Territorial Control in Violent Armed Conflict." *Transactions in GIS,* 20 (3): 413–425.

Taylor, Charles Fernandes, Jon CW Pevehouse, and Scott Straus. 2017. "Perils of Pluralism: Electoral Violence and Incumbency in Sub-Saharan Africa." *Journal of Peace Research* 54 (3): 374–411.

Tendi, Blessing-Miles. 2013. "Robert Mugabe's 2013 Presidential Election Campaign." *Journal of Southern African Studies* 39 (4): 963–970.

Tevera, D.S. 1989. "Voting Patters in Zimbabwe's Elections of 1980 and 1985." *Geography* 74 (2): 162–165.

Throup, David and Charles Hornsby. 1997. *Multi-Party Politics in Kenya: The Kenyatta and Moi States and the Triumph of the System in the 1992 Election.* Oxford: James Currey.

Travaglianti, Manuela. 2017. "Malawi: Widespread Tension, Limited Violence," in Claes, Jonas (Ed.) *Electing Peace: Violence Prevention and Impact at the Polls.* Washington DC: US Institute for Peace.

Tsoka, Maxton. 2009. "A Country Turning Blue? Political Party Support and the End of Regionalism in Malawi." *Afrobarometer Briefing Paper* No. 75:2009.

Turnbull, Megan. 2020. "Elite Competition, Social Movements, and Election Violence in Nigeria." *International Security* 45 (3): 40–78.

Van de Walle. 2006. "'Tipping Games' When Do Opposition Parties Coalesce?" in Schedler, Andreas (Ed.) *Electoral Authoritarianism, the Dynamics of Unfree Competition*. Boulder: Lynne Rienner.

VonDoepp, Peter. 2005. "The Problem of Judicial Control in Africa's Neopatrimonial Democracies: Malawi and Zambia." *Political Science Quarterly* 120 (2): 275–301.

VonDoepp, Peter and Daniel J. Young. 2013. "Assaults on the Fourth Estate: Explaining Media Harassment in Africa." *Journal of Politics* 75 (1): 36–51.

Wahman, Michael. 2011. "Offices and Policies- Why Do Oppositional Parties form Pre-Electoral Coalitions in Competitive Authoritarian Regimes?" *Electoral Studies* 30 (4): 642–657.

Wahman, Michael. 2014. "Electoral Coordination in Anglophone Africa." *Commonwealth & Comparative Politics* 52 (2): 187–211.

Wahman, Michael. 2016. "Opposition Coordination in Africa." *APSA Comparative Democratization Newsletter* 14 (1): 1–7.

Wahman, Michael. 2017. "Nationalized Incumbents and Regionalized Challengers: Opposition- and Incumbent-Party Nationalization in Africa." *Party Politics* 23 (3): 309–322.

Wahman, Michael. 2022. *Zambia Candidate Survey*. Michigan State University.

Wahman, Michael and Catherine Boone. 2018. "Captured Countryside? Stability and Change in Sub-National Support for African Incumbent Parties." *Comparative Politics* 50 (2): 189–209.

Wahman, Michael and Layla Brooks. 2022. "A Statistical Analysis of the 2019 Malawi Presidential and Parliamentary Vote: Persistence, Change, and Electoral Geography," in Patel, Nandini and Fidelis Edge Kanyongolo (Eds.) *Democracy Tested: Malawi's 2019 Tripartite Elections*. Pretoria: Pretoria University Law Press, pp. 358–393.

Wahman, Michael and Daniel Chapman. 2015. "The Persistent and Increasing Problem of Unequal Representation in Malawi: A Statistical Argumet for Redistricting," in Patel, Nandini and Michael Wahman (Eds.) *The Malawi 2014 Election: Is Democracy Maturing?* Lilongwe: National initiative for Civic Education, pp. 35–69.

Wahman, Michael and A. Cooper Drury. 2018. "Leverage, Diplomacy, and African Lesbian, Gay, Bisexual, Transgendered, and Intersex Rights: Malawi and Zambia Compared." *Journal of Human Rights* 17 (5): 622–641.

Wahman, Michael, Nikolaos Frantzeskakis, and Tevfik Murat Yildirim. 2021. "From Thin to Thick Representation: How A Female President Shapes Female Parliamentary Behavior." *American Political Science Review* 115 (2): 360–378.

Wahman, Michael and Merete Bech Seeberg. 2022. "Paying to Play: How Parliamentary Candidates Fund Ruling Party Campaigns in Malawi." *Comparative Politics* 55 (1): 95–118.

Van de Walle, Nicolas. 2007. "Meet the New Boss, Same as the Old Boss? The Evolution of Political Clientelism in Africa," in Kitchelt, Herbert and Steven I. Wilkinson (Eds.) *Patrons, Clients, and Policies: Patterns of Democratic Accountability and Political Competition*. Cambridge: Cambridge University Press, pp. 50–67.

Van Donge, Jan Kees. 1995. "Kamuzu's Legacy: The Democratization of Malawi or Searching for the Rules of the Game in African Politics." *African Affairs* 94 (375): 227–257.

Van Donge, Jan Kees. 1998. "Reflections on Donors, Opposition, and Popular Will in the 1996 Zambian Elections." *Journal of Modern African Studies* 36 (1): 71–99.

Weghorst, Keith, R. and Michael Bernhard. 2014. "From Formlessness to Structure? The Institutionalization of Competitive Party Systems in Africa." *Comparative Political Studies* 47 (12): 1707–1737.

Weghorst, Keith R. and Staffan I. Lindberg. 2013. "What Drives the Swing Voter in Africa." *American Journal of Political Science* 57 (3): 717–734.

Weidmann, Nils B. and Sebastian Schutte. 2016. "Using Night Light Emissions for the Prediction of Local Wealth." *Journal of Peace Research* 54 (2): 125–140.

Wilkinson, Steven I. 2004. *Votes and Violence.* Cambridge: Cambridge University Press.

Wong, Stan Hok-Wui. 2019. "Gerrymandering in Electoral Autocracies: Evidence from Hong Kong." *British Journal of Political Science* 49 (2): 579–610.

Wroe, Daniel. 2012. "Donors, Dependency, and Political Crisis in Malawi." *African Affairs* 111 (442): 135–144.

Wuhs, Steven T. 2016. "Paths and Places of Party Formation: The Post-Unification Development of Germany's Christian Democracy." *Comparative Politics* 49 (1): 43–62.

Young, Lauren. 2020. "Who Dissents? Self-efficiency and Opposition Action After State-sponsored Election Violence." *Journal of Peace Research* 57 (1): 62–76.

Zambia Reports. 2016. "Zambia: UPND Say Lusaka, Namwala Campaign Freeze Illegal." July 12, 2016. https://allafrica.com/stories/201607120133.html [Last viewed 10/28/2022].

Zamchiya, Phillan. 2013. "The MDC-T's (Un)Seeing Eye in Zimbabwe's Harmonised Elections: A Technical Knockout." *Journal of Southern African Studies* 39 (4): 955–962.

Ziblatt, Daniel. 2009. "Shaping Democratic Practice and the Causes of Electoral Fraud: The Case of Nineteenth Century Germany." *American Political Science Review* 103 (1): 1–21.

Zimmerman, Brigitte. 2015. "Voter Response to Scandal: Cashgate," in Patel, Nandini and Michael Wahman (Eds.) *The Malawi 2014 Election: Is Democracy Maturing?* Lilongwe: National initiative for Civic Education, pp. 215–234.

Subject Index

For the benefit of digital users, indexed terms that span two pages (e.g., 52–53) may, on occasion, appear on only one of those pages.

Notes

vs. indicates a comparison